THIS STUDY concentrates upon a period in Iranian history, 1870–80, when the country's self-sufficiency seemed to be crumbling beneath the challenges of severe internal stress and threats from abroad. It was a time for retrenchment and reassessment, for innovative thought and action in internal affairs and for bold new openness toward the progress then experienced beyond its borders. To no one was the country's position more clearly evident than to Mirza Huseyn Khan, who, when given the opportunity, launched upon a crusade to implement improvements he felt were necessary in all aspects of the life and affairs of the Iranian nation.

The book begins with a glimpse of Iran as it was—from its early roots, through its prosperity and splendor, to its late nineteenth-century decline. It then presents a detailed examination of Mirza Huseyn Khan's involvement in the governmental affairs of Iran. It concludes that, even though Mirza Huseyn Khan's actual successes were limited, he deserves to be recognized for having renewed the sense of national pride and for having done the spadework that eventually resulted in the constitutional revolution of the early twentieth century.

This is a drama not only of national survival, but also of personalities—of all who were caught up in the nation's struggle. Each contributed in an individual way to the nation's legacy, by means of humanity or inhumanity, strength or weakness, altruism or self-seeking.

Much of the wealth of primary sources drawn upon for this book has been hitherto untapped. This includes contemporary governmental documents, records, and reports; correspondence between major figures of the period; journalistic features and reports; and observations of contemporary travelers. To assist others interested in Iranian and Middle Eastern studies, an appendix has been included that identifies, evaluates, and places the main sources consulted in their historical context. Some of these sources, unfortunately, are no longer available outside of Iran due to the recent revolution there.

Guity Nashat was born into an Iranian family that was engaged in public service under the Qajars. She came to the United States to pursue advanced studies and was awarded a B.A. degree in English literature by Barnard College in 1958 and a Ph.D. degree in Middle Eastern history by the University of Chicago in 1973. She is currently a member of the history faculty at the University of Illinois at Chicago.

THE ORIGINS OF MODERN REFORM IN IRAN, 1870–80

*Publication of this book has been made possible
in part by a grant from the Iran-America Foundation*

THE ORIGINS OF
MODERN REFORM
IN IRAN, 1870–80

Guity Nashat

UNIVERSITY OF ILLINOIS PRESS
Urbana Chicago London

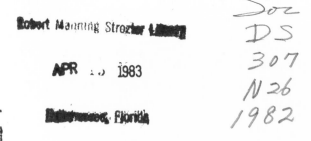
LIBRARY OF CONGRESS CATALOGING IN PUBLICATION DATA

Nashat, Guity
    The origins of modern reform in Iran.

    Based on the author's thesis (Ph. D.—University
of Chicago, 1973) presented under the title: The
beginnings of modernization in Iran.
    Bibliography: p.
    Includes index.
    1. Iran—History—19th century. 2. Husayn Khān
Mushīr-al-Dawlah, 1827 or 8–1881. 3. Statesmen—Iran—
Biography. I. Title.
DS307.N26   955'.04   81-3343
ISBN 0-252-00822-7   AACR2

To my sons MICHAEL *and* CYRUS
for their patience and cheerfulness

NOTE ON TRANSLATION AND TRANSLITERATION

ALL PASSAGES from works in languages other than English appear in translations by this author.

For uniformity of style, since most of the sources used in this work are in Persian, all names and words, even those of Arabic origin, have been transliterated in the Persian manner, e.g., Rabīʿ al-Thānī appears as Rabīʿ us-Sānī.

The vowels are *a, i, u* (short), *ā, ī, ū* (long), and *eh* for words ending with h *havvaz*, e.g., khāneh, Makkeh. The diphthongs are *ow* and *ey*, e.g., dowlat, Huseyn.

Initial *hamzeh* is not indicated, but in middle or final position it is indicated by ', e.g., inshā', mir'at.

The letter ع is noted as ʿ, e.g., ʿAlī, Iʿtimād. The letter ق is noted as *q*, and غ as *gh*. Other consonants are indicated گ as *g*, ج as *j*, and خ as *kh*.

In the text, diacritical marks appear at the first use of a word or name only, although an attempt was made to use the diacritical marks throughout in the footnotes, bibliography, and index.

CONTENTS

ILLUSTRATIONS

PREFACE

MOST WESTERN HISTORIANS of Iran in the nineteenth century agree
that during the Qajar period (1796–1924), Iran was transformed
"from a medieval Islamic monarchy with an administration following the traditional pattern that had prevailed in the eastern
provinces of the ʿAbbasid Caliphate, to a constitutional monarchy
with the outward forms of a western European representative
government." [1] The popular uprising that followed the granting
of the Tobacco Concession in 1890 has been generally regarded
as the starting point for the movement that led to this transformation, culminating in the Constitutional Revolution of 1905–7.

It is the intention of this study to demonstrate that some of the
groundwork for this transformation was laid in the decade of the
1870s. Furthermore, this decade witnessed a systematic, if partially
aborted, attempt on the part of a handful of Iranian leaders to
introduce reform and European ideas into the country.

The obscurity that has surrounded this period is due not so
much to a lack of historical material as to a need for the collation
and exposition of the materials that are available.[2] Moreover, the
events of the decade are less dramatic than those that went before,
with the meteoric career of Amir Kabir (1848–51), and those that
came after, with the Tobacco Concession and Constitutional Revolution. I believe the obscurity can be cleared somewhat by an
examination of the reforms initiated by Mirza Huseyn Khan Mushir ud-Dowleh, the outstanding statesman of his day.

For my analysis I have been able to draw on a number of sources
that are to a large extent unpublished. The most important of
these were (1) the private correspondence between Mirza Huseyn
Khan and Nasir ed-Din Shah, as well as other important figures
of the period, in the Farhad Collection, the Ghani Collection, and

the Majlis Collection; (2) the newspapers of the period: *Iran, Ruz-nameh-yi ʿAdliyeh, Ruznameh-yi Nizami, Mirrikh,* and *Ruznameh-yi ʿIlmiyeh;* (3) biographies and chronicles written by contemporary witnesses and participants in the events of the decade, such as Iʿtimad us-Saltaneh; Amin ud-Dowleh; Drs. Polak and Feuverier, two of the shah's private physicians; and the documents of the British Foreign Office.

I have attempted to analyze the events of this decade within the larger context of Iranian history, particularly that of the nineteenth century as a whole. I first examine a major factor affecting Iranian history—its geography—which has resulted in certain peculiarities in the development of the country in all its aspects, political, economic, social, and historical. The description presented in the first chapter closes with a panoramic view of the conditions prevailing in Iran as the decade of the 1870s opens and of the career of Mirza Huseyn Khan up to that point. The next seven chapters describe and analyze reforms initiated by Mirza Huseyn Khan in the judiciary, military, political, and economic spheres, ending with his attempts to introduce new ideas and modes of behavior that were European in inspiration. In the last section I have undertaken to evaluate Mirza Huseyn Khan's reform efforts and their impact on subsequent reform attempts in Iran.

It is hoped that the detailed exposition of Mirza Huseyn Khan's meaningful, if abortive, efforts presented here will illuminate much of Iran's history during and after the 1870s, as well as the nature of the modernization process in Iran.

The nucleus of this study is a Ph.D. dissertation that was presented to the University of Chicago in 1973. In the preparation and revision of this work many persons have been of great help. I should like to thank my dissertation committee—Halil Inalcik, William R. Polk, and John Woods—and others who made valuable comments on the work—Leonard Binder, Reubin Smith, Marilyn Waldman, and Marvin Zonis. I would also like to thank the late Marshall G. S. Hodgson for stimulating my interest in Islamic studies.

I am grateful, also, to Dr. Fereydoun Adamiyat, who guided my research during my stay in Tehran in 1970–71 and put at my disposal his collection of Qajar documents and manuscripts, in addition to reading the first version of this study and offering valuable suggestions. I am indebted, too, to the late Mahmud Farhad-Muʿtamid and his daughters Guli Mustowfi and Shahri

Nashat for their generous permission to use their vast collection of Qajar documents, including much hitherto unpublished correspondence of Mirza Huseyn Khan, Nasir ed-Din Shah, and other major statesmen of the period. I also acknowledge with thanks Dr. Hisam ud-Din Khurumi's generosity in allowing me access to his extensive collection of rare newspapers of this period.

I wish to express my appreciation to the Iran-America Foundation, which has helped to defray the costs of publication of this study. To Frank O. Williams of the University of Illinois Press I am grateful for his helpful comments. My thanks to Rita Zelewsky for meticulous copyediting of the manuscript.

To my parents I owe a special debt for providing me with an environment in Iran in which a woman could pursue higher education. Without the support and encouragement of my husband Gary S. Becker this study would not have come into being.

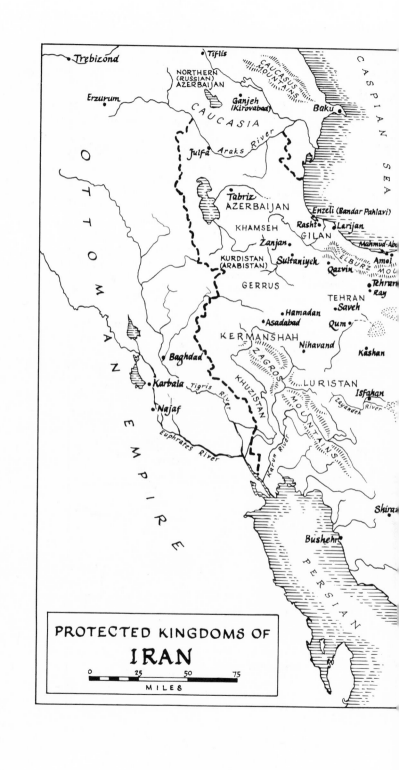

PROTECTED KINGDOMS OF

IRAN

0   25   50   75

MILES

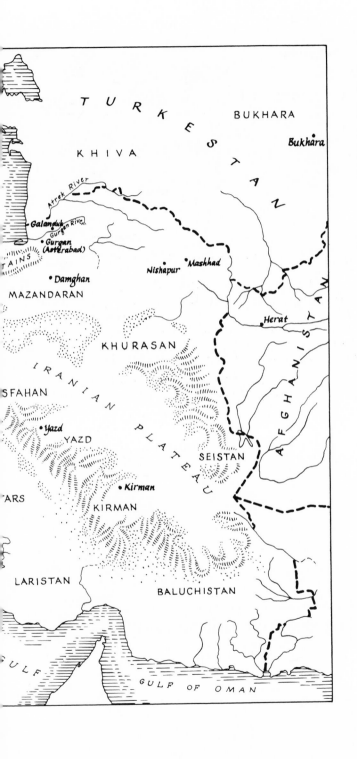

Camels had not been seen or known in the countries of Mazandaran and Gilan until six years ago, because camels could not cross the Sarkulā and Mankulā Hizārcham, Khazarān, and other mountains. When six years ago the roads of Hizārcham and Kandūn were built with the help of Albert Kastig [Albert Castiger], the German, it became possible to take camels there, and it was regarded as a rarity and object of wonderment.

Taqī Khān Ansārī-yi Kāshānī, "Jānivarnāmeh," 1287/1870, Majlis Library, Tehran, Iran

INTRODUCTION

In 1870 a young Iranian of modest background, Mīrzā Huseyn Khān, was presented with an opportunity to regenerate Iran. During the next ten years he introduced regulations that were designed to transform the country's traditional political, military, and judicial institutions to resemble Western models. He also attempted to introduce Western cultural innovations and Westernized modes of thought. His efforts are the main focus of this study, but it will be useful first to look at the traditions he sought to change, to see the country as it was in 1870.

Geography and General Historical Trends

By 1870 the Protected Kingdoms of Iran covered an area almost equal in size to the present state of Iran, an area of 628,000 miles— about three times the size of France. The frontiers were well defined, except in the east. In the north, Iran shared with the Russian Empire a long border along the Caucasus, the Caspian Sea, and Turkmenistan. On the southern frontier, the Persian Gulf and the Gulf of Oman provided access to the open seas. To the east was Afghanistan, and the southeastern border was still in dispute between Iran and British India.[1]

In that vast area, which included all of the Iranian Plateau, only about 20 percent of the total land surface was arable.[2] The Elburz and Zagros Mountain ranges, which run along the country's borders, prevented moisture from the Caspian and other seas from reaching the interior; and two impenetrable deserts covered about 70 percent of the inner plateau. With the exception of the Caspian coast and a small area along the Karun River in Khuzistan, only scattered valleys near the mountains and occasional oases had sufficient water from rain or *qanāts* for settlements.[3] Qanats or underground conduits supplied 75 percent of Iran's water for irrigation and household consumption. For thousands of years the irrigation system had counterbalanced the disadvantage of scanty and highly seasonal rainfall (only about six inches a year in central and southeastern Iran).[4]

Most Iranian towns, like Isfahan, Shiraz, Kashan, Yazd, Kirman, Hamadan, Qazvin, Tabriz, Ray (the predecessor of Tehran), and Nishapur (the predecessor of Mashhad) were built on the sites of much earlier settlements. Throughout the centuries the crucial factor in the siting of towns was the availability of water; to a large extent that is still true.

If Iranian towns owed their origin to the availability of water, they owed their greatness to trade, which transformed simple settlements into renowned and prosperous cities recognizable in the early and middle Islamic periods. The Iranian Plateau was at the crossroads of trade between China and India to the east and Africa, the Fertile Crescent, and an increasingly prosperous Europe to the south and west. The two most important trade routes, the Silk Routes, ran through Iranian cities: the northern route from Asia Minor (Mesopotamia) over the Zagros and east through Qazvin, Tehran, Damghan, and Mashhad; the southern route from Tehran in the north through Qum, Khashan, Isfahan, Yazd, and Kirman to the Indian subcontinent.[5]

Terrain and location on the trade routes also influenced the types of settlements formed in Iran. Distance forced most early settlers to become self-sufficient. As life in the settlements became more complex and specialization developed, one particular point in the settled area gained ascendancy and dominated its hinterland, taking all its surplus production in exchange for administration, protection, and handicrafts.[6] Trade did the rest, reaching a height during the early and middle Islamic periods, when in the late eleventh century the city of Nishapur rivaled Baghdad in wealth, population, and culture.[7]

Location on the trade routes encouraged Iranian cities to develop commodities that could be transported to far-off markets. Most of the cities became craft centers. So valuable and beautiful were Iranian products that craftsmen were the only segment of the population to be spared by the Mongols in their repeated attacks on Iranian cities during the first part of the thirteenth century. That the Iranian Plateau owed its prosperity to trade is clear from the fact that even after the Mongols had irreparably damaged the irrigation system, especially in Khurasan, the richest province, the country's economic base was strong enough to support the creation of the Safavid Empire, which equaled in wealth and cultural achievement any of the pre-Mongol states.

Two events of great significance for subsequent periods occurred during the reign of the Safavids. The first was the imposition of Shiʿism on Iranians, most of whom were Sunnis, by Shah Ismaʿil (1501–24), the founder of the dynasty. Shiʿism, which had hitherto consisted of a body of religious doctrines, now became identified with a political entity. It took some time for Shiʿism to become widely accepted by the people within the official boundaries of Iran. But those living within Shiʿi boundaries were isolated by the opposition and enmity of the surrounding Turkish-speaking Sunni states, the Uzbeks to the north and the Ottomans to the west, who regarded the Safavid brand of Shiʿism heretical and politically dangerous. By the time of the Qajars, this forced isolation had resulted in the emergence of a religious, cultural, and linguistic identity that set the people of the Iranian Plateau apart from their neighbors and, indeed, from any other Muslim land. The people of Qajar Iran thought of themselves as Persians.[8]

The second development of consequence was the discovery of the sea routes by the Portuguese at the end of the fifteenth century. Increased dependence on the sea meant a lessened dependence on the land for interregional trade. Gradually but steadily the cities of the Iranian Plateau declined, especially those to the north, like Bukhara and Samarqand. But this process did not affect the prosperity of Iranian cities while the Safavid dynasty was in power.

By the end of the eighteenth century, however, the damage from loss of trade was apparent. The fall of the Safavids in 1624 and the resultant intermittent war for the rest of the century accelerated the decline of Iranian cities, with the exception of Mashhad and Shiraz, the capitals of the Afshar and Zand dynasties. When the first Qajar ruler, Āghā Muhammad Khān, ascended the throne in 1794, he found the country less prosperous and smaller in territory than it had been a century earlier. In the interim, Europe had emerged as the superior force on the world scene, and any country that did not share its civilization, including Iran, was at a disadvantage.

During the nineteenth century, following a world-wide trend, Iran's foreign trade began to expand slowly and steadily. Though the rate of expansion was only twelvefold, compared with twentyfold for the Ottoman Empire and sixtyfold for Egypt, this development nevertheless had important repercussions for Iran's social and economic conditions.[9]

One of the important consequences of this expansion of foreign trade was the country's increased dependence upon cheaply made manufactured goods—especially various types of cloth—from England. Those local crafts and industries that could not compete effectively suffered, as did the towns that relied on those crafts. The fate of Isfahan was typical. At the beginning of the nineteenth century, Isfahan was still "the greatest city in Iran, a population of approximately 200,000, and having no rival."[10] By 1870 travelers were reporting empty bazaars and a population of 70,000. Cloth manufacture, the most important cottage industry in the country, was hardest hit. "In Shiraz, formerly there were five hundred weavers' factories; there are now only about ten, and these make a coarse fabric called Kerbas."[11]

Another factor that contributed to the decline of cities such as Isfahan and Shiraz and the southern provinces was the opening of the Trebizond-Tabriz route. This new route attracted much of the trade that had hitherto passed through the Persian Gulf, a shift that proved beneficial to the towns located along its course. One of the most prosperous of these towns was Tabriz, which was "situated at the junction of the high roads leading to Tehran, from Tiflis on the north and Trebizond on the West."[12] It had become the depot for European trade with most of Iran. With a population of 200,000, by the 1870s it had become the largest city in Iran.[13]

During the first part of the nineteenth century, Iran, because of its remoteness from Europe, its impoverishment, and its mountains, held no attraction for outside powers. Except for the loss of northern Azerbaijan to Russia in the wars of 1815 and 1828 and brief skirmishes with Britain over Herat, Iran, despite its weakened military power, was left relatively undisturbed. Though the Qajars never acquired sufficient resources to establish a strong central administration and military power, their rule over the country was not seriously challenged. To be sure, other contenders opposed every new ruler after Agha Muhammad Khan, but no adversary succeeded in raising an army large enough to challenge the heir effectively. Therefore, the fourth Qajar ruler Nāsir ed-Dīn Shah seemed relatively safe when the 1870s began, in spite of a lack of two prerequisites for a strong government: a powerful army and a full treasury.

However, especially during the first part of the nineteenth century, this political weakness prevented the government from acquiring the resources to build an effective central control and a military capability to maintain that control. Figures at several intervals during the nineteenth century show a decline in the revenue of the central government. This was placed at £2.9 million sterling when Sir John Malcolm visited the country in 1810–11. Fraser's estimate of 2.5 million tumans (£1.5 million sterling) for fixed revenue in 1820 was perhaps much smaller due to the Russo-Persian wars. Fifty years later, in 1869, the total fixed revenue was placed at about 5 million tumans (£1,965,000 sterling). In real terms, the fixed revenue between 1810 and 1869 remained the same in terms of sterling; but, in spite of the evident numerical increase in tumans, the fixed revenue actually declined due to the depreciation of Iranian currency. The decrease in government revenue occurred at a time when the size of the bueaucracy had expanded considerably. It is not surprising, therefore, that those who depended upon the government for their livelihood could not make ends meet: "The Nobles, and particularly the officers of government, are in truth kept wretchedly poor! There is hardly one of them who is not deeply and ruinously in debt." [14]

Although Fath-ʿAlī Shah impressed European visitors with his legendary crown jewels, his central treasury rarely had adequate funds to meet all necessary expenses. Toward the end of his reign, the cost of the lengthy wars with Russia and the inability of the central government to collect sufficient revenue caused a great shortage of funds. This shortage was also characteristic of the reign of Muhammad Shah, who had to deal with repeated financial crises. [15]

Nasir ed-Din Shah's parsimony reversed this trend temporarily; and around 1869 Thompson, the secretary of the British legation, remarked that the shah's treasury received an annual surplus of £200,000 sterling. However, as the seventies began, the future of the state's finances looked precarious. A series of failures of the silk crop, Iran's main export, had drastically reduced the production of silk in Gilan, the main silk-producing region. Export figures reveal the severity of the decline: in 1864 Iran's total export was estimated at £600,000, of which £502,000 was for the sale of silk; in 1871 the total export volume was £340,000, and only £119,000 was for the sale of silk. [16]

Furthermore, the country had suffered two consecutive years of drought that had destroyed the agriculture in many regions and had caused serious famine in the land. This was an added and more serious cause of the decline in government revenue, which came primarily from the peasantry.[17] As the famine worsened and the tax collectors attempted to get anything possible from the starving population, thousands of peasants and artisans migrated to neighboring countries.[18] This created a vicious circle—most noticeably in agriculture—which did not abate for at least another decade. An Iranian engineer traveling in Khuzistan in the late 1870s commented that due to the migration of many farmers much of the fertile land in that province had been laid waste.[19]

Iran could ill afford a drain on its able-bodied manpower. Though there were no census data, the population in 1870 was estimated to be between 4,400,000 and 7,000,000.[20] In comparison with England's population of 310 per square mile, Iran's population was only 7 to 10 per square mile. About 25 percent of the population of Iran lived in urban centers with more than 5,000 inhabitants. Tabriz had 200,000 inhabitants, Tehran—the capital—about 85,000, and Isfahan and a few other towns 70,000. The rest were little more than villages.[21] Another 25 percent of the population were members of nomadic and seminomadic tribes, who lived mainly in Fars and Isfahan and were virtually independent of any control by the central authorities of the capital. The remainder lived in villages and hamlets.

The village formed the basic social and economic unit because agriculture and related activities provided occupation for 90 percent of the population. Most of the tax revenue (less than £2 million annually) came from the land, either through taxation or the sale of export products such as cotton, raw silk, wool, opium, fruit, and tobacco. The revenue was supplied by the lowest classes of society—artisans, shopkeepers, and agriculturists—whether settled or nomad.[22] The population of a village consisted of small landowners, peasant proprietors, agricultural laborers, shopkeepers, and members of the clergy. However, most villages and the surrounding lands belonged not to the villagers but to the government or absentee landlords who usually lived in the capital.

At this time all villages and land in the country fell into three categories of ownership. The first and largest landholder was the crown. Sometimes, as in the case of Khuzistan, an entire province could be considered *khāsseh* or crown land. In practice the crown usually allowed local grandees to act as owners as long as the rent was paid.[23] Some of the khasseh land was granted to tribes in return for the provision of soldiers. It was also fairly common to grant the revenues of a specific district to a high government official or prince in lieu of salary.

A second type of landholding called *vaqf* was in some cases extensive, as in Khurasan. The vaqf or dedication of revenues from land or property for religious purposes was an old Islamic tradition and was exempt from taxation. Many families designated their land as vaqf and appointed their descendants as trustees, thus safeguarding their possessions and securing exemption from taxation.[24]

The third type of landholding was private ownership of land that had been acquired by inheritance, purchase, gift of the crown, or reclamation from the desert. Most of this land belonged to a small number of absentee landlords, who managed their estates through *mubāshirs* or overseers. Small landowners were few, but most villagers cultivated the land either as subtenants or as agricultural workers.[25]

Most villages were located near a town that controlled the land and its produce. A small town was in turn controlled by a larger town, usually the main town in the province. Iran was divided into five *mamlikats* or provinces and thirty subprovinces, hence the name *Mamālik-i Mahrūseh-yi Irān* or Protected Kingdoms of Iran.[26]

Although the capital towns within the provinces and subprovinces controlled their areas, they in turn were controlled by certain groups within their populations, including the merchants, the ⁽ulamā or clergy, and the political elite. Lines of demarcation between these groups were indefinite; intermarriage between the ⁽ulama and the other groups was common, and mutual interest connected them at various points in the network they formed. The main point of similarity between them, as an English traveler noted, was that "the great nobles and wealthy merchants pay nothing to the exchequer." [27] This exemption from taxation applied as well to the ⁽ulama and the vaqf properties they supervised. Members of these three groups were among Iran's major landowning families. An examination of each group in turn may improve our understanding of them.

Perhaps the most respected part of Iranian society was the merchant class. Unlike Egypt and the Ottoman Empire, Iranian trade remained in indigenous hands. Consequently, as the country's trade with the outside world expanded, merchants and other urban groups, who either controlled or were involved in trade, were able to enhance their position of wealth and social power.[28]

During the last quarter of the nineteenth century in Iran, an increase in activity within the merchant class led to the creation of substantial capitalists. Most notable among these was Hājjī Muhammad Hasan Amīn uz-Zarb, who had agents in all major Iranian towns and also engaged in widespread trade abroad.[29] Even though not all traders were of Amin uz-Zarb's caliber, they still played a significant role in the life of the country.

The line dividing large landowners from large merchants was blurred. Large landowners sometimes personally supervised the sale of their products. Rich merchants in their turn might invest surplus capital in land; this gave them greater control over the means of production and also brought them additional social prestige.

Small and medium traders connected the villages and towns; large traders connected the towns and the outside world. Since merchants held a considerable portion of Iran's liquid assets, they served as bankers for rich and poor alike, even supplying capital to members of the ruling class. It was also usually the merchant who, through one of his agents, relayed monies to those government employees who had been granted the taxes of an area in lieu of salary.[30]

High officials were usually recruited from families with great landholdings or with a long tradition of civil service.[31] Humble origin did not prevent men of ability from rising, as did Amīr Kabīr, Nasir ed-Din Shah's first *sadr-i aʿzam* or grand vizier;[32] however, the right connections were helpful. Appointment to high office usually required know-how—which most bureaucratic families guarded jealously—and enough wealth to present to the sovereign and other high officials a substantial sum at the time of appointment.

The most powerful group in society was undoubtedly the ʿulama. If the merchants owed their importance to their wealth and usefulness, the ʿulama's power sprang from their spiritual and moral ascendancy. In the absence of the *twelfth iman,* whom the Shiʿites regarded as their rightful temporal and spiritual leader, the ʿulama acted as his regents. The Shiʿites believed that Muhammad al-Muntazar, who was their twelfth *imam*—leader of prayer and of the Islamic community—had disappeared from public view in 273 A.D. and would one day reappear to fill the world with justice.

Like the Catholic Church of the Middle Ages, the Shiʿite ʿulama of the Qajar period had resigned themselves to rendering to Caesar his dues and had no pretensions to worldly sovereignty.[33] On the other hand, the rulers had resolved, out of convenience or conviction, to respect the moral authority of the ʿulama as their spiritual mentors. Yet conflict arose, as it did during the reign of Muhammad Shah, Nasir ed-Din's father, or when Amir Kabir was in power, when the state tried to subordinate the ʿulama to its authority.[34] By 1870 a truce was established, and the state agreed to forego both its intention to promote the secular ʿurf courts at the expense of the religious sharʿ courts and the close control over vaqf revenues instituted by Amir Kabir.[35]

The ʿulama derived their power from two sources: (1) their role as spiritual leaders, in which they interpreted the shariʿa or religious law, administered the sharʿ courts, and controlled the schools; and (2) their role as administrators of the wealth of religious institutions, which included revenues from the vaqf, the zakāt and khums, both forms of religious taxation, and private contributions. The ʿulama were, on the whole, a tightly knit group and probably the largest professional group in Iran. All these factors added up to a potential for considerable power. For instance, Nasir ed-Din Shah, upon hearing of the death of Mīrzā Siyyid Muhammad, imam jumʿeh of Isfahan,[36] is reported to have said, "Praise be to God; today I can claim that Isfahan belongs to me." [37]

Certain members of the ʿulama used their power to amass great wealth, which they invested in land. Siyyid Muhammad Bāqir Shaftī Hujjat ul-Islām, who dominated the life of Isfahan until his death during the reign of Muhammad Shah, accumulated four hundred caravansaries, two thousand shops in Isfahan, and many villages not only near Isfahan but also in nearby regions. Rather than detracting from the esteem in which he was held, his great wealth enhanced it.[38] The reason for the apparent contradiction was that the great mujtahids, men of exceptional religious learning, avoided connection with those in power. The people regarded the mujtahids as their protectors, men who intervened on their behalf with government officials up to the shah.[39]

Finally, we turn to the social group that held political control. This group consisted of the ruler, his household, ranking members of the administration, and tribal leaders. They controlled the process of taxation and were the main beneficiaries of its revenues. Like members of the other two groups, they paid no taxes, and most of the privately owned land belonged to them.

Control of power and control of land were easily reconciled. Since it was customary to present the king or his provincial representative, the governor, with a present in the form of cash for most appointments to political office, only those with means, usually drawn from the land, could afford to seek office. Since such appointment was also the surest way to increase wealth for investment in more land, landowners were anxious to be appointed, and most of those who possessed large estates participated in political success.

This situation contradicts the notion, popular with European travelers in nineteenth century Iran, that the Qajar rulers were despots who held unlimited power over the life and property of their subjects. Although the government was, and had long been, an absolute monarchy that was in theory unlimited, in actual practice the monarch's power was substantially limited. As a Muslim he had to abide by the injunctions of the sharīʿa. He had to tread carefully where interests of the ʿulama might be endangered, for they were a powerful pressure group. He also had to take into account the interests of those upon whom he relied for control of his realm, the large landowners, princes of the Qajar tribe, and other tribal leaders.

By the second half of the nineteenth century, as revenues from trade dwindled and dependence upon the land for tax monies increased, the ruler needed the cooperation of these powerful groups more than ever to maintain his authority. To make matters worse, Nasir ed-Din Shah's effective military force was limited to his own bodyguards and one artillery regiment, a total of about seven thousand men.[40] Under the circumstances, the real condition of the ruler was far removed from the pomp that surrounded his person and the precious verbal homage paid him by his courtiers. Only the fact that the elite were not really unified in goal but, rather, were split into factions prevented the shah from being nothing more than a puppet.

One faction consisted of the leading families of the great tribes, the Afshārs, the Bakhtīyarīs, the Qashqāʾīs, the Kurds, the Arabs, and the Turkomans. These families actually controlled one-fourth of the population of Iran, the nomads. A visitor commented: "Their chiefs are possessed of great authority over the tribesmen, and all dealings between the government and the tribes are carried on through the heads of these divisions. Through the chief the taxes, whether in money or in kind, are paid, and through him the regiments which his tribe may furnish are recruited."[41] These tribes had played a role in Iranian history since the eleventh century; their support had brought the Qajars to the throne after the civil wars in the second half of the eighteenth century. Tribal militia continued to be important in the Iranian armed forces. Maintenance of good relations with tribal leaders was vital. Powerless to subordinate the tribes, the ruler was forced to grant their leaders virtual autonomy in exchange for cooperation.[42]

Nasir ed-Din Shah's relationship with Huseynqulī Khān Bakhtīyarī was typical. The Bakhtiyari tribe inhabited parts of Isfahan and Fars provinces. When Huseynquli Khan emerged as *ilbīgī* or tribal leader after destroying all contenders, Nasir ed-Din Shah officially invested him with that title. The shah was not able to expel the tribe from their new grazing grounds in Khuzistan, even though their presence created much hardship for the smaller Arab tribes settled there.[43] Although Huseynquli Khan was no threat to the throne, in the areas under Bakhtiyari control he could act in virtual independence, and the shah was content to receive the surplus taxation. (*Coercion*)

Another faction that exerted considerable political and social influence was the official class, which assisted the sovereign in governing the state. During this period, the bureaucratic machinery, which was similar in organization and function to that of the Safavid and earlier periods but smaller, was usually, but not always, headed by a sadr-i aᶜzam or grand vizier. Just below the grand vizier were several ministers, the most important of them the *mustowfī ul-mamālik,* who headed the department of finance.

Most members of the bureaucracy resided, like the shah, in the capital. This concentration of power, based on wealth, administrative experience, and numbers, could be a threat to the authority of any ruler, but several factors offset the inherent danger. Because the functions and responsibilities of offices and departments were not clearly defined, an official derived his status from his closeness to the ruler, who determined all appointments, no matter how minor. Furthermore, there was no coordination in the work of the various ministers, each of whom had to refer to the monarch in all affairs of state. The situation caused great confusion as well as jealousy and rivalry, but it worked in the shah's favor by giving him ultimate control. Nasir ed-Din Shah resorted to the ancient practice of spying to ensure the loyalty of his officials.[44]

The final faction consisted of high princes of the Qajar tribe, some of whom occupied positions of great wealth and power. Of Turkic origin, the tribe had come to the Iranian Plateau during or shortly after the Mongol invasions; it is mentioned in the *Il Khanid* and the *Timurid* chronicles.[45] But it was during the Safavid period that the Qajars, helping to secure Safavid power, came into prominence. With the fall of the Safavids in 1724, the Qajar leaders became principal contenders for the throne. When Agha Muhammad Khan Qajar proclaimed himself ruler in 1794, the main body of the tribe withdrew to their ancestral pasture grounds in Asterabad, near Gurgan, leaving many of their leaders in the new capital, Tehran.

Although members of the Qajar aristocracy were assimilated fairly readily into the landed and bureaucratic families with which they became associated, some tribal customs lingered and affected their manner of government. Important to the nomadic tradition was the insistence that any territory controlled by the tribe belonged to all of its members. Like the Saljuqs and other pre-Safavid tribal dynasties, the Qajars appointed their own important princes and provincial governors. In 1870 the provinces of Azerbaijan, Khurasan, Isfahan, Fars, and Kurdistan were all governed by sons or uncles of the shah. Each governor controlled taxation and was commander of the provincial army. Power combined with inaccessibility gave each governor virtual autonomy. All princes, with the exception of Muzaffar ed-Dīn Mīrzā, the crown prince and governor of Azerbaijan, used their privileged positions to amass great wealth. Although by 1870 Nasir ed-Din Shah was established as the legitimate ruler, in the absence of definitive rules of succession, he could never feel totally secure. Both he and his predecessors had had to put down several contenders before accession.[46] His younger brother, ʿAbbās Mīrzā, who was living in exile in Baghdad under Ottoman protection, might well have been appointed the heir had their father lived longer. Perhaps the reason no Iranian ruler had dared travel to Europe was that "the risk of finding his throne threatened by others is at all times too great to admit of the Shah venturing to leave Persia." [47]

The position of Nasir ed-Din Shah was far from enviable. He lacked the means to assert control over all these factions, but he also knew he needed their help in maintaining a semblance of sovereignty. The shah's predicament was observed by his private physician:

> Despite the numerous men in his service, Nasir ed-Din Shah is the worst served master. No one follows his injunctions, and none of his rules, announced in the official newspaper are heeded. Of course, all his orders are met with the formula, "Yes, Sir, may I be your sacrifice." But often his men evade his orders by various excuses. He is very well aware of this,

but to avoid having to punish evaders, he rarely enquires whether or not his orders have been executed. He purposely takes refuge in the obviously contrary notion that he is an independent sovereign; whereas in reality, he is a ball in the hands of other players.[48]

The shah devoted most of his energy to keeping the various forces in balance. A man of stronger character might have attempted to rise above this state, but Nasir ed-Din Shah had a tendency to put his safety above all other considerations. His inability to initiate any action or to take any risks had an important bearing on the sequence of events in the 1870s. It is therefore helpful to understand the shah and his motivations to understand those events.

The Shah

Muhammad Shah's first son, Nasir ed-Din Shah, was born in 1247/1831, in a small village near Tabriz.[49] Although his mother, Mahd-i ʿUlyā, was a Qajar princess, his father "disliked both the young prince and his mother." [50] According to Polak, who has left us a valuable account of the early period of Nasir ed-Din's reign, Muhammad Shah doubted that he was the prince's father. Nasir ed-Din "was rarely allowed to come to his father's presence, and was ill-treated by everyone." [51] When Nasir ed-Din reached adolescence, he was appointed governor of Azerbaijan, where Qajar crown princes were sent to gain experience in rulership. But, in the view of Polak and perhaps Nasir ed-Din, it was more a form of banishment, since the prince was totally forgotten by his father after he left Tehran. During his stay in Tabriz, the provincial capital, Nasir ed-Din was not paid an adequate allowance, and he lived in abject poverty. "He was so poor that he could hardly afford to pay his servants or to refurbish their worn uniforms. The few friends who had gathered around him in the hope of future gain suffered from poverty like the prince." [52]

Several contemporaries have suggested that Muhammad Shah intended to pass the succession to his younger son, ʿAbbas Mirza, who was only nine when his father died suddenly in 1848.[53] These rumors and his father's general attitude left an indelible scar on Nasir ed-Din. The years of poverty and humiliation might also account for his later parsimony and love of precious stones.[54]

Nasir ed-Din often recalled his childhood with bitterness. "One day the shah portrayed the caricature of an ugly-looking child to his courtiers and asked them to identify that boy. No one dared express an opinion. Finally the shah said, "That was the way I looked as a child.' " [55] Since various portraits of him at different periods show that he was handsome throughout his life, the incident says more about how he felt about himself than about how he looked.[56] His uncertainty and lack of self-confidence during the early years of his reign made Nasir ed-Din Shah shy and awkward. He later learned to hide his shyness under an air of reserve, but he continued to waver in character and to have difficulty in making decisions. His private correspondence often contains appeals like "You know how difficult it is for me to decide. Tell me what should be done." [57]

Because of the early neglect and humiliation he suffered, Nasir ed-Din Shah found it difficult to love or trust anyone. Polak remarked, "He does not love anyone, neither his wives, with the exception of one, nor any of his men." [58] In Polak's opinion the shah held a low opinion of most men, "In his view, men are solely motivated by personal interests." [59] The exceptions were the shah's wife Jayrān and his first sadr-i aʿzam, Mīrzā Taqī Khān Amīr Kabīr.

Amir Kabir, who was twenty-five years older than the shah, met him in the days of banishment in Tabriz. Although little is known of the early history of the relationship, it is clear that Amir's efficient handling of the events following Muhammad Shah's death in 1848 secured the throne for Nasir ed-Din Shah. His statesmanship also averted civil war and bankruptcy and helped to develop a strong central government with an adequate army.[60] Yet none of these services, great though they were, can explain adequately the great devotion of the young ruler for his minister. Amir Kabir may well have fulfilled the needs that were not met in Nasir ed-Din's relationship with his father. Fereydoun Adamiyat, the authority on Amir Kabir and his period, has noted: "Amir's relationship with the shah was that of a father with a son, characterized by deep affection without any trace of formality. In Amir's correspondence with the shah, the harshest reproofs and deepest affection are expressed." [61]

The shah gave his only full sister, ʿIzzat ud-Dowleh, to Amir in marriage, but the unusual relationship between the two men aroused the jealousy of many courtiers, including the shah's mother, Mahd-i ʿUlya, and her favorite, Mīrzā Āqā Khān Nūrī. For three years they tried without success to cloud the mind of the young ruler before they finally found the Achilles heel in the relationship. They accused Amir of conspiring to bring ʿAbbas Mirza to the throne.[62] In less than a month Amir was removed from his post and put to death. The shah wept copiously as he signed the death warrant, which the opposition made certain was carried out within a few hours, on 17 Rabiʿ ul-Avval/10 January 1852.[63] So hasty a decision to do away with a man who was deeply loved and totally trusted is difficult to comprehend, yet it is not totally out of character. Polak remarked: "[The shah] is not cruel by nature. But whenever his person or the interests of the country are endangered, he does not hesitate to shed blood, as was the case with the execution of his beloved tutor and benefactor." [64]

Nasir ed-Din Shah never ceased to regret the death of Amir, which he attributed to his own youthful folly;[65] for many years he wore black on the anniversary of the death.[66] The experience made him doubly cynical of the courtiers "with whom he was surrounded after Amir's fall from power and death. To gain their pettiest favors, they resorted to untold excesses in flattering the shah; and to promote their slightest ends, they encouraged the shah to act with the greatest degree of whim in the affairs of state." [67] The shah was extremely sensitive and intelligent, but he flattered his courtiers in return and granted their favors, "so that they would not betray or hurt him." [68]

Although he diverted himself with women, hunting, traveling, and reform experiments, he must have suffered deeply from isolation and the lack of someone trustworthy, with whom he could share his thoughts. Then, twenty years after Amir's death, about 1870, he seemed to have found a new friend in Mīrzā Huseyn Khān Mushīr ud-Dowleh, his ambassador to the Ottoman Empire. After a brief trial of this new man's ability, he entrusted all the affairs of his ancient though decaying kingdom to him, giving him extensive authority to revive the country. Mirza Huseyn Khan proposed to transform the country and recreate it in the image of the West.

Early Reforms. Earlier attempts had been made to lay foundations Western in origin and manner to improve conditions in Iran and extend contact with the Western world. But throughout most of the eighteenth century, Iranian leaders were involved with internal problems and consequently were oblivious to developments that were changing the face of Europe. Not until the reign of the second Qajar ruler, Fath-ʿAli Shah (1797–1834), did Iranians become aware of the emergence of a new type of power in the West.[69] This awareness was brought home by Russia's two defeats of Iran, which resulted in the Treaty of Gulistan in 1813 and the Treaty of Turkmanchay in 1828, both of which required the surrender of territories in the rich northwestern part of Iran.

These defeats naturally alerted the Iranian leaders who had directed the wars against Russia—notably crown prince ʿAbbas Mirza and his minister, Qāʼimmaqām—to the superiority of Western military techniques. These two men hired European instructors and sent seven students in two missions to study in England; however, not much came of this because of the prince's premature death in 1834. Neither Fath-ʿAli Shah nor his heir, Muhammad Shah (1834–48), showed any predilection for European reforms, and the interest in reform was not revived until the reign of Nasir ed-Din Shah (1848–96).

This renewal of interest under Nasir ed-Din Shah was initiated by Amir Kabir, who had been raised in the household of Qāʼimmaqām. He had also visited Russia as a member of a mission that was sent to present formal apologies for the death of the Russian ambassador, Griboidov, at the hands of mobs in Tehran in 1244/1828–29.[70] That mission spent eighteen months in Moscow, visiting scientific institutions, factories, schools, and military academies. Recording the impressions of the group, the secretary of the mission, Mīrzā Mustafā Khan Afshār, compared Russian progress with Iranian backwardness and commented on the indifference of his country's leaders:

> It is a pity that we should witness with our own eyes the advancement and order that our neighbor has achieved in a short period and should not do the same, but merely to continue our visits to foreign lands, our heads bent with shame at seeing our countrymen sold in the bazaars of Khiva and Bukhara. . . . A chronicle has no business talking in this vein, but since this humble servant has the love of the fatherland [*vatan*] and concern for religion [*taʼassub-i dīn*] at heart, he has allowed himself the liberty of expressing these opinions, in the hope that they would help increase the might of his government and religion.[71]

Amir Kabir's knowledge of the reforms undertaken by Iran's neighbors increased during a four-year stay in the Ottoman Empire. He went there as Iran's representative to the Erzurum Conference, held from 1259/1844 to 1263/1848, to try to solve the Irano-Ottoman border disputes.[72] His apprenticeship with Qāʼimmaqām and his observations in Russia and the Ottoman Empire inspired him with ideas for reform.[73] However, his efforts were also a response to an increasingly felt need for reform that had intermittently expressed itself in violent eruptions on the seemingly calm surface of Iranian society in the 1840s.

These demands for reform found expression in religious form, as had also been true in the preceding Islamic society. The most important of these was the Babi movement, which originated in 1260/1844 with the claim of Siyyid ʿAlī-Muhammad of Shiraz to be the long-awaited *mahdī*, the twelfth Shiʿite imam, who according to Shiʿi belief would appear when the world was filled with injustice. Siyyid ʿAli-Muhammad, more commonly known as the Bāb, was of merchant stock.[74] After receiving some religious education in Karbala, he returned to his native Shiraz and at the age of twenty-four proclaimed himself the initiator of a new social and religious era, thereby claiming the right to interpret religion in a different fashion.

Although it is difficult to determine the extent of the Bab's following, his adherents in the urban centers were numerous enough to cause concern in the government.[75] To combat the spread of Babism, Muhammad Shah had the Bab arrested and imprisoned, but this did not abate the popularity of the new prophet. Nasir ed-Din Shah's accession to the throne provided the followers of the Bab, who had broken away from Islam in that year, with an opportunity to declare war on Islam. The provinces of Yazd, Kirman, and Mazandaran became centers of Babi activity and insurrection, while the city of Zanjan became a Babi stronghold. The Bab was finally shot in 1850, and thousands of his followers were killed before the movement was contained. However, its extraordinary, if short-lived, success among the urban population and the messianic nature of the Babi claims indicate dissatisfaction with the state of affairs in Iran, particularly in the cities.

Amir Kabir's reforms were motivated by a keen awareness of the country's mood. It was not an accident that his policies were especially favorable to the commercial class.[76] To alleviate the condition of those craftsmen who had suffered from foreign competition he tried, with some degree of success, to protect the domestic crafts, especially the manufacture of cloth, and to set up new factories for the production of consumer goods such as glass and sugar. The high esteem in which he was held by the various classes of society attests his sensitivity to the needs of the period.

With his appointment to the office of sadr-i aʿzam in 1264/1848, a period of accelerated reform began in Iran. When Amir Kabir accompanied the seventeen-year-old Nasir ed-Din Shah to Tehran, the country was facing civil war, the treasury was empty, and there was no army to speak of. Amir Kabir put down the rebellion; straightened out the country's finances; strengthened and reorganized the army; founded factories for the production of such goods as ammunition, sugar, glass, and cloth; built many dams; enforced the laws of the country; and passed strict measures to end corruption and bribery within the government. All this he achieved in less than three years. But his most important contribution was the emphasis he placed upon the acquisition of European knowledge and science.[77]

To promote the spread of modern knowledge, Amir Kabir founded the first modern school, Dār ul-Funūn, the House of the Arts, which opened in 1851, shortly after the death of its founder. With one hundred fifty students and a six- to eight-year course, the school was designed to teach military science, engineering, mathematics, drafting, mining, physics, pharmacology, and medicine—a curriculum completely outside the control of the ʿulama. European instructors were hired. The school's name and curriculum were similar to those of a school opened in Istanbul in 1845.[78] The similarity was not accidental. The Ottoman Empire was one important channel through which European ideas were transmitted to Iran in the nineteenth century, and Iranian advocates of reform like ʿAbbas Mirza, Qa'immaqam, Amir Kabir, and those who succeeded them (such as Malkam Khān, Mīrzā Yūsuf Khan Mustashār ud-Dowleh, and Mirza Huseyn Khan) used their coreligionists and rivals, the Ottomans, as the inspiration and model for some of their programs.[79] The Dar ul-Funun may not have been impressive on European terms, but its social and intellectual consequences were considerable. It set new standards by which traditional knowledge and methods of education could be judged, revealing deficiencies in the old methods. It accelerated the translation of books from European languages into Persian, thus introducing new ideas to a wider section of the society.

Amir Kabir set an impressive record during his three years in power. But he made no attempt to fundamentally change the country's institutions or totally transform its systems, as later advocates of reform proposed. Instead, he tried only to render the existing system more efficient by ending abusive practices in the judicial system and by introducing a few European technical innovations and institutions. Although he went much further than Qa'immaqam or ʿAbbas Mirza, the European features of his reforms, as in the earlier phase, fitted easily into the existing framework. Perhaps the reason his reforms were so greatly admired by contemporaries and later generations was simply that they did not attempt to create sharp departures from the accepted practices of Iranian society.

Amir Kabir's successor, Mirza Aqa Khan Nuri, was more interested in promoting his own and his family's welfare than that of the state. He encouraged Nasir ed-Din Shah to be merry, advising him, "May I be Your Sacrifice, why do you want to bother with watching the army practicing? Take a few women and go have a good time." [80] For a while the shah complied with the advice of his sadr-i a°zam, who had appointed most of his relatives, including two sons, to high office. But although the shah could be influenced, he was an astute man; and he was aware that the reforms of his friend and tutor Amir Kabir were gradually being undone. In a letter to Mirza Aqa Khan, he expressed concern over the deterioration of the affairs of government and pointed out the change in attitude of the British minister, who had grown increasingly less respectful.[81] Then, in 1858, when the sadr-i a°zam failed to convince the British to allow Iran to keep the newly conquered city of Herat, Nasir ed-Din Shah dismissed Aqa Khan and banished him from Tehran.

After Aqa Khan's dismissal, the shah showed renewed interest in reform. His mood was reflected in the choice of Mīrzā Ja°far Khān Mushīr ud-Dowleh, an elder statesman with a European education known for his liberal views, as his trusted adviser.[82]

Mirza Ja°far Khan was a member of the second group of students sent to England by °Abbas Mirza in 1815. After his return to Iran, he served in the department dealing with foreign affairs. In 1836 he was sent to the Ottoman court as ambassador and remained there until 1842. In 1848 Amir Kabir assigned him a post dealing with foreign envoys in Azerbaijan and a few months later appointed him to the four-nation commission (Iran, Britain, France, and the Ottoman Empire) that was attempting to settle the Irano-Ottoman border. When he returned to Tehran in 1853, he was shunned by Amir Kabir's successor and remained unemployed until Mirza Aqa Khan's dismissal in 1858. He was then appointed president of the Government Advisory Council.[83]

The shah's new interest in reform may be accounted for in part by the loss of Herat. Both he and his father had tried to reestablish suzerainty over this city, and each had been forced by British pressure to retreat after conquering it. Then in the 1857 Treaty of Paris between Iran and Britain, Iran had to relinquish all claims to the city. The shah must have felt this loss deeply. Iranians had always regarded Herat as part of Khurasan. The shah's despondency can be judged by his physician's remark that the only thing for which Nasir ed-Din Shah was happy to spend money "was reviving the ancient borders of Iran." [84] The incident undoubtedly made the shah aware of his country's weakness and stirred in him a desire for reform.

The shah's interest in change coincided with the return to Iran of a young Iranian of Armenian descent, Malkam Khan, who had been studying in France. Malkam had been appointed instructor at the Dar ul-Funun and also did translating for the government. He was probably brought to the shah's attention by Mirza Ja'far Khan. Malkam claimed to be able to solve the problem of Iran's weakness. His solution, elaborately and eloquently argued in essays, was that Iran must adopt not only European techniques but also European institutions. If it did not follow this course, it would fall under the domination of the ever-expanding European powers who were always in search of new economic resources. [85]

The shah, who was deeply despondent over the loss of Herat and disillusioned with his sadr-i a'zam, welcomed Malkam's ideas. He abolished the post of sadr-i a'zam and replaced it in 1275/1858 with the Majlis-i Showrā-yi Dowlat or Government Advisory Council, a body consisting of a president and six ministers. [86] The ministers were to act independently of each other and to report directly to the shah, consulting each other on important matters of state. However, the duties of the ministers, the limits of their authority, and their relationship with each other were not discussed in the text of the decree announcing creation of the council. This was Iran's first attempt at cabinet government. Although it lacked a prime minister to coordinate the work of the ministers and bear final responsibility, the council was still a departure from the tradition of appointing a sadr-i a'zam and two or three officials in charge of finances and foreign affairs. It was a search for new ways.

Even more conspicuous was the creation of the Majlis-i Maslihat Khāneh (Advisory Council) or Mashvirat Khāneh-yi 'Ammeh-yi Dowlatī (General Advisory Council of the State) in 1276/1859. [87] The decree appointed twenty-five high-ranking officials and courtiers to the council, which had the authority to discuss any matter of importance to the state, with the exception of diplomatic treaties. Once a bill met the approval of the majority of the council members, it was to be viewed by the ministers. If approved by the ministers, it was to be put into effect. Despite various efforts, however, it was not until the Constitutional Revolution occurred nearly fifty years later that a lawmaking body with such wide legislative power came into existence. The decree also stated that any citizen who might present the council with a worthwhile opinion beneficial to the country or the welfare of the people would be duly rewarded by the government. This was an obvious effort to encourage public interest and participation in the affairs of the council.

The inspiration for the creation of such a council, which had no precedent in Iran's political heritage or system of government, came from Malkam Khan. The decree bears a great similarity to his essay "Tanzīm-i Lashkar va Majlis-i Idāreh," "The Organization of the Army and Administrative Council," probably written in 1273/1858. In the essay Malkam argued that the unlimited and irresponsible exercise of power, to which he attributed the unfavorable conditions in all Eastern nations, harmed not only the people but also the ruler. Although the ruler at first appeared to possess much power, he was in fact subject to the whim of his ministers and subordinates. Malkam reasoned that, since the responsibility and authority of these men were unclear, they could easily disregard the ruler's wishes and orders or abuse their power.[88] To remedy this, Malkam suggested that laws defining the authority and responsibility of members of the government be written by a council similar in conception and responsibility to the Majlis-i Tanzimat or Organizational Council. Unfortunately no contemporary sources give any information about whether the majlis was put into effect. Its fate may have been decided when the Farāmūshkhāneh, a secret society Malkam formed in 1859 or 1860, was accused of being subversive, of plotting to overthrow the monarchy, and of attempting to establish a republican form of government in Iran.[89]

Malkam, his father and brothers, and a few leaders of the society were exiled to Baghdad.[90] Shortly afterward Malkam went to Istanbul, and with the help of the Iranian ambassador there, Mirza Huseyn Khan, he regained the favor of the shah. But the allegedly subversive activities of the Faramushkhaneh had alienated Nasir ed-Din Shah from the educated classes who had made up its membership, and for nearly a decade afterward he was suspicious of anyone who advocated reform.[91] The shah's disillusionment was also detrimental to the cause of modern education. One contemporary observed:

> Nasir ed-Din Shah rarely went out for a ride without stopping at the School [Dar ul-Funun], going into the classrooms, encouraging [the students], and giving [them] presents. But after that premature event, he could not bear to hear the name of the school. . . . Nasir ed-Din Shah, who had been so eager to send students to Europe and had made that speech at the appointment of the first prefect of the school, became indifferent to European education.[92]

The shah's appointments to major positions during most of the sixties reflected this attitude. In 1279/1863 Mirza Ja°far Khan, the liberal elder statesman, was unofficially banished to Khurasan as trustee of the Shrine of Imam Riza, the eighth Shi°ite imam; and he died there.[93] The shah then appointed a triumvirate and left to it the affairs of government. The members of the group, Mīrzā Muhammad Khan Qajar Davallū, Mīrzā Yūsuf Khan Mustowfī ul-Mamālik, and Mīrzā Sa°īd Khan Ansārī, were all opposed to new ideas. In 1281/1864, Mīrzā Muhammad Khan, whom the shah's secretary, Amīn ul-Mulk, described as an "uninformed illiterate," was named sadr-i a°zam.[94] After his death the following year, his duties but not his title were given to Mirza Yusuf Khan Mustowfi ul-Mamalik.

The shah, in the meantime, returned to his leisure pursuits, especially hunting and traveling for pleasure throughout his kingdom. He grew increasingly negligent in his official duties, and his disenchantment with the educated drove him steadily closer to the ignorant, "who knew nothing, not even their birthdates, and lacked total knowledge of their country." According to Amīn ul-Mulk, they had discovered the shah's weakness, "his love of praise." [95]

Conditions within the country grew steadily worse, governors and officials became increasingly oppressive, and public discontent began to mount.[96] Finally, in 1869 a severe drought brought famine and death to thousands in the towns and villages and precipitated a crisis. This crisis shocked Nasir ed-Din Shah into a realization of the condition of his country. For his solution he turned to Mirza Huseyn Khan, his ambassador to the Ottoman court.

2

MIRZA HUSEYN KHAN: EARLY CAREER

MIRZA HUSEYN KHAN returned to Iran in December 1870 at the invitation of Nasir ed-Din Shah to help restore his waning domain.[1] At the age of forty-three Mirza Huseyn Khan had been out of the country for twenty-two years, studying in France and on government missions to India, Russia, and the Ottoman Empire. This prolonged stay in societies where man either had achieved some mastery of his fate by effectively harnessing the human and material resources available, as in the West, or was trying to emulate others who had attained that end had altered Mirza Huseyn Khan's vision of the world and of his own country, which seemed in a state of stagnation and in need of radical change. From abroad Mirza Huseyn Khan had sent home elaborate reports alerting the country's leadership to the dangers that lay ahead if they made no attempt to shake off their lethargy. He also reported the efforts being made by the Ottoman government to overcome a similar predicament.

Mirza Huseyn Khan was born in 1827. His genealogy reflects the mobility of Qajar society. His grandfather was a masseur from Qazvin, for which Mirza Huseyn Khan was ridiculed by his enemies and termed an upstart.[2] His father, Mīrzā Nabī Khān, joined the household of Rukn ud-Dowleh, the governor of Qazvin, who recognized his intelligence and honesty and undertook to train and educate him.

Mirza Nabi Khan made rapid progress in his career. During the reign of Muhammad Shah (1835–58), he was appointed *amīr-i dīvan-khāneh-yi ʿadlīyeh,* later known as minister of justice. He became governor of Fars and married one of Fath-ʿAli Shah's daughters. He continued to enjoy his favored position at court during the reign of the new king, Nasir ed-Din Shah (1848–96). Mirza

Taqi Khan Amir Kabir apparently also liked him, for in 1848 Amir Kabir entrusted him with the task of preparing for his marriage to the shah's sister, the princess ʿIzzat ud-Dowleh.[3]

We know little about Mirza Huseyn Khan's early childhood and upbringing, but the few allusions to him during this period reveal some important facts. An incident that points out his great ambition is related by his official biographer: "One day during his father's lifetime and Amir Kabir's period, when Mirza Huseyn Khan was with his brothers and cousins in Azgal village near Shimīrān, he told them, 'Last night I had to pawn my comb so that I could have dinner. But you will see, some day I will take the place of this Farahānī,' meaning Mirza Taqi Khan."[4] The name by which his friends knew him—*Huseyn Bīnī* or Huseyn the Nose[5]—is also suggestive. Such taunting references to his large nose by peers during his early years may account for his later extreme sensitivity.

This sensitivity is often evident in his correspondence with the shah and in a group of private letters written to Nasīr ud-Dowleh, an intimate friend. The latter, written near the end of his life, reveal a man extremely lacking in confidence and unsure of himself. He repeatedly appeals to his friend for reassurance of his friendship and interprets the slightest negative word as a sign of rejection.[6]

Due to his extreme sensitivity, Mirza Huseyn Khan was not always in control of himself. Under pressure he would break into a tirade or tears. His correspondence contains occasional references to times when a difficult situation or slight from the shah caused him to shed tears.

None of our sources mentions anything about his early education. We can assume that, like other upper-class children, he was instructed at home by a private tutor.[7] Children under twelve were commonly taught the Qur'an, Persian literature and grammar, arithmetic, calligraphy, and composition. Judging by the spelling and grammatical mistakes occasionally found in his later correspondence, he could not have been a brilliant student. His poor knowledge of the language is confirmed by Iʿtimad us-Saltaneh: "He wrote Persian badly and had a hard time writing from right to left, so he wrote very slowly."[8] He recorded, also, that Mirza Huseyn Khan was poor in mathematics.[9]

The most important event of these early years was his father's decision to send him to France to study. The dates of his travel and stay in France are not certain. We are told that he went to France at the beginning of Nasir ed-Din Shah's reign.[10] We also know that in 1851 he was chosen by Amir Kabir as head of Iran's newly established consulate in Bombay. We can assume that he went to France in 1848 and spent two or three years there. His stay must have been long enough to have enabled him to learn French well. Samples of his writing in French, such as his correspondence with members of the European delegations in Tehran, and the testimony of foreign visitors suggest that he was more assiduous in his study of French than he had been in the study of Persian. Mme Carla Serena, who met him in 1879 in Tehran, reported, "*Doué d-une intélligence superieure, il parlaît plusieurs langues avec une grande pureté.*" [11]

This early introduction to Europe left a deep impression on Mirza Huseyn Khan and influenced his personality and thought significantly. He became a great admirer of Europeans and their civilization and he tried to introduce them to his fellow countrymen. His admiration of Europe was also manifest in his lifestyle. He exchanged traditional Iranian clothing—a long or knee-length robe, wide pants, several vests, and tall conical hat—for a dark suit—jacket and narrow pants. Later, when he became prime minister, he made this the official style of dress for all government employees. After a visit to his home in Tehran, Mme Serena reported that the house was "*un charmant palais, mis-européen, mis-persan*" and that European furniture appeared there. Household eunuchs had been replaced by ten- to twelve-year-old page boys, who wore semimilitary uniforms.[12]

A more significant aspect of Mirza Huseyn Khan's stay in France was that it coincided with the increase in political and revolutionary activity there that led to the establishment of the short-lived Second Republic in 1848. We can only surmise the effect these events had on Mirza Huseyn Khan, since he makes no reference to them. We do know, however, that another Persian student who was in Paris at the same time became so deeply involved that he actively participated in the defense of the National Assembly when it was attacked by the mob in May 1848.[13] We cannot be sure that the atmosphere of Paris had the same effect on Mirza Huseyn Khan, but some of his reforming zeal and liberal ideas may have been shaped by his experiences there. Perhaps that was why, years later, he was so anxious to take the shah to Europe and expose him to the results of progress and reform.

Mirza Huseyn Khan
Courtesy of Asghar Muhajir

Love of Europe and admiration for European civilization were only part of the impact of this early European experience on Mirza Huseyn Khan. It also made him a member of one of the most exclusive groups in Iran, those with a European education. The exact number of Iranians who studied in Europe during this period cannot be determined with certainty, but they could not have been more than a few in the early 1850s.[14] Although they were so few, members of the group were regarded with suspicion and distrust. R. G. Watson, the British minister in Iran in the late 1850s, explained: "Several of these have come back to Persia, but they are looked on with an eye of distrust by the majority of their less instructed countrymen, who take care to do all in their power to prevent them from having the opportunity of putting in practice anything they may have learned, and thereby throwing others into the shade." [15]

This mistrust of those with European educations played a decisive role in the fate of Mirza Huseyn Khan's later reforms and contributed substantially to the hostility they aroused. The fact that, in addition to his European education, he had spent many more years abroad in the diplomatic service intensified the mistrust of his contemporaries at home.

However, not every Iranian man of affairs mistrusted a European education. Some, like Amir Kabir, Nasir ed-Din Shah's first sadr-i a'zam, valued such training highly; and, when the Iranian government was permitted to open a consulate in Bombay, he chose Mirza Huseyn Khan for the post. It is reported that Amir Kabir thought highly of Mirza Huseyn Khan's abilities. He was quoted as saying, "This son of Mirza Nabi Khan will some day become sadr-i a'zam." [16] That Mirza Huseyn Khan was only twenty-three when the task was entrusted to him confirms this high opinion. The Indian consulate, like the other new diplomatic mission in London, was part of Amir Kabir's policy of protecting Iranians and improving foreign relations.

The Bombay assignment was especially important, because many Iranian merchants resided in India and there was much trade between the two countries. Mirza Huseyn Khan was instructed to pay special attention to "protecting and lending support to them [the Iranians in India], allowing no harm to come to them, and keeping them happy and satisfied with steps taken by their government." [17] His most important task was setting up the mission itself under the terms of a commercial treaty between Persia and Britain. He was also charged with mediating disputes between

Iranian nationals and Indian merchants, with the issuance of official passports, and with the recording of all commercial transactions of Iranians in India.

The interval between his return from France and his departure for Bombay gave Mirza Huseyn Khan a chance to witness Amir Kabir's reforms at close quarters. The latter's comment about Mirza Huseyn Khan becoming the sadr suggests that some familiarity existed between the two. It is, therefore, not surprising that Mirza Huseyn Khan should have been influenced by Amir Kabir, and that he should have tried to emulate his predecessor.

There were some similarities between the two men's ideas and policies. Both denounced bribery and were concerned about the prestige and good name of Iran. Both were concerned with enforcing existing laws and administering justice for all citizens. They also professed an intense love for their country and were distressed by its chaotic internal condition and its inability to defend itself against the increasing pressures of Russia and Britain. Because of these similarities, Mirza Huseyn Khan can be regarded as a true heir of Amir Kabir. However, Mirza Huseyn Khan did not merely follow in Amir Kabir's footsteps. His aims were to regulate all the affairs of government with laws that could not be tampered with by any individual, including the monarch, and to create a strong central government that could protect these laws. The sources of inspiration for the laws he hoped to enact were the "civilized" governments of the Europeans and the Ottomans.

The ability and efficiency Mirza Huseyn Khan brought to his commission are evident in the official letter of commendation he received from Amir's successor, Mirza Aqa Khan Nuri, in 1852:

> The services you have rendered to the Government and its subjects, your success in raising the flag, and your success with the other duties entrusted to you, whether small or big, have been noticed and admired by His Majesty, and have caused an increase in my affection for you. If God wills, therefore, as a result of these services, your reward will be so great that you will be envied by your peers.[18]

Upon his return to Tehran, Mirza Huseyn Khan was rewarded by promotion to the post of consul general in Tiflis in 1852. The most notable event of his life in Tiflis was the friendship he formed with Mīrzā Fath-ᶜAlī Akhundzādeh, a vociferous advocate of social reform and one of the earliest exponents of Iranian nationalism.

Mirza Fath-ᶜAli Akhundzadeh was born in Tabriz in 1812 and remained there until he was twelve years old; then his family emigrated to Ganjeh, a city in Russian Azerbaijan. When he was twenty-two, he moved to Tiflis, the cultural and intellectual capital of Caucasia. Its remoteness from St. Petersburg made the city a haven for revolutionary activity and propaganda against the czarist regime.[19] Mirza Fath-ʿAli came to be deeply influenced by the various currents of thought in Tiflis. Because he knew Persian as well as Arabic and Turkish, he found employment as a translator in the office of the Caucasian governor general. But he devoted most of his energies to writing plays and social and political essays, which were widely read in Russian Azerbaijan and Iran.[20]

His political essays were concerned mainly with Iranian nationalism, the reasons for Iran's defeat by Russia, and Iran's decline. He attributed the weakness of Iran to two causes: the Islamic conquest and despotism. Although the radical views he expressed in some of his essays prevented their publication in either Iran or Caucasia, Mirza Fath-ʿAli distributed enough handwritten copies among friends to make his views well known. In his private correspondence with friends and government officials, he did not hesitate to reiterate his views, including his criticism of the government, the shah, and despotism.[21]

We may safely conclude that the friendship between Mirza Huseyn Khan, a government representative, and Mirza Fath-ʿAli, a man openly critical of that government, involved some risk and that Mirza Huseyn Khan would not have taken that risk unless he cherished the friendship and shared some of the views. After leaving Tiflis for Istanbul in 1858, he kept in touch with Mirza Fath-ʿAli and invited him for a visit. During his stay in Istanbul, Mirza Fath-ʿAli lived as a guest of the Iranian mission.

It is not difficult to see why Mirza Fath-ʿAli might have influenced Mirza Huseyn Khan. When Mirza Huseyn Khan arrived in Tiflis at the age of twenty-five, Mirza Fath-ʿAli was already forty, an established playwright and author, accepted by the younger generation of reformers as a guide and teacher. He was also a close friend of Mirza Yusuf Khan Mustashar ud-Dowleh, whom Mirza Huseyn Khan later entrusted with continuing his reforms in the ministry of justice after his own promotion to the office of sadr-i aʿzam. Mirza Yusuf Khan carried on a lengthy correspondence with Mirza Fath-ʿAli, consulting him about his plans. The latter's role as teacher is illuminated in one reply:

> The Sheykh ul-Islam and I see fit that all questions pertaining to disputes should be removed from the control of the ʿulama and should be placed under the control of the Ministry of

Justice. Henceforth, the ʿulama should not interfere with disputes and should limit their meddling to matters related to religious practices, such as prayer, fasting, preaching, marriage, divorce, burials, and the like, in the same way it is done in Europe.[22]

Mirza Fath-ʿAli was an outspoken advocate of secularism, and it is probably he who converted Mirza Huseyn Khan and Mirza Yusuf Khan to this view. Though neither of the two tampered openly with the power of the ʿulama, both tried to curb clerical power whenever there was an opportunity.[23] However, Mirza Huseyn Khan's attitude toward religion should not be judged by his attitude toward organized religion. Much existing evidence, his private correspondence, and the testimony of friends and foes strongly suggest that he was a devout Muslim. Iʿtimad us-Saltaneh, who certainly is not a friendly critic, reported that Mirza Huseyn Khan prayed long hours, fasted regularly, and never touched wine or other alcoholic beverages. During his stay in Istanbul he joined the circle of a well-known Persian mystic, Ḥājjī Mīrzā Safā, who had taken residence there.[24] Before returning to Iran in 1870, he made his pilgrimage to the holy cities of Mecca and Medina; and in 1879, the last year of his life, he helped build the Sipahsālār Mosque in Tehran.

Mirza Huseyn Khan spent six years in Tiflis. When he returned to Iran, he was named head of the Iranian mission in Istanbul. The new appointment demonstrates the great trust his superiors, especially the shah, had in his ability. He was the first resident Iranian representative to the Ottoman Empire, whose relations with Iran, from the Iranian point of view, had been characterized by bad faith, hostility, aggression, and arrogance. The hostility between the Iranians and Ottomans could be traced to Safavid times, when Shah Ismaʿil, the founder of the dynasty, chose Shiʿism as the official religion of Iran. Thereafter the two sides had fought many indecisive battles, and the constantly shifting boundaries between the countries created grounds for renewed hostility.

This hostility between the two countries existed until the mid-nineteenth century, when a commission participated in by Russia and Britain resolved the border controversy.[25] The commission came to an agreement, with minor differences, and the Treaty of Erzurum in 1848 fixed the borders.[26] But relations between the two states were still far from satisfactory. The Ottomans were too involved on the European front to breach the treaty, although during their war with Russia in 1853–56, they tried to keep Iran from lending support to the enemy. Yet during peacetime they exerted pressure on Iran to amend the terms of the treaty. They were most insistent on changing the provision that returned the district of Qatour to Iran, a district that had been occupied by the Ottomans since 1848.[27]

In the conflict between the Ottomans and the Iranians, several factors gave the former the upper hand. They controlled the holy cities of Mecca and Medina in Arabia as well as the Shiʿi shrines in Iraq. They could stir up the ʿulama living in Iraq and make life difficult for many Iranian subjects who were living in Karbala and Najaf or who wanted to make the holy pilgrimages. Moreover, the Ottomans controlled one of the two major trade routes between Iran and Europe; the other route went through Russia.

When Mirza Huseyn Khan was appointed minister to Istanbul, he had an additional problem. This was the presence in Baghdad of ʿAbbas Mirza, Nasir ed-Din Shah's younger brother, whom the shah considered to be a potential threat to his throne. ʿAbbas Mirza had been living quietly in exile in Baghdad since 1851. Though he had a peaceful temperament, the British had tried to make use of him in 1857 when the shah undertook his expedition to retrieve Herat; but the shah had foiled the British by sending gifts to his brother and increasing his pension. There was no guarantee, however, that other enemies, internal or external, would not try again. It was therefore necessary either that ʿAbbas Mirza return to Iran or that the Ottomans guarantee he would remain peaceful.

Mirza Huseyn Khan faced many problems when he arrived in Istanbul in 1858. The Ottoman officials seemed openly hostile to him, and they attempted systematically to make him feel unwelcome. He had a great deal of difficulty finding a place for the mission, since proprietors were discouraged from renting to this first Iranian minister. Indeed, he was forced to rent under an assumed name until he was granted permission by the shah to purchase a house.[28]

Nevertheless, his stay proved significant for him and beneficial for Iranian-Ottoman relations. He arrived in Istanbul at the beginning of an energetic phase of the Tanzīmāt reforms in the Ottoman Empire. Throughout the 1860s there was increasingly heated debate about establishing a constitutional form of government. Mirza Huseyn Khan knew Ottoman Turkish quite well and became friendly with a number of high officials. These included the two main planners of the Tanzimat, Fu'ād and Ālī Pasha, and this placed him in a position to watch the developments closely.

Many of his critics, who later held it against him that he had been so familiar with Ottoman conditions, argued that: "His upbringing and knowledge of Iran were deficient. He spent most of his years in the Ottoman Empire. So when he returned to Iran he decided to carry out Ottoman-type reforms in the Protected Kingdoms. But the intentions of that great man were not realized and had opposite results."[29]

The dispatches that Mirza Huseyn Khan sent to Tehran reveal his keen interest in Ottoman reforms. He considered sending these dispatches not merely a routine task but also a duty. Writing to the shah, he said: "Just as God has given man eyes with which to see and has ordained that man should look around him with these eyes, in order to be informed of the intentions of those around him and to protect himself if need be, so has God done with the government envoys, giving them sight. They must report without delay to the government . . . what they see and observe and detect. If they should keep silent and hide what they see, they have failed in their duty. In my opinion, failing in one's duty to the government is a major sin." [30]

The Tanzimat reforms seem to have had a deep impact on Mirza Huseyn Khan. His experiences in Istanbul impressed upon him the need to apply Western solutions to Iran's problems and convinced him that reforms carried out in the Ottoman Empire could be carried out in Iran. He did not seem to realize that the Tanzimat reforms in Turkey were a continuation of earlier reforms and that no such preparation had been made in Iran. Perhaps the greatest weakness of Mirza Huseyn Khan's reforms was that they departed radically from the Iranian way of life. While a handful of vocal westernized individuals like Malkam complained that he went too slowly, most Iranians who advocated reform could not support his program.

A recurrent topic in his dispatches was the spread of constitutional ideas in Turkey. By describing the Ottoman discussions about parliamentary government, Mirza Huseyn Khan hoped to familiarize the Iranian ruling class, including the shah, with the idea of a parliament and to dispel their fears of this form of government. He once sent the Iranian foreign minister the full text of a letter written by Mustafā Fazil Pasha, a leader of the Young Ottomans, to Sultan Abdulaziz. Mustafa Fazil Pasha was

informing the sultan of the weakened state of the empire and
suggesting that the introduction of parliamentary government
would solve all the empire's ills. Mirza Huseyn Khan recommended
that his foreign minister "prepare a careful translation of Mustafa
Pasha's letter, for it would prove beneficial." [31]

He often adopted the arguments of Ottoman parliamentary
enthusiasts who were Muslims. In one report to the foreign ministry, he quoted their contention that the quality of the sultan's
advisors had deteriorated, causing the empire to weaken: "Instead
of having the management of thirty million people left to four
or five individuals, would it not be better to entrust it to four or
five hundred representatives of the people? Would it also not be
better for the councillors of state, i.e., the ministers, to be answerable to a parliament? Then if a councillor of state should
commit any wrong, he would be dismissed and another would be
appointed to take his place in serving the government and the
people." [32]

He did understand that the system would pose a threat to the
supremacy of the Muslim population: "Since the Ottoman Empire
is composed of various nations and adherents of different religions, and the non-Muslims will have the right to appoint representatives, in a short time the Christians, who are better versed
in politics and greater in number, will gain supremacy over the
Muslims." [33] However, like many European liberals, Mirza Huseyn
Khan believed optimistically that change necessarily brought improvement. Despite the risk involved, replacing older political institutions with new ones like parliaments was therefore a step
forward—it was progress. He was convinced that it was the duty
of governments, especially in the weaker states like the Ottoman
Empire and Iran, to keep abreast of changes in the more advanced
nations of Europe so they could introduce similar changes at home.
"Each period requires an organization suited to its needs. If these
needs are neglected, there may be reason for regret." [34]

What distressed Mirza Huseyn Khan deeply was that in his own
country, which "once had a glorious name," hardly anything was
being done to improve conditions. He wrote to the foreign ministry
in a dispatch:

I am grieved and know that I am seeking the impossible. I
know that what I wish for my country cannot be achieved
overnight, and must be attained gradually. But the reason for
my sadness is that not only have we made no effort in this
direction yet, but that we do not even believe there is anything

wrong with our state, or that our affairs need improvement. To the contrary, we believe that we have reached the highest degree of progress, and there is nothing we have to do or to worry about.[35]

In the same dispatch he tried to explicate what he thought as his duty to the state and his fellow countrymen:

In my view, if a person is not willing to sacrifice himself, and if he does not give priority to what pertains to the public over and above what concerns him personally, and if he does not state, write, and repeat that which the ears are not accustomed to hear, that individual has not fulfilled his love of the state, and his love of his country, and his love of his countrymen.[36]

Realizing that his concern for his country and his pained understanding of its condition would seem unfamiliar to many of his countrymen, he used an analogy to clarify his position: "Supposing that during a trip on the sea, a few individuals discover that the ship has suffered a great damage, of which the rest of the passengers, who merely spend their time in seeking private pleasure, are unaware. Is not the duty of the few to tell the rest of the impending danger?" [37]

Having taken such pains to prepare his reports, Mirza Huseyn Khan was deeply grieved by the indifference that greeted them in Iran. He tried to shake his colleagues out of their apathy:

It causes me great pain to learn that my dispatches, insisting that the government avail itself of the time of peace and initiate programs to improve the country's condition, have been treated as the reading of fiction: they are read once and then forgotten forever. These dispatches contain suggestions suitable for the present needs of the country. But they never receive attention and remain in oblivion.[38]

Time and again he pointed out Iran's backwardness in dispatches direct to the shah. Sometimes he appealed to the shah's sense of pride:

When I had just arrived in Istanbul, the foreigners showed great interest in the Iranian government and nation, and they predicted a great future for us. Often they used the reform projects of the Iranian government as a means of chiding the Ottoman government. The European newspapers were filled with our praise, while blaming the Ottomans. But I have noticed with great regret that lately this situation has changed.

These nations have become disappointed with us and lost hope in the progress of our nation. They consider us devoid of civilization, they are no longer seeking our friendship and do not consider us worthy of equality with the countries of Europe. In short, they consider us worthless, and whoever says the contrary is telling a lie.[39]

But Iran could yet restore herself in the eyes of Europe—if her leaders set out on the path of progress.[40]

If Iran made an effort to overcome her backwardness and achieve the same level of progress as the European nations, Mirza Huseyn Khan declared in another report, she would not only solve her internal problems but would also ensure her territorial integrity. Her neighbors would no longer have an excuse to tell her what to do; and if they did so, a strong Iran could silence them easily.[41]

In his dispatches Mirza Huseyn Khan repeatedly returned to the European attitudes toward the reforms undertaken by the Ottoman government. He no doubt hoped that by expounding on the encouragement of the Ottoman government by such powers as Britain and France he would inspire his own leaders to seek European support for reform projects in Iran. The French and British governments, he thought, "were exerting a great deal of pressure on Ottoman authorities to carry out numerous reforms in the political institutions of the Empire"[42] because, he conjectured, they were concerned about Ottoman stability and territorial integrity: "Russia, secretly and in the open, is opposed to these reforms, whereas the two governments of France and Britain are insistent that these reforms be carried out . . . because these two governments wish for the survival and strength of the Ottoman government, but the Russians would like to see it disappear or at least be weak and humiliated."[43] The Iranian ambassador astutely pointed out that France and Britain had their own self-interest in mind in encouraging Ottoman reforms. The two governments were afraid that if the Ottomans did not arrest the decline of their country, Istanbul would be occupied by Russia, causing a serious disruption in the European balance of power.

During his long stay in Istanbul (1858–69), Mirza Huseyn Khan witnessed both the systematic French and British pressure for Ottoman reform and their encouragement whenever reform was attempted. The self-interest of these two powers, he felt, coincided with the well-being of the Ottoman government and people, so their role in Ottoman affairs was constructive. He wrote, "Their pressure on the Ottomans to introduce reform will benefit the Ottoman government and nation." [44]

His sympathy for the British attitude toward reform was increased by his close personal friendship with Sir Henry Layard, British ambassador to the Porte, who spent six months at the Iranian embassy at Istanbul during a period of convalescence.[45] It is important to keep in mind the favorable impression Mirza Huseyn Khan had of the two European powers, especially Britain, in appraising his role in the Reuter Concession in 1873. The concession granted Baron de Reuter a seventy-year right to exploit Iran's natural resources. Mirza Huseyn Khan's role in bringing this about has been roundly condemned and ridiculed by some historians, but he honestly, if somewhat naïvely, believed that Iran could be transformed as he had dreamed, with the help of "a benevolent European power"; his hope of overnight reform blinded him to the weaknesses of the contract.[46]

It is not surprising that Mirza Huseyn Khan should have welcomed the friendship of Malkam Khan when the latter was banished to Istanbul in 1864 at the order of the shah. The two men were naturally drawn together by their intellectual interests, European education, and zeal for reforming Iran. Mirza Huseyn Khan made no secret of their friendship and, indeed, succeeded in reinstating Malkam in the shah's favor. Malkam could then be employed at the embassy; and when Mirza Huseyn Khan was called back to Tehran to assume higher office, he took Malkam with him. There can be little doubt that he was pleased to find a kindred spirit.

Mirza Huseyn Khan used his twelve years in Istanbul to advantage. He won the friendship of many top Ottoman officials, and those friendships helped him to resolve almost seventy areas of disagreement that had been long outstanding for lack of Ottoman willingness to negotiate. The most important of these concerned the treatment of Iranian Shi'i subjects in various parts of the Ottoman Empire and the treatment of Iranian travelers on pilgrimage to the holy cities.[47]

What was most appreciated, however, was that Mirza Huseyn Khan was able to secure Ottoman consent for the shah to visit the shrine of the Shi'ite imams at Najaf and Karbala in Iraq. Ottoman opposition to the visit had a political basis. The population of Iraq was divided along sectarian lines. The majority of the inhabitants were Shi'ites, many of whom felt a strong sympathy for Iran. Most of the administrative and political positions in Iraq were controlled by the Sunnites, however, since they belonged to the same sect as the Ottoman ruling class.

The Ottomans managed in general to keep peace between the two factions. Periodically Shi'ite resentment at privileges accorded Sunnites or at Sunnite attempts to plunder the Shi'ites, who were the main beneficiaries of the stream of pilgrims from Iran to the shrines, would lead to actual fighting.[48] The Ottomans sought to avoid a visit from Nasir ed-Din Shah as a factor that might tip the balance in favor of the Shi'ites, who had been the victims of the most recent disturbance.[49]

These difficulties only increased the shah's ardor. In reply to an explanation of the problems from Mirza Huseyn Khan, he asked, "Is it fair that you . . . should have gone to Mecca on pilgrimage, but that I should not be allowed to go to the Shrines of the Imams?"[50] Mirza Huseyn Khan tried to divert him to Europe, where he could study reforms, but he was adamant: "I will go to Europe later, after I have gone on pilgrimage to the shrines of the Imams. I would like my subjects to get used to the idea of my traveling gradually."[51] When Mirza Huseyn Khan secured an official invitation for him, he was jubilant. His courtiers, however, were not so jubilant; they felt their sovereign had chosen a time to travel that was far from opportune. Their apprehensions were based upon troubles within Iran and by the threat of Russian expansion from Turkestan into Iran.

The immediate internal problem was a severe famine caused by years of drought. Zill us-Sultan, the shah's oldest son, gives an eyewitness account of its ravages:

> The trip I made to Tehran, on the occasion of Kāmrān Mirza's wedding, was the most awful, the worst, and vilest trip I have ever made in my whole life. From the beginning of 1286 [1869] to 1289 [1871], a famine was raging all over Iran. Tehran, Isfahan, and 'Irāq-i'Ajam were the worst off. . . . People were so desperate that they ate cats and dogs, even human corpses. . . . From our first stop in Fars till Tehran, we passed by only the dead; we saw corpses strewn along the road, or people who had been murdered by the hungry, in hopes of getting whatever they had; we saw those about to die. . . . In Isfahan, about 100,000 had died. . . . Most stores were closed and the bazaars were derelict. I saw with my own eyes a well dug in the middle of the Zāyandeh-rūd [River] and they would try to pull water from out of there. But the moment the pail would reach the surface, people, cats, dogs,

even birds would attack the pail. I cannot possibly describe
the misery of the people. . . . Kashan seemed a thousand times
worse than Isfahan. . . . Qum was a hundred times worse.[52]

Court officials pleaded with the shah that: "Misfortune has befallen
most provinces, and famine and scarcity have spread everywhere. . . . It would not be prudent to leave the throne vacant,
for the king's absence might increase the anxiety and fear would
spread. It is possible for evils to ensue as a result. . . . But His
Majesty did not pay heed." [53]

It was characteristic of Nasir ed-Din Shah to remove himself
from a troubled situation by taking a trip. Yet if his purpose in
taking the trip was to find respite, it was not effective. On his way,
the shah saw that:

> The subjects had given up all pretenses of civilization, had
> abandoned work, and, due to poverty and great need, had
> left their homes. Men and women, young and old had gone
> to the roads and the cry of misery was reaching up to Heaven.
> In every town he saw a group of beggars, clad in rags and
> appearing as if they were going to welcome him. Instead they
> brought forth wailing and disturbed the happiness, appetite,
> and sleep of His Majesty.[54]

However, in the shah's own account of the trip, he gave no hint
of being disturbed by what he saw on the roads to the border. He
describes only routine ceremonial events and natural sights. It was
on this trip, though, that he asked Mirza Huseyn Khan to return
with him to Tehran to assume the post of minister of justice.

This appointment appears to have been merely a trial of his
abilities. Nine months later, in September 1871, having apparently
proved his competence, Mirza Huseyn Khan was named minister
of war. Then, within a few weeks, on October 16, he was appointed
to the post of sadr-i aᶜzam or prime minister.

Strong evidence suggests that the shah had been contemplating
reform for some time and that his promotion of Mirza Huseyn
Khan was intended to put it into effect. While Mirza Huseyn Khan
was still in Istanbul, the shah had written him of his desire to
improve conditions in Iran:

> I am so happy to have someone like you in Iran who knows
> what is wrong and what needs to be done, who is concerned
> about the welfare of the state, who is wise and knowledgeable,
> who knows what he is doing, and who understands what he
> is told. This kind of person is very rare in Iran—nay, there

has never been such a person. So shouldn't I be happy at finding him?[55]

Though the shah felt the need for reform, he could not trust any of the men at court to carry it out:

> Repeatedly there has been discussion about reforming the government, and proposals by Malkam Khan and others have been read. Our ministers and servants discuss this among themselves and in the Majlis-i Dār ush-Showrā-yi Kubra. But they never come up with any constructive suggestions that might be beneficial for the state. They spend their time telling stories, exchanging jokes, criticizing, or talking nonsense.[56]

Mirza Huseyn Khan's dispatches through the years surely had the effect of awakening in the shah an interest in reform, but the famine and the advance of the Russians into Muslim lands northeast of Iran were undoubtedly contributing factors.

As the Russians advanced in the Transcaucasus early in the nineteenth century, Iran lost its Caucasian territories. After the Treaty of Turkmanchay in 1828, Russia turned from Iran to Turkestan and Central Asia, areas in which her borders were not defined, and then spent most of the 1840s exploring both of these areas. Raids by the Turkomans and other inhabitants of the region, such as the Khivans, gave the Russians an excuse to send expeditions into the area. They began to build forts along a line that extended from the south end of the Aral Sea toward Khiva at its southernmost point. Factors that helped the Russian advance were the area's sparse population and the internal weakness and constant warring between the three Muslim khanates of Khuqand, Bukhara, and Khiva.[57]

In 1864 a small force of Russians took the two cities of Turkestan and Chimkent. The next year they took Tashkent, the principal city of Khuqand, which was formally annexed to the Russian Empire in 1866. The khanate of Bukhara suffered a similar fate. In 1866 and 1868 Russian troops fought the Bukharans and forced their ruler, Amīr Muzaffar ed-Dīn, to accept a Russian protectorate and cede parts of the khanate, including the city of Samarqand, to them.[58] Khiva's turn was next; it was conquered in 1873, though its ruling dynasty was retained.[59]

Meanwhile, Iran and Britain watched apprehensively as Russia extended her hold over the region. Her pretext for expansion was the protection of her frontiers from unruly nomads. The British protested to the Russian ambassador in London and the Russian foreign minister in St. Petersburg. Each protest throughout the 1860s was met with assurances from the Russian foreign minister that they would advance no further, only to have each assurance abrogated by the Russian Asiatic and War departments.

While Russia and Britain exchanged diplomatic notes, Iran grew more and more anxious. As far as the shah was concerned, there was nothing to stop Russia from turning southward once she had finished annexing the small tract of land separating her from Khurasan. The fear recurred a few years later when General Falkenhagen, a retired Russian general sought a railway concession from the Iranian government. The shah urged Mirza Huseyn Khan to answer no to the Russian minister, who was intervening on his behalf. "Otherwise," he said, "the state will be in danger." [60] He also told Mirza Huseyn Khan that "If the Russians come to Tabriz, we must say the last prayer for Iran; we must perform the last rites for Iran." [61]

The shah had learned many lessons when he was forced to surrender all rights to the city of Herat because Iranian statesmen did not understand international politics. The most important of these lessons were the need for caution in trusting the abilities of his own men and the need for knowledge of the outside world in dealing with such powerful neighbors as Russia and Britain. Under the circumstances, the choice of Mirza Huseyn Khan was logical and prudent. Mirza Huseyn Khan was distressed by the disturbed state of his country and deeply committed to reform. He had proved his abilities as a diplomat, and Nasir ed-Din Shah felt he could trust him.

3

JUDICIAL REFORM

MIRZA HUSEYN KHAN was appointed minister of justice, pensions, and religious endowments on 29 Ramazān 1287/23 December 1870. During the ten months he held this post, he tried to provide the country with independent tribunals and a unified code of laws. He also set new standards for law enforcement, proving himself to be an energetic and diligent administrator who emphasized equal treatment for all.[1] He also tried to enhance the authority of the central government by creating greater central control in the judicial process.

Any reforms in secular law and justice had to be pursued with tact and shrewdness, since they were bound to affect the sharᶜ law administered by the ᶜulama, who opposed any project that might infringe upon their privileges. The Iranian judicial system was divided into two branches, the ᶜurf or customary law administered by the civil authorities and the sharᶜ or religious law administered by the ᶜulama. The ᶜurf law governed in criminal cases, including any offense against the state, and the sharᶜ law in cases of a personal or commercial nature. Although the two systems were theoretically separate, their jurisdictions often overlapped.[2]

ᶜUrf law, which was based on precedents and customs, varied greatly from one city or locale to another. The ᶜurf system was administered by a hakīm or governor in the cities and a kadkhudā or village head in the villages. Although the lack of a written code left a miscreant at the mercy of the ruling official, the ᶜurf system was not completely lacking in safeguards against the abuse of justice. Each province, including Tehran, had a dīvān-i ᶜadlīyeh or office of justice, which was in effect a court of equity. These divans were supervised by the governors general in the provinces and by the sovereign in the capital.

The court in Tehran was theoretically the highest court of appeal. It was uncommon for the shah to officiate there; instead, a deputy amīr-i dīvān or chief of the office acted on his behalf.[3] Although the right of appeal existed in theory, in practice it was difficult to appeal to a governor against a city magistrate or to the shah against a governor. This was one reason why most people preferred to relegate their disputes to the sharᶜ courts. It also was not uncommon for the civil authorities themselves to refer difficult cases to the religious courts.

Sharᶜ law was based on Shīᶜī fiqh or Shiᶜite jurisprudence; hence, it derived from the Qur'an, the Sunna, the opinion of the twelve imams, and the pronouncements of the leading mujtahids of each period. Over the years a vast collection of regulations had accumulated concerning every conceivable aspect of daily life. Yet, despite this elaborate and explicit body of law, sharᶜ tribunals were severely handicapped by their lack of power to execute their decisions; they were dependent on civil authorities to do so.[4]

A dual system controlled by two basically opposed forces, the civil authorities on the one hand and the religious authorities on the other, did not seem the most efficient instrument for rendering personal justice. It also contained the inherent possibility of conflict between the civil and religious classes. Furthermore, this control of the judicial system by the provincial governors and the religious leaders interfered with Mirza Huseyn Khan's main objective—the creation of a strong central government—without which no reform could be lasting. Even though the dual nature of the judicial system was more theoretical than real, it furnished Mirza Huseyn Khan with a starting point from which to launch his reforms.

One earlier attempt to reorganize the system of justice had been made in the reign of Nasir ed-Din Shah. The Ministry of Justice itself had been created in 1858, when the shah, in an attempt to improve conditions for his people, had divided the affairs of government among six ministries. However, this was a creation in name only. The minister of justice, for example, was merely the amir-i divan with a new title, and his function continued to be the supervision of the Dīvān-i ᶜAdlīyeh Aᶜzam, the High Court of Justice.

In 1279/1863 an ordinance was issued proclaiming the superiority of the Divan-i ᶜAdliyeh Aᶜzam over all other divans, i.e., those in the provinces, and describing its functions. But more significant was the section concerning the trial of foreign subjects, which was relegated to the Ministry of Foreign Affairs and not to the Divan-i ʿAdliyeh Aʿzam. The minister of justice was to be no more than a supervisor of the high court.[5]

The creation of this ministry is typical of Nasir ed-Din Shah's method of introducing reforms before Mirza Huseyn Khan came to power. His private secretary, Amīn ul-Mulk (later the Amīn ud-Dowleh), testifies that the shah, whose knowledge of things Western was lacking, had tried, with the help of others equally ignorant of the West, to introduce Western-style institutions into the country.[6] It is not surprising, therefore, that the efforts did not bring about the desired transformation into European-style knowledge and progress.

Three months after Mirza Huseyn Khan assumed the position of minister of justice, on 15 Ziqaʿdeh 1287/9 March 1871 he issued his first ordinance. The text appeared in a new weekly newspaper, *Vaqāyiʿ-i ʿAdlīyeh* or *Judiciary News*, which was founded to report on administrative reforms and new regulations decreed by the Ministry of Justice. The shah's sentiments and his minister's zeal for reform are reflected in the preamble to the ordinance:

> His Majesty, desirous that justice should be extended, that his subjects be protected, that his people should be educated, and that his country attain flourishing condition, has always directed his sincere endeavor toward establishing and consolidating the means of improving the state of his people so that they should all alike enjoy the benefits of his noble institutions. His Majesty is therefore anxious that the improvement and comfort of his subjects and the good organization of his dominion should attain a higher degree of advancement; that institutions, which have been unsuitable by hindering justice, and which are in truth forbidden by the pure religious laws, should be abolished; that right should be distinguished from wrong; so that in their increased tranquility, good order and wisdom, the Persian nation and the ancient kingdom of Persia may emulate their older times. In the same way should be rendered the means of enlightening and enobling their minds.[7]

The most important announcement in the first issue of the newspaper concerned the division of the High Court of Justice into four specialized courts: (1) a court of investigation to receive petitions, discriminate between right and wrong, and report in writing to the minister of justice; (2) a legislative court to draw up regulations equally applicable to every case and to all classes; (3) a criminal court to investigate cases of assault, identify the

Nasir ed-Din Shah
Source: Historical Pictures Service, Chicago

culprit and nature of the offense, and deal with the decision issued by the judge; and (4) an execution court to carry out all decisions proceeding from the Ministry of Justice.[8]

Two weeks later two more courts were announced: a commercial court to supervise commercial transactions and disputes, and a land court to investigate old leases and land claims.[9] The announcement was brief and did not state what types of law would be applied in the commercial courts. The extant sources unfortunately do not shed any light on such questions as whether these courts were intended to use laws of Western origin as the Ottomans had done earlier or whether the commercial code would be drawn from existing shar^c and ^{c}urf laws.

The same uncertainty surrounds the type of law intended for the legislative court, which was clearly the most important of the new courts, since it was empowered to legislate. It is equally difficult to determine whether this court did in fact enact any laws. We are also uncertain of the meaning of the statements defining this court's role: "This court will institute regulations applicable to any case and all classes." According to W. T. Thompson, the British minister in Tehran, Mirza Huseyn Khan intended to formulate laws pronouncing the equality of all Iranian citizens, i.e., Muslims, Christians, Jews, and Zoroastrians.[10] If this had been the sole function of the legislative court, its impact, despite the favorable reaction it had on liberal European governments, would have been negligible, since the proportion of religious minorities in Iran was very small.[11] The intended function of this court, like the Ottoman predecessors upon which it was undoubtedly modeled, was much greater: it was intended to assure the right of the central government to legislate. Implicit in its creation also was a closer control of the ^{c}ulama by the central government, since the former were active in running the shar^c courts.

Heretofore the government had indirectly, through the ^{c}urf system, cooperated in implementing the rulings of the shar^c courts, but it did not have any jurisdiction over these courts. Under the new system successfully implemented, the government would have been the active partner in running the judiciary. Although the creation of the new courts does not seem to have gone beyond the planning stage, the implied threat in Mirza Huseyn Khan's attempt, which would have undermined ^{c}ulama power, could not have escaped their attention. This might well have constituted the beginning of their apprehension of Mirza Huseyn Khan and his policies, which met with increasing hostility and opposition from this powerful group.[12]

The ᶜulama's suspicions of Mirza Huseyn Khan's intention were well grounded. Although Mirza Huseyn Khan did not explicitly state his goal, there is sufficient evidence of his intention to limit ᶜulama power by reducing their role in the judiciary and curtailing their control of vaqf holdings or endowments.[13] His intent to create a strong central government would have, of necessity, curtailed the power of any organized group, such as the ᶜulama, that claimed ascendancy and independence within the state.

Mirza Huseyn Khan was diplomatic enough not to oppose the ᶜulama openly. On occasion he tried to win their friendship. But he expressed his real view of ᶜulama power in a letter to an intimate friend: "I believe that the *mullās* [clergy] should be entrusted with all matters that pertain to them, such as leading the prayer, preaching, performing marriage and divorce ceremonies, answering religious questions, and the like, so long as that does not contradict the interest of the State."[14] He reiterated this viewpoint in a letter to the shah two years after his removal from the post of sadr-i aᶜzam, which was brought about in part by the opposition of the religious leaders: "As for the mullas, I swear that they were never treated with as much respect as they were in the day of my *sidārat* [prime ministership]. But I did not permit them to interfere with the affairs of government."[15]

The active opposition of the ᶜulama to Mirza Huseyn Khan was, however, in the future, and it was not their hostility that prevented the successful implementation of the judicial reform program proposed by the new minister of justice. Although the sources do not shed light on the reasons why these plans failed, the most likely reason probably should be sought in their foreignness and the lack of prior preparation. Perhaps more than any of the later reforms of Mirza Huseyn Khan, the judicial reforms bear a resemblance to Ottoman and Western models. The nomenclature, function, and spirit of the new courts are strongly reminiscent of Ottoman judicial reforms.

The Western orientation of the judicial system instituted by Mirza Huseyn Khan is found in the procedural details of the various courts. Here in embryonic form are such Western judicial concepts as trial by jury, respect for the rights of the individual, the application of scientific methods in establishing evidence, and a formalized trial procedure. Other stipulations are: that court proceedings be recorded in special registers; that a defendant, unless accused of murder or grand robbery, be set free on bail; that the victim of a crime be examined by a qualified physician; that a judge's verdict be in agreement with the views of two court officials; and, finally, that the conduct of defendant and plaintiff in the presence of the judge be regulated.[16] These innovations are brought into perspective by an observer's description of what had preceded them: "As a rule plaintiff and defendant, accompanied by all their relations, present themselves at the public audience of the provincial governor; they and all their followers speak at once; they rave, they tear their hair, clothes, and beards. Pandemonium let loose is a joke compared to the scene at the first appearance in court of rival suitors." [17]

The preamble to the new laws and regulations stated that they were designed to ensure better protection for the citizens. The creation of the courts had been a move in this direction, and the passage of additional laws further attempted to achieve that end. One of the first new regulations stated: "No servant of the Ministry of Justice may summon a defendant to that office without a special printed warrant. No servant or official, unless thus authorized, is entitled to obedience." [18] This was an attack on the traditional arbitrariness of proceedings and the accompanying extortion practiced by officials.

Two weeks later another decree appeared, prohibiting all private individuals from exercising jurisdiction over subordinates. This important decree declared: "Heretofore, everyone has taken the liberty of trying subordinates and has willfully brought on them damage and suffering. To put an end to this injustice, His Majesty has decreed that from now on imprisonment and other types of punishment must be stopped." [19] It then proceeded to lay down the fundamental principle that the power to exercise jurisdiction was restricted to the Ministry of Justice in Tehran and its representatives in the provinces, i.e., the governors of provinces and towns, and heads of districts and villages.[20] This was directed at the large landowners and *tuyūldars*—the holders of *tuyūls* or land grants—two of the most powerful groups in the country, both of which had exercised authority to judge all disputes among the population of the villages.[21]

The tuyul was inherited by the Qajars from earlier times. By it the state granted to an official the authority to levy his salary or pension against the taxes of a particular district, which consisted of one or more villages.[22] The tuyul was usually given for life; but, increasingly during the second half of the nineteenth century, many tuyuls were transformed into private property. Since the tuyuldar paid no tax into the central treasury, large parts of the country were outside the direct control of the central government. For example, one estimate held that tuyul holdings in the province of Zanjan made up over one-third of the villages.[23]

Tuyuls were usually granted to high officials of state or to those favored by the sovereign as an additional source of income and influence. It would be naïve, therefore, to expect that this decree aiming to curb the power of the tuyuldars would meet with much success. Nevertheless, the decree contributed significantly to the cause of justice in Iran, if only by its statement of the principle that law and justice should be protected by the authority of the government rather than left to the whim of the individual. Even more significant was the assertion that only the central authority or those to whom it delegated its power had the authority to enforce the law.

A third decree deprived governors of the power to impose the death penalty, authority for which was reserved to the sovereign. The decree also prohibited infliction of any type of punishment on mere suspects. It attacked one of the mainstays of the arbitrary power of governors, who presided in the name of the sovereign over the execution of justice in the provinces. Seeking redress from the shah was in practice extremely difficult, so the governors had free use of this power. If a governor wished, he could exert pressure on any citizen with a threat of death, indefinite punishment, or torture. A subject could rarely protect himself against the whim and extortion of a powerful governor.[24]

This decree appeared as a circular addressed to the crown prince, Muzaffar ed-Din Mirza, the governor of Azerbaijan. Its introductory passage describes the conditions that prevailed in the provinces:

> Heretofore, in each province, it was customary for the governors to impose punishment on ignorant subjects on the slightest pretext; for the smallest reasons, overseers of districts and governors would inflict the severest punishments. Sometimes the real culprit would be set free without punishment, and at other times innocent people would pay the price.[25]

To end this abuse of justice, the decree stated, it was decided that only His Majesty should have the authority to determine punishment. "From now on, when a culprit is caught, he should only be put in prison and his case reported to His Majesty through the Ministry of Justice, so that His Majesty may decide on the case." [26]

For the first time in Iran the principle of the sacredness of human life was recognized. This was one of the few laws that were not abrogated after Mirza Huseyn Khan's dismissal; it remained as a testimony to his efforts to improve the rule of justice in Iran: "For this act, Mushir ud-Dowleh deserves the gratitude of the Iranian nation. As a result of his action and his care, no governor was able to kill anyone on the slightest pretext or to shed blood by mere accusation." [27] So said one of his critics many years after his death.

Mirza Huseyn Khan's concern for justice did not cease with his promotion to the post of sadr-i aᶜzam. He appointed as assistant minister of justice Mirza Yusuf Khan Mustashar ud-Dowleh, one of his trusted friends and the author of *Yik Kalimeh*. *Yik Kalimeh* was written while Mirza Yusuf Khan was in Paris as the Iranian charge d'affaires. In it Mirza Yusuf attributed European progress to one word—*law*. He explained in detail the French constitution, which he likened to the *shariᶜa* or canon law of Islam, calling it the shariᶜat of France. To allay the fears of the ᶜulama, he tried to show that all the articles of the constitution had parallel Qur'anic injunctions.[28] When the pamphlet was published in Tehran in 1287/1869, it was not well received by the shah, who ordered its author back from Paris. It is remarkable, therefore, that Mirza Yusuf received the appointment as assistant minister of justice. His appointment indicates Mirza Huseyn Khan's determination to safeguard the reforms he himself had initiated as minister of justice. The documents available do not shed much light on Mirza Yusuf's career, but do provide evidence of Mirza Huseyn Khan's continuing interest in the affairs of the Ministry of Justice long after he left it.

The official newspaper *Irān* on one occasion mentioned that Mirza Huseyn Khan, the newly appointed prime minister, attached great importance to the regulations he instituted in the Ministry of Justice. The report added:

> His Highness said to Amin ud-Dowleh [Mirza Huseyn Khan's successor as minister of justice], "You must consider your power and the sway of the rule of justice above any other consideration. You must not allow anything to stay the execution of your ordinances in the defense of justice. For example, once you have passed a verdict, it should be binding

on everyone, from the prime minister to the most humble citizen." [29]

Although Mirza Huseyn Khan was no longer able to directly supervise the affairs of the Ministry of Justice and the courts after his removal from the post of sadr-i aᶜzam in 1290/1873, he still held a position of trust with the shah and continued to urge him to initiate reforms, some of them in the judiciary. One of the latter was the introduction of *sandūq-i ᶜadālat,* the box of justice, in Tehran and the provincial capitals. These were sealed boxes, changed at regular intervals (twice weekly in Tehran and twice monthly in the provinces), installed in a central location and guarded to ensure that even the poorest citizen had free access to them. It was hoped that they would provide "those who have suffered an injustice which has not been redressed" with a means of appeal directly to the sovereign. [30]

A committee that included Mirza Huseyn Khan reviewed the complaints received through these boxes. Reports of W. T. Thompson, the British minister, concerning the arrest of a servant of the British consulate at Rasht indicate that the letters reaching the central government through these boxes were given serious attention. [31] The people flooded the boxes with requests and complaints, yet the boxes were quietly removed after several months and no specific reason given for their withdrawal. "The reluctance of governors to send the boxes back to the capital" [32] may have been one of the reasons.

A far more significant bill was the Code of the *Tanzīmāt-i Hasaneh* (the beneficent reorganization), which was promulgated in 1292/1875. [33] Although the code was concerned primarily with the reform of taxation and conscription, it also included provisions for judicial reform. It created a five-man council that included a representative from the Ministry of Justice, whose task was to "supervise the affairs of the subjects." [34] This vague phraseology is elaborated in the appendix to the code, which specifies the duties of the governors: "Whatever happens in the province, be it a dispute, an argument of a Sharᶜi or non-Sharᶜi nature, or disagreement concerning property, it should be referred to the Council of Tanzimat. The governor should bring forth to the council whomever the members should demand." [35] Thus, surreptitiously the code tried to remove the judicial authority remaining to the governors by transferring control of the jurisdiction of the ᶜurf courts to the *Majlis-i Tanzīmāt* or Council of Tanzimat, attempting to complete the process begun with the act of 1289/1872, which transferred to the sovereign the power to impose the death penalty.

Although the Tanzimat code did not explicitly interfere with the function of the shar^c courts, it tried to exert indirect control over them. Parties to a suit were required to inform the council of their choice of a shar^c court. The code stated further:

> Whatever the verdict of the shar^c court, the Majlis-i Tanzimat would issue the order for its execution, to be carried out by the governor. If by any chance the defendant or the plaintiff should produce another ruling, after the shar^c court has passed a verdict, it would not be binding. However, if at the beginning of the litigation, each side should produce a ruling in his favor, then the majlis would refer them to a third court. If both sides should disagree over the jurisdiction of that court or there should be any difficulty in assigning a third court, then the case will be reviewed by the majlis.[36]

By specifying that the shar^c court had to be approved by both sides, that the Majlis-i Tanzimat had to be notified of the choice, and that only the ruling of that court would be binding, the code closed many of the loopholes that had been manipulated to the advantage of the stronger party or used by unscrupulous officials for extortion from the lower classes. By affording appeal to the Majlis-i Tanzimat, the code further protected the weak and provided more equal protection than had been available until then.

The shar^c courts had never had the power to execute their rulings, and in theory at least the Tanzimat code did not deprive the religious class of any of its prerogatives. But the ^{c}ulama opposed the code, recognizing an attempt to impose tighter control over the judiciary including the shar^c courts. They may also have been alarmed at article 43 of the code, which brought some of vaqf property under the control of the majlis. The vaqf properties were a principal source of the power and independence of the clerical class. Any attempt by the government to loosen clerical control of these would naturally have evoked their hostility.

The ^{c}ulama were supported in their opposition by the governors, who were equally resentful of the central government's curtailment of their power.[37] The combined resistance of these two powerful groups proved disastrous. The code was abruptly abandoned by the shah and Mirza Huseyn Khan, both of whom feared that even more strenuous opposition was in the offing.[38]

Mirza Huseyn Khan's final effort to smooth the path of justice in Iran occurred in 1295/1878, shortly before the shah returned to Europe for a visit. After an alleged attempt on his life, the shah ordered the summary punishment of ten innocent men. To rectify the bad impression this action would have on the shah's image, Mirza Huseyn Khan recommended that a decree be passed, under which: "The Iranian government would guarantee the protection of the life and property of all its subjects. The rights of the people will be protected according to the tenets of the holy Shariʿa; and to ensure and strengthen the principle of justice, no order [for search] will be issued from any government office without prior and thorough investigation." [39] Nasir ed-Din Shah at first agreed to sign the statement into law, but he reversed this decision soon afterward. Yet eight years after Mirza Huseyn Khan's death, he did sign a similar law.[40]

It would be naïve to suppose that Mirza Huseyn Khan cured many of the ailments of the Iranian judicial system. Most people continued to refer their problems to the sharʿ courts, which were less costly and offered quicker decisions than the ʿurf courts, besides being more familiar. Furthermore, Mirza Huseyn Khan was minister of justice for only ten months, hardly time enough in which to remold that ministry into an effective organ for the administration of equal justice. Yet his achievement was not altogether negligible. Not since the time of Amir Kabir had the law and its enforcement had such a consistent advocate as it had in Mirza Huseyn Khan, whose attempts to codify the law objectively set an important precedent that found fulfillment in the Civil Code of 1911.[41]

4

MILITARY REFORM

Mirza Huseyn Khan was appointed minister of war on 13 Rajab 1288/29 September 1871. He was removed briefly in 1290/1873, but was reinstated a year later, and continued to head the ministry until his final dismissal in 1297/1880. During his years in office, he introduced extensive plans to reorganize the army: to regulate the army budget, systematize conscription, develop a new organizational model, hire European instructors, put new emphasis on the education of officers, and expand arms and ammunition factories. He expressed his aspirations for the army succinctly: "We hope the Exalted Government would possess an army, which by virtue not only of its bravery, its endurance both physical and spiritual, its obedience, but by virtue also of its new sciences and newly invented arms could be considered one of the greatest armies in the world."[1] Such an army was an important element in Mirza Huseyn Khan's overall plan to create a strong central government.

Mirza Huseyn Khan was appointed to the Ministry of War on a national holiday commemorating the birth of Imam ʿAli, the first Shiʿite imam. In the public speech announcing the appointment, the shah said:

> You may be wondering why I am wearing this military uniform today. . . . You are all aware that in these last few years we have not made progress worthy of the Iranian government in military and civil affairs; in particular, the kind of progress Europeans have achieved in modern weapons, in military drill, and in education has not reached Iran. Commanders and officers of high and low rank have neglected their duties, have exceeded their authority, and have destroyed the prestige of their profession. Commanders and high officers have become

accustomed to improper practices and have forgotten military regulations. Troops stationed on the borders and inside the country have become inactive—indolent instead of continuously drilling.... Therefore I have decided to assume the task of ordering and regulating the army in person. As an intermediary between us and the army, we appoint Hajji Mirza Huseyn Khan Mushir ud-Dowleh, who is present here, as our deputy, and we designate him as *sipah-sālār-i a'zam* [commander in chief] and minister of war. We give him these two books of law formerly written to execute to the last letter. From this date, promotion shall be based on service and not on heredity or patronage.[2]

In his speech the shah pointed out the principal shortcomings of the military system. By specifying that the decline had occurred in recent years, he implicitly expressed his approval of conditions in the early part of his reign when reforms were being carried out by Amir Kabir.

During the three years Amir Kabir was in power (1848–51), he tried to end unfair recruitment practices by instituting the *bunīcheh* system, which made conscription proportionate to the amount of taxation levied on a province, district, or village. He expanded and improved ammunition and arms factories, bought new arms from Europe, hired Austrian and Italian instructors to train Iranian army officers, and included military education in the curriculum of the Dar ul-Funun academy.[3] In those three years he created an army of 137,248 men, of whom 94,570 were in the infantry.[4] One observer well acquainted with Iran commented, "Had he [Amir] lived, the army of Persia might today have been a very different body than that which it now is."[5] After his dismissal and death, however, the army declined steadily. As the shah pointed out, due to the inefficiency and neglect of the commanding officers who were led by Kamran Mirza, the minister of war, and the shah's third son, the Iranian army at that time consisted of a vast irregular infantry and a small irregular cavalry. The only troops with regular training were the shah's personal guards.[6]

The shah's announcement made it clear that changes were in the offing. For once there was no harking back to a golden past from which the present had deviated; instead there was a forecast of new laws to come. If the shah wrote the declaration, he was surely guided by his new minister of war. The proclamation stated:

Since we are desirous of the progress of government, especially of the army; and since we now have decided to institute a new order and new regulations in this field, so that it will in no way resemble what it has been in the past, and so that, if God wills, all matters pertaining to the military will be conducted according to laws and regulations, we appoint Mirza Huseyn Khan Mushir ud-Dowleh, who is one of the special ministers and who is loyal to this state, as high minister of victorious armies and designate him as sipah-salar-i aᶜzam. He will have a free hand in executing beneficial regulations, and he is empowered by us to do what he deems necessary.[7]

Two months later the shah elevated Mirza Huseyn Khan to the post of prime minister, entrusting him with even greater powers.[8] Immediate crises had to be coped with, especially the famine throughout the country; but, although these required a great expenditure of energy, Mirza Huseyn Khan also retained the post of minister of war and continued to press for reform of the army.

Before Mirza Huseyn Khan could proceed with his plans, he had to determine the state of the existing army, its finances, and the ammunition and arms in the arsenals. The post of the army minister of finance, *vazīr-i lashkar,* had previously been most lucrative. When it became generally known that Mirza Huseyn Khan was looking for a new vazir-i lashkar, "some of the ministers and courtiers made attempts to win his friendship by offering him presents, so that he would appoint them to the post," [9] but he was not to be swayed. He wrote the shah that the choice should be made on the basis of "honesty and loyalty to the government, and complete obedience to his Majesty's commands. He should not be tempted by greed or intimidated by fear to perform what is unlawful." [10]

For this post, as for so many other key positions in his drive for reform, Mirza Huseyn Khan faced a shortage of qualified personnel, men who were both sympathetic to his ideals and determined to carry them out. His final choice as army minister of finance was Mīrzā Mūsā Āshtīyānī, one of a long line of bureaucrats in the Ministry of Finance. What commended him for the post were his great honesty and integrity, with which Mirza Huseyn Khan had had personal experience. In his early years of experience, he wrote the shah, he himself had tried to force Mirza Musa to lower taxes on one of his own villages, first by bribery, then by threats. "Then I left him with great annoyance," he wrote, "but at this critical time, I would like to entrust the army affairs to him." [11]

Not only was Mirza Musa honest, he was also thoroughly experienced in finance. When Mirza Huseyn Khan recommended him for the post of vazir-i lashkar, he informed the shah that

Mirza Yusuf Khan Mustowfi ul-Mamalik
Source: Khān Malik Sāsānī, *Sīyāsatgarān-i Dowreh-yi Qājār*, 2 vols.
(Tehran: Tahūrī, 1337S/1958), vol. 1

under him no one, not even Mīrzā Yahyā Khān Muᶜtamid ul-Mulk
(his own brother and the shah's brother-in-law), could get by with
incomplete or suspicious ledgers.[12] The shah approved the choice,
and Mirza Musa held the post of vazir-i lashkar—army minister
of finance—until his death in 1298/1880. During the intervening
years, he repeatedly proved himself worthy of Mirza Huseyn
Khan's trust.

Mirza Musa began his office by thoroughly investigating the
main arsenal in Tehran and its registers. He discovered that during
the eighteen years since Amir Kabir's dismissal no regular accounts
or registers had been kept. The registers had usually been com-
piled after each previous officer's term as head of the arsenal had
terminated. He found that the current head of the arsenal, who
had been appointed in 1276/1859, had reports that were seriously
deficient. An early report of Mirza Musa to the shah gives an
indication of the enormous problems the reformers faced: "For
several years the performance of the arsenal has been disrupted,
everyone has meddled with its affairs, no one has paid any indemnity or knows about what has been going on." [13] He made no
promises, except to do everything he could. When he finally succeeded in reconstructing the account books, he recommended an
annual investigation to prevent future confusion.

After the accounts had been organized and the contents of the
arsenal had been inventoried, Mirza Huseyn Khan directed the
energies of the Ministry of War to the ammunition and arms
factories. The Safavids had established elaborate factories. In the
Qajar period, ᶜAbbas Mirza, the son of Fath-ᶜAli Shah, had set up
facilities in Tabriz for making heavy artillery and ammunition.
Amir Kabir had built several arsenals and small cannon factories
in Tehran and the provinces.[14] Under the ministries of Mirza Aqa
Khan Nuri and Mīrzā Muhammad Khān Sipahsālār, the factories
had deteriorated; and under Kamran Mirza they had come to a
standstill.[15] The factories were now ordered back into production.
Mirza Huseyn Khan paid them a number of surprise visits. After
one of these, he wrote the shah a letter that reveals the working
habits of the time and his own impatience with the inefficiency
of his subordinates:

> I went to the arms factory without prior notice. Production
> has begun after it had stopped completely for two years. They
> are not performing as well as I would like them to. A hundred
> men were busy making cartridges in four rooms. . . . In several
> other rooms they were making cannon parts. . . . After care-

fully examining them [the cannons], I asked for Jahāngīr
Khān [head of the factory] and told him, "I advise you to take
heed. You have become accustomed to accepting obligations
and promising to fulfill them. Since you have never been held
accountable, you have not suffered from not keeping your
word. But now my reputation is at stake, and I have undertaken to finish making these fifty cannons by the time His
Majesty returns. . . . Try to get this work done, while there
is still time. I do not attach any value to words; only good
work can prove service.[16]

Mirza Musa's investigations revealed extensive misappropriation
of funds not only in the arsenal accounts but also in the method
by which soldiers were paid, which provided dishonest officials
with abundant opportunity to enrich themselves at the army's
expense—especially in the provinces, where the military budget,
like all others, was under the direct control of the governor. Mirza
Huseyn Khan wrote to the shah, pointing out the deficiencies of
the arrangement, "It was not easy to determine how much of these
funds reached the soldiery, and what amount was divided between
the commander and the governor." [17]

To amend the situation at least in part, Mirza Huseyn Khan
created, with the shah's approval, an independent treasury for the
Ministry of War, which collected what was allotted to the army
from the various provinces. Control of each provincial budget was
placed in the hands of the provincial commander, who was answerable to the ministry. With the governor thus eliminated as
middleman between the revenues and their dispersal, the soldiers
got a better share of their due.

Except for the creation of this treasury, Mirza Huseyn Khan's
efforts during his first term as minister of war were concentrated
on improving prevailing conditions for the army, especially for
the common soldiers. His initiation of a program serving hot food
in the Tehran barracks and nearby posts was so successful that
the shah ordered that hot food be likewise served even in the
remotest border areas.[18]

Mirza Huseyn Khan showed concern not only for the well-being
of his soldiers but also for their behavior toward civilians, especially
peasants. From Mongol times villagers had regarded the passage
of an army as a menace. There was no way to predict or prevent
the destruction wrought on villages, homes, and farms by troops
who were themselves mistreated, underpaid, and ill-fed. As late
as 1840 one observer remarked after the passage of the army:
"Hamadan looked as if it had been taken and sacked in war." [19]

Mirza Huseyn Khan apparently warned his men about such conduct. He reported to the shah:

> I sent for a few inhabitants from Galanduk and the surround-
> ing villages. They brought over a few of the elders. I inquired
> whether any damage had been done by the soldiers to the
> cultivation of their farms. If so, they should tell me, and I
> would render justice to them. They all swore that they had
> not been bothered by the soldiers, and in fact, the arrival of
> the regiment has been profitable and has helped them sell
> their products.[20]

In the same letter he said, "But no one seems to notice this,
except your Majesty, to whom no trouble or service goes by unnoticed." [21] Events would soon reveal, however, that it was not so
much that Mirza Huseyn Khan's performance went unnoticed as
that what he was doing was seen too clearly by some who were
threatened by it. They rallied to unseat him and, indeed, succeeded; but the shah remembered and, although threatened himself, reinstated him.

Mirza Huseyn Khan's first term as minister of war ended abruptly in September 1873 with his forced resignation. Although
he was appointed foreign minister a few months later and by
November 1874 was once more the minister of war, the shah's
attitude had changed fundamentally. Having become aware of the
strength of the opposition to new ideas, the shah no longer supported his minister of war actively. Even when in agreement with
him, he left Mirza Huseyn Khan to fight his own battles.[22] This
should be kept in mind as we discuss Mirza Huseyn Khan's various
projects for reorganizing the army.

During the first term of his war ministry, Mirza Huseyn Khan
had only had time to ameliorate the existing conditions of the
army; during his second term he began to work on major reor-
ganizations. High on the list of priorities was a guarantee of regular
pay for the soldiers. In one of the first letters he wrote to the shah
after his second appointment, he said, "In European countries,
progress has been achieved as a result of effort made to pay the
army on time." [23]

He was also immediately concerned with reforming conscription,
which he made part of his comprehensive code for reconstruction
of the provincial administration, the Tanzimat-i Hasaneh promulgated in 1874.[24] Thirteen of its forty-seven articles dealt with
conscription. Amir Kabir had introduced bunicheh, which made
recruitment proportionate to the taxation levied on a province,

district, or village. But length of service was usually for life, unless a soldier could buy a discharge from his superior. Under the conditions prevailing at that time, military service was not an attractive prospect for able-bodied villagers, and army life drew only the less able and unruly members of the population.[25]

To make service more acceptable, several measures were adopted under Mirza Huseyn Khan. The bunicheh was retained, but the measure (art. 16) stipulated that recruits be chosen by lot. This theoretically ended any unfair pressure the recruitment officer could exert on village notables by threatening to enlist their sons. The compulsory service term was limited to ten years rather than life (art. 18), although reenlistment at the end of ten years' service was made possible. The government was obligated to provide uniforms, arms, and rations for periods of drill; the soldier was entitled to regular pay of five tumans (£2.5) per month while on duty and half that while at rest (arts. 18 and 19). To protect enlisted men from unfair treatment by superiors, the verdict issued by the commander of the regiment for all major offenses, such as theft or murder, had to be reported to the Ministry of War for approval before enforcement (art. 19). Moreover, to protect civilians from the soldiery, disputes between soldiers and local populations had to be dealt with by the Majlis-i Tanzimat, a five-member council assigned by the central government to provincial and district centers to enforce the code (art. 20). Other articles pertaining to the military were mere elaborations of these sections.

The military reforms might have fared better had they been implemented separately. There seems to be little evidence that they elicited major hostility. But, unfortunately, pressure from groups with special interests, especially the ʿulama, forced the Tanzimat-i Hasaneh code to be set aside in 1875.

Though undoubtedly discouraged, Mirza Huseyn Khan was not daunted, and he persisted in carrying out some of the more important measures in the code through special enactments. One of these was the measure guaranteeing regular pay to soldiers. The issue appears regularly in his correspondence with the shah throughout 1874 and 1875. His rationale for regular wages was:

> The security, order, and power of the state, the collection of taxes inside the country, and the maintenance of the rights, and prestige of the government abroad all are dependent on a well-organized army. But the army cannot be organized unless its dues—including rations, wages, clothing, tent, and other necessities—are given regularly and promptly. Then you can demand it [to perform] and give it orders.[26]

This rationale was a sound one in the eyes of at least one foreign observer of Iranian events during the last decades of the nineteenth century, who agreed that: "The secret of a reorganization of the Persian forces would be a government guarantee of regular pay. In peace the army is now a loose aggregation of slovenly units, in war it degenerates on the least provocation into rabble. But by such simple means, and with capable officers, it might in a few years be converted into a creditable body of men." [27]

Shortly before the shah's first trip to Europe, the minister of war had pointed out the need for additional funds to enable the ministry to pay the soldiers regularly.[28] The lack of funds was one of the chronic problems Mirza Huseyn Khan faced in implementing his reforms; it was part of a larger problem that needed to be solved before any reform measures could be successfully implemented. The solution would be an extensive reorganization of the finances of the state, a task he did not have the expertise to undertake; instead he proposed partial and piecemeal measures. He now requested that a certain amount of custom revenue and some of the provincial revenue be assigned to this purpose. He also demanded a certain portion of the taxation in kind be turned over to the Ministry of War to create a central military granary in the capital. He argued in several letters that if the revenue sources were not specified and the needed sums appropriated on time, the ministry would not be able to regulate its affairs, including prompt payment of the military.[29] The shah agreed in principle, but he was reluctant to do so openly. He wrote:

> Assigning revenues for the army, as you have said, is necessary. Obviously the army needs money, and we are willing to give it. . . . Why don't you discuss the matter with the Aqā [Mirza Yusuf Khan, the minister of finance] and decide among yourselves where the revenue should come from. If the matter were still up to me, I would have assigned a place. However, the affairs of taxation and the provincial treasury have been entrusted to Mustowfi ul-Mamalik [Mirza Yusuf Khan]. Therefore, it would be unlawful of me to give an order.[30]

To appease the opposition, the shah had indeed divided the responsibility for all government affairs between Mirza Yusuf Khan and Mirza Huseyn Khan after his return from Europe.[31] But his reluctance to commit himself in this case was probably more a desire to maintain neutrality than to obey regulations. Recognizing this, Mirza Huseyn Khan pressed for the shah's active support; without it a steady source of income would be blocked by the minister of finance, who was his staunch adversary and chief rival.

Again he appealed to the shah, "If you do not support this: first, the new plans will remain incomplete; second, an army without funds and without definite sources of revenue is tantamount to disorder." He then turned to the question of Mirza Yusuf Khan's opposition. The shah advised Mirza Huseyn Khan to forget his differences with that venerable gentleman. He wrote: "Agreement is the beginning of order. From the start of this new arrangement, I want you and the Aqa to work in harmony." [32] In response Mirza Huseyn Khan asked to be spared from dealing directly with the Aqa. He replied: "The only problem that could create discord between us is this question of assignment [of revenues for the military treasury]. If this is removed, there will be no disagreement between us till the day of judgment." [33]

At last the shah ordered Mirza Yusuf Khan to assign to the Ministry of War the revenues from the provinces of Gilan and Isfahan, a portion of the proceeds from the customs, and some of the grains received in lieu of taxation.[34] The army could get the funds it needed, but the point was not completely won. Mirza Huseyn Khan had asked the sovereign for an independent and permanent source of revenue for which he would be responsible and account directly to the shah. But by addressing the order to Mirza Yusuf Khan, the shah had in fact implicitly given control of these funds, as well as supervision over their expenditure, to the minister of finance.

It might be argued that here Mirza Huseyn Khan was asking for the sort of unlimited power he had repeatedly denounced for others. In response it might be pointed out that the type of extensive reforms he wanted to initiate demanded freedom from the control of the opposition if his plans were not to be sabotaged. In a more formally regulated government, with more structure, it might be helpful to have one arm such as the Ministry of Finance checking on the Ministry of War. But under the conditions prevailing in Iran at that time, no law regulated the limits of the responsibility of any minister or body within the government, except perhaps the control of the sovereign. Most issues were determined primarily on the basis of personal considerations by those who were involved directly. Such control could easily become obstructive. This was why Mirza Huseyn Khan objected to Mirza Yusuf's involvement in the Ministry of War. Furthermore, the aging minister of finance had been one of the earliest and most

active members in the opposition to Mirza Huseyn Khan. Under
these circumstances, it was not surprising that the latter was wary
of Mirza Yusuf's control over the army's budget.[35]

Later events made it clear that his fears were not unfounded.
While Mirza Huseyn Khan rode high in the shah's favor, he had
no problems with the minister of finance. But as soon as the
opposition, which Mirza Yusuf headed, sensed that friction had
developed, they tried to cast a shadow on his personal integrity
by raising numerous objections to his accounts. Mirza Huseyn
Khan, who had nothing to fear in this respect, usually took the
matter up with the shah. He wrote on one occasion:

> In the last few days, they [the opposition] seem to have nothing
> else to do. They have been spending all their time trying to
> find just or unjust faults with my accounts. If they were mo-
> tivated by a sense of welfare of the state, may God be my
> witness, I would have been grateful. But I see that when they
> review the questionable accounts of Jahangir Khan [head of
> the arsenal], they openly and clearly say during the meetings
> of the Darbar-i Aᶜzam that his word is sufficient proof, and
> they write the drafts for whatever amount he asks for. But
> when it comes to my accounts, they raise a thousand objec-
> tions, which they think might result in my loss of reputation.[36]

In response, the shah indicated that whatever objections he might
have had to Mirza Huseyn Khan were not on grounds of dishon-
esty: "This is not the time for me to talk about your honesty," he
replied. "Of course, I have known you personally to such a degree
that I feel certain that you have not wasted even a penny of the
government's money. Since I know this, you should not be upset
by what others might say." [37] Some of the funds acquired in the
face of this opposition did go to the army, and much effort was
spent in seeing that this was done regularly and promptly. In
Tehran and contiguous areas, this was, no doubt, carried out with
considerable success;[38] but the minister of war was unable to exercise direct and effective control in the distant provinces.

Shortly after he succeeded in obtaining at least a semi-inde-
pendent source of revenue for the army, Mirza Huseyn Khan
prepared a code that would further limit any interference by
provincial governors with the funds allotted to the militia stationed
in their provinces.[39] This code, signed by the shah in Muharram
1294/January 1877, also defined and regulated the relationship
between the governor and the commander of the provincial troops.
Though quite limited in scope, it appears to have been a contin-

uation of the ill-fated Tanzimat-i Hasaneh, attempting to hold these two officials accountable for their breach of law or neglect in its enforcement and thus defining and limiting their responsibilities.

The new code established the principle of the superiority of the governor to the military commander (art. 2) and left to the governor responsibility for launching an attack on disruptive elements within the province. "If this action occurred without justification, then he [the governor] would be answerable to the government" (art. 3). Another important provision concerned separation of the duties of the two offices (art. 4) in its statement that, even if the same person held both posts, their functions should be kept apart.

The article dealing with the provincial army budget (art. 5) sheds light on how the provincial military budget was administered: "The tax, both in cash and in kind, which is levied on the province, according to the instruction sheet, must be paid without any interference [by the governor] to the official appointed by the minister of war; the receipt given [to him] by the official [of the ministry] is the only voucher needed." [40] Another (art. 6) stated that military expenses should be given priority over the other expenses of the province. This was, no doubt, to stave off any attempt by the governor to avoid paying the full amount of tax levied on his provinces.

The remaining ten articles of the code that deal with the army are elaborations of the points already mentioned. Even though the code theoretically ended the governors' misuse of military funds, it would be naïve to suppose that the funds collected were used as prescribed. Contemporary accounts of the misuse of funds by army officials controlling the budget abound. In one case the official in charge of collecting the military tax in Qazvin first lent the soldiers the money that was collected for their pay and collected interest on it before actually paying it to them. [41] The code, like other reforms, was further hampered by a lack of trained personnel to assure its implementation.

The training of the army, both of officers and soldiers, was another area that received attention from Mirza Huseyn Khan. At his initiative, in 1291/1873, in his first attempt to improve training and provide better qualified officers, the État Major College for officers was founded. Military subjects such as mathematics, engineering, artillery, and cavalry tactics were already being taught at the Dar ul-Funun, but the shah had not felt kindly toward that college since 1279/1862, when some of its teachers and students were implicated in a plot against him and his government. The new college was situated on the premises of the old; but, unlike Dar ul-Funun, it had a curriculum restricted to military subjects.

On the basis of available information, consisting of occasional references to the État Major College in the military newspapers *Rūznāmeh-yi Nizāmī* and *Mirrīkh*, it is difficult to determine the later development of this institution or the role it played in Mirza Huseyn Khan's military scheme. The Iranian officers who assisted the Austrian instructors in 1296/1877 were products of this school. After Mirza Huseyn Khan's fall from power in 1880, it was replaced by the Military College, which was founded by Kamran Mirza in 1885.

Of more lasting impact was the creation of two corps trained by foreign officers, one by Austrians, the other by a Russian. Attempts to hire foreign instructors began in 1873 during or soon after the shah's trip to Europe. Mirza Huseyn Khan broached the subject with the British authorities, but his request for British officers for this purpose coincided with what Curzon termed "the criminal reign of masterly inactivity" on the part of the British toward Iran, and the request was ignored.[42]

On the shah's second trip to Europe, thirteen Austrian officers and a Russian colonel were hired to train military personnel in Iran. Two weeks before their arrival, an article about modern warfare appeared in *Mirrikh*, which was published under Mirza Huseyn Khan's direction, as if to justify the need to hire them. The article, undoubtedly written at Mirza Huseyn Khan's instruction, discussed the differences between present and past methods of warfare. "In the past, victory was due to personal bravery," it said. "But now courage does not suffice, and war has become a science like other branches of knowledge, except that it is more difficult."[43]

The article attributed the conquests of the Mongols, Timur, and Nadir as much to their courage as to the weakness of their adversaries. But it pointed out that reliance on the element of chance could no longer be counted on because of the new scientific organization of war. Today's armies, it stated, depend on three elements: the efficiency, knowledge, and experience of the commanding officers; the unflinching loyalty and obedience of the soldiers toward their commander; and excellent armament. In

conclusion it added, "Any army possessing these qualities, even
if it is inferior to the enemy in numbers, will overcome its
adversary." [44]

Two weeks later the same newspaper announced the arrival of
one Russian and fourteen Austrian instructors. The Russian, Colonel Domantovich, was put in charge of creating a small cavalry
force of four hundred men, who were to be trained in the manner
of the Russian Cossacks, whose appearance had impressed the
shah on his visit to Russia.[45] At first the members of this group,
who came to be known as the Cossack Brigade, were made up
entirely of *muhájirs*, descendants of emigrants from Transcaucasia
after its annexation by Russia early in the nineteenth century; but
later other volunteers were admitted.[46]

Mirza Huseyn Khan allocated 10,000 tumans (about £5,000) to
the brigade for such initial expenses as purchasing tents, uniforms,
and horses.[47] With the aid of five additional Russian officers who
were hired later, Colonel Domantovich succeeded in creating a
force that became the most organized detachment in the Iranian
army. Ironically in later years the Cossack Brigade was used to
promote Russian aims in Iran. Even worse, it was the principal
force used by Muhammad-Alī Shah to crush the nascent constitutional movement in 1907.

The Austrian Corps's role in Iranian history was much less
significant than that of the Cossacks.[48] At first it was larger and
better organized than the Cossack Brigade. Among the Austrians
were infantry and artillery instructors, and even musicians to create a European-style army band. They were "to train seven thousand men who will be used as a model for the reorganization of
other battalions." [49] The corps was to consist of artillery and infantry regiments. In its first stage the model army was to consist
of 1,200 men, who were to be recruited from the central provinces
between Tehran and Hamadan. New recruits were to be added
every three months until the full complement was reached. An
Austrian instructor went with each Iranian officer to the provinces
to ensure the recruitment of qualified men.[50]

It seemed for a while that the regeneration of the Iranian army,
to which Mirza Huseyn Khan was devoting most of his time, was
about to be realized. Judging by the shah's frequent visits to the
training camp, which were reported in every issue of *Mirrikh*, he
also seems to have taken a great interest in the work of the Austrian
instructors. *Mirrikh* was filled with reports on the new army: its

training, division into regiments, uniforms, barracks, individual room assignments, furnishings, and similar details. The most novel of these developments was the creation of a military hospital and pharmacy under the supervision of a trained European doctor.[51]

These lengthy reports had two motivations. The first was to inform the public, to generate interest in the new army. The second and more important was a desire on the part of Mirza Huseyn Khan to impress the shah and fortify his own position. He must have been aware that his influence with the shah was on the wane and that the man who was replacing him in the shah's favor had sympathy for neither new ideas nor him. "Though the Shah has divided the power between the two men [Mirza Huseyn Khan and Mirza Yusuf Khan], it is Mīrzā Ibrāhīm [Amīn us-Sultan] who runs the show." [52]

The intimations of catastrophe proved well grounded. In Shavval 1297/September 1880, Mirza Huseyn Khan was suddenly removed from all official duties, including his post in the Ministry of War, and was appointed governor of Qazvin.[53] His stay in Qazvin was brief, however, for a few weeks later the shah ordered him to Azerbaijan to put down the rebellion of Shaykh ʿUbiydullāh, a Kurdish leader who had wrought havoc on western Azerbaijan. This done he was appointed *pishkār* or overseer of that province. He stayed there until 1881, when he was sent as Iran's representative to the funeral of Czar Alexander II in Russia.

Mirza Huseyn Khan's appointments as commander of the army to crush the rebellious Kurdish leader and as pishkar of Azerbaijan suggest that his removal from power a few months earlier was not for lack of confidence in him on the part of the shah.[54] But, as his enemies had hoped, many of the projects he had begun suffered considerably as a result of his departure. The Austrian Corps, for example, underwent a radical change. It became, instead of a model for the reorganization of the other regiments, a mere part of the existing army. It was enlarged to thirty thousand men and for some years constituted the most effective section of the Iranian army.[55] But under the apathetic new minister of war, Kamran Mirza, the shah's third son, the corps gradually disintegrated, as also did the other regiments. The only memory of Mirza Huseyn Khan's efforts to create a new army was the Russian-controlled Cossack Brigade.

One other aspect of Mirza Huseyn Khan's military reforms deserves attention: the expansion of ammunition and arms factories and the purchase of modern armament. His early efforts to put existing factories back into production were stepped up considerably during his second term as minister of war. While the shah was on his first trip to Europe, some five thousand transformed muzzle-loaders were bought from Germany.[56] More arms were ordered later from the Krupp factories.[57] Arms were also bought from Austria during the shah's visit there in 1878.[58]

The first steam-powered cannon foundry was set up in Tehran in 1879; it began production a few months before Mirza Huseyn Khan's dismissal from the Ministry of War. The glowing account of the shah's first visit to this factory suggests that Mirza Huseyn Khan found great satisfaction in the facility, for steam power to him was the symbol of European progress.[59] These factories were among Mirza Huseyn Khan's most lasting contributions to the Iranian army. When Curzon visited Iran in 1889, he discovered that most of the ammunition and arms used there were of local manufacture.[60]

Mirza Huseyn Khan also deserves at least partial credit for instituting the Tehran police force, which was created in 1296/1879 under the supervision of Austrian Count de Mont Fret. A contemporary account records that "Now the task of guarding the city, its houses, and the bazaars of the capital is in the hands of this large group. Verily, this office has had great success in putting an end to robbers and in preserving the general order of the city." [61]

In terms of the goals he set for himself, the success of Mirza Huseyn Khan's military reforms seems negligible. After his departure the main part of the Iranian army was in as great a state of disarray as when he came to power, and his hope for the creation of a modern army as the focal point of a strong central government went unrealized. But the Austrian Corps and the Cossack Brigade proved their effectiveness in 1896 after the assassination of Nasir ed-Din Shah. In guiding their creation, Mirza Huseyn Khan had rendered the country a great service.

In the panic that ensued after the shah's death, the statesmen in the capital feared the possibility of a move by Zill us-Sultan to usurp the throne. He himself had been bypassed in the succession because his mother was not one of the shah's legal wives, and he had never been reconciled to this and had tried to win the succession in his father's lifetime. Now he had a private army of seven thousand well-equipped men in Isfahan and was much closer to the capital than the crown prince, who had to come from Tabriz to assume power.[62] Yet Zill us-Sultan did not move to upset his father's decision, and for the first time in Qajar history a king ascended the throne without bloodshed.

The ease with which Muzaffar ed-Din Shah came to power was due mainly to the "semi-regular army of infantry, cavalry, and artillery, equipped, clothed, and drilled more or less along European lines and constituting the bulk of the defensive forces of the kingdom, "[63] which had been the creation of Mirza Huseyn Khan. This force might not have been great enough to fend off an attack by Britain or Russia, but it was sufficient to save Iran from the drain of civil war.

5

POLITICAL REFORM BEFORE 1873

WHEN Mirza Huseyn Khan was appointed sadr-i a'zam or prime minister in Sha'bān 1288/November 1871, his appointment set new trends in motion. The most obvious sign of change was the use of a new vocabulary reminiscent of the Ottoman Tanzimat. Emulation of the advanced nations of Europe was the goal of most government reforms. But the new mood went beyond new terms. Under Mirza Huseyn Khan, a great effort was made to replace an informal system of administration with a more bureaucratic system that would render government efficient and rational.

More significant was Mirza Huseyn Khan's attempt to regulate government affairs "by praiseworthy laws similar to those prevalent in the civilized governments, to which laws they owe their great progress." [1] He introduced regulations to create a cabinet system to coordinate and control all government affairs, set up provincial councils to curb the power of provincial governors, and instituted a consultative council to advise the sovereign.

His clear objective was to arrest the decline of the country, which was beset by disorder and corruption at all levels of government, and to create a state "in which all the affairs are conducted in the manner of the great states." [2] The successful implementation of his efforts would also have resulted in increased authority for the central government, where power would have been concentrated in the hands of a few men who had European orientation and training. To prevent this, a coalition began to form among all who found Mirza Huseyn Khan's reforms detrimental to their own power: the provincial governors who were accustomed to autonomy, the official class with its traditional training and outlook, and the 'ulama who were suspicious of any effort that might encroach on their domain.

Despite attempts at reform made by Amir Kabir between 1848 and 1851 and by Nasir ed-Din Shah beginning in 1858, Qajar government had generally been administered like one vast household. The pattern of administration resulted both from the origins of the dynasty and from its having come to power in 1796 after seventy years of internecine warfare that followed the fall of the Safavids in 1724.

Agha Muhammad Khan, the first Qajar king, "spent his early years at Asterabad [a small town in the Gurgan Steppes] and grew up among the nomadic Turkoman tribes." [3] He proclaimed himself ruler after the death of Karīm Khan Zand (1755–79) but did not ascend the throne until 1794, after he finally established control over the entire country. He defeated his challengers primarily in his capacity as the leader of his own tribe. These wars, especially those with the descendants of Karim Khan Zand, were really tribal feuds prompted by a desire to avenge the deaths of Qajar leaders at the hands of Karim Khan. [4] Agha Muhammad Khan's tribal origins and his close association with his tribe deeply influenced his style of ruling.

The first Qajar ruler chose Tehran as his capital because it was close to the tribe's grazing lands in the Gurgan Steppes on the northeastern frontier. His administration consisted only of a sadr-i aᶜzam, two ministers, and a number of scribes, most of whom had served earlier ruling houses. [5] He took the members of his administration with him on campaigns and closely controlled their management of the affairs of the empire. He alone cared for the crown jewels, for which he had a special fondness; he spent his leisure time playing with them. [6]

Soon after the Qajars had established themselves as legitimate rulers, the ranks of their administration began to swell under the demands of running a large country. But the basic nature of the administration remained personal and informal. Fath-ᶜAli Shah is a case in point. The splendors of his court and his large retinue revived memories of the Arabian Nights in the minds of travelers who had audience with him, yet he entrusted care of the crown jewels to one of his daughters, Khāzin ud-Dowleh, and responsibility for important correspondence to another, Anīs ud-Dowleh. [7]

Only in the reign of Nasir ed-Din Shah did a more formal type of government begin to appear once more. After dismissing Mirza Aqa Khan Nuri in 1858, the shah appointed six ministers and divided the work of government among them. He abandoned this arrangement, however, when he became disenchanted with the advocates of reform; and despite a great number of officials with myriad titles, state business continued to be conducted informally. The importance of an office depended on its holder and the degree of his closeness to the sovereign; the holder of a relatively insignificant office might surpass all others in power and prestige.

Through the 1860s, Nasir ed-Din Shah continued to exercise close control of government affairs, but as the decade closed he once more became interested in changing the old order. One reason was a two-year drought, together with widespread famine and cholera, which caused the death of a large number of people. Another reason was the rapid encroachment of the Russian Empire into the territories northeast of Iran, a fate the shah feared might befall his own kingdom. Finally, the shah had come to have increasing confidence in the ability of Mirza Huseyn Khan to carry out wide-ranging reforms that might save the country from total collapse. Soon after Mirza Huseyn Khan had proved his ability, first as minister of justice and then as minister of war, the shah elevated him to the post of sadr-i aᶜzam on 29 Sha'bān 1288/12 November 1871.

The extensive power given to the new prime minister indicated the shah's great trust in him. In the long decree announcing the appointment of Mirza Huseyn Khan, Nasir ed-Din Shah announced his intention to depart from the past, "when from everywhere and on every minor issue, reports were sent to the Royal Presence." [8] To spare himself "the inconveniences of the past," the shah stated that "In all government affairs, ranging from internal, military, and foreign, the sadr-i aᶜzam will personally direct the government," [9] including the supervision of the shah's household. In short, "The seal of the sadr-i aᶜzam shall signify royal assent." [10]

All officials, except a military adjutant and the deputy of the ministry of justice, were to send their reports to the sadr-i aᶜzam, including the ministers, governors of towns and provinces, and military commanders. The sadr-i aᶜzam, in turn, was to present to the shah a summary of what had been reported to him, along with his own suggestions for dealing with the matters. Finally, the decree added, the sadr-i aᶜzam would carry out His Majesty's wishes concerning the reports. [11]

Despite the wide-ranging powers entrusted to the sadr-i aᶜzam as the newly authorized head of government, his role and relationship with the ruler did not differ fundamentally from the traditional role of his predecessors, whose authority was merely

Muzaffar ed-Din Mirza, crown prince,
successor to Nasir ed-Din Shah
Source: S. G. W. Benjamin, *Persia and the Persians*
(London: John Murray, 1887)

an extension of that of the ruler; however, the new sadr-i a'zam soon made his impact felt. Traditionally, in Iran as in other pre-modern Islamic societies, natural calamities and problems of community or social welfare were considered to be private matters. When rulers built roads or established charitable foundations, they did so as private individuals who were prompted by religious or humanitarian sentiments. But in the face of the famine and cholera epidemic, the most serious challenges that faced Iran, Mirza Huseyn Khan involved the government. He organized a council of prominent officials and resident members of the foreign delegations to collect contributions and supervise relief work.[12]

The government organized several temporary settlements in and near the capital to accommodate the streams of refugees to Tehran.[13] Mirza Huseyn Khan made a considerable personal contribution, hoping to encourage other wealthy members of the court to do likewise. To acquaint the people with efforts of the Council on Famine Relief, regular articles were written in *Irān*, the official newspaper. During his first few months in office, the famine and the cholera epidemic required a great deal of Mirza Huseyn Khan's attention; but by the summer of 1289/1872, conditions had improved enough so that he was free to turn his attention to more fundamental issues.

His approach to issues like reform of the political structure differed radically from that of Amir Kabir, whose objective had been to make existing institutions viable. Amir's attempt to create a strong central government with a strong army and full treasury was based upon a pattern recommended by the Saljuqid vizier Nizam ul-Mulk (1017–92) in his manual for government, the *Sīyāsatnāmeh*. Nizam ul-Mulk was primarily concerned with the rule of one man. Whatever he recommended was meant to enhance the power, authority, and wealth of a single ruler. His recommendations were prompted primarily by expedience, with the well-being of the community a remote secondary consideration. He advised the ruler to be just because justice would result in the prosperity of his subjects, upon whom he depended for revenue.

Nizam ul-Mulk provided the ruler with a personal code of behavior, a code that did not extend to the generality of the people or the state. He felt that the shari'a would provide sufficient protection for the people. Whatever the reasons for not taking into account the welfare of the population and the state, Nizam ul-Mulk's attitude became the prevailing one among rulers and governments in Iran and other Muslim states. Furthermore, because of the personal nature of the code, it could not be used as a basis for protecting the welfare of rulers. Each ruler had to wage his own battle to assert control. This is exactly what Amir Kabir had attempted to do for Nasir ed-Din Shah. Although Amir Kabir had greater awareness of the state and of the welfare of the people than Nizam ul-Mulk, he was still primarily serving the interests of the ruler. Whatever reforms he undertook, including the importation of military technology and science from Europe, were designed to serve the ruler.

Mirza Huseyn Khan, however, had a totally different attitude. Although he was loyal to the ruler, for him the state came first, and the ruler was primarily an agent who served the state. Mirza Huseyn Khan believed in the preeminence of the state and the welfare of its people. In a letter to the shah, he referred to the lack of this orientation among most of his colleagues:

> The reason for the quarrel of Nizām ud-Dowleh and the others with me is only one point: whereas I say, "We should look after the welfare of the State," they say, "We should look after the welfare of the individual." I want order, they want disorder so that they can promote their individual interests. In the opinion of your humble servant, if we continue in this manner we shall fall apart and soon be enslaved [by our neighbors].[14]

The major regulations instituted by Mirza Huseyn Khan were an attempt to protect the state against individuals. The laws devised to regulate the relationship between various members of the government and each other and between the government and the people were an attempt to prevent certain individuals from jeopardizing the welfare of all. The regulations were meant, first, to create a body within the government that would coordinate, control, and bear final responsibility for all important matters within the country; and second, to institute laws that would govern the relationship between the provincial governors and the central government and thereby enhance central control over the provinces. These objectives were indicated in an article that dealt with Ottoman reforms, which stated, "Recently the Ottoman government has been reorganizing its internal affairs, and the Ottoman sadr-i acẓam is carrying out beneficial laws and regulations [qavānīn-i Hasaneh va Tanzīmāt-i Mustahsaneh]." [15]

This perhaps refers to the thorough revision of the Vilāyat Law issued in 1864.[16] The revised law had regulated the provincial administration by setting up an integrated hierarchy, "stretching from the sultan down to the rural community." In this hierarchy the *valī* or governor controlled the police, political affairs, financial affairs, and the execution of justice and the imperial laws.[17] The administrative councils to be set up under the law were to have members who were elected by local communities as a first step toward some kind of electoral system. The chief aim of the revised law was to eliminate some of the ambiguities of the previous law. One of the consequences of the revision was to increase the power of the governor.[18] These are important points to bear in mind when reviewing the article about Ottoman reforms, which stated further:

> The purpose of that government is to change the tradition [*rasm*] of government and the law of the country. Hence an ordinance has been issued by His Majesty the Sultan to the sadr-i aʿzam stating that innovative laws and new regulations have become prevalent. The people of the country have carefully considered this and have realized the advantages of the new regulations and have recognized the shortcomings of the old laws. Not until such unpraiseworthy manners and such unpropitious foundations have been uprooted can the affairs of government prosper and the affairs of the people move toward progress. The change in the affairs and manner of government is a prerequisite for the progress and education of the government and the nation.[19]

Clearly then, Mirza Huseyn Khan's intention was not so much to inform his readers about Ottoman reforms as to prepare them for what he himself intended to do—to completely reorganize the Iranian government. He cited the Ottoman example to clear the way for acceptance of his own reforms.[20] The article does, however, reveal Mirza Huseyn Khan's continued interest in Ottoman reforms.

These objectives were presented in the form of two major regulations: the Edict of the Darbar-i Aʿzam, issued in Zīhajjeh 1289/ January 1873, and the code of Tanzimat-i Hasaneh, issued in Safar 1291/March 1874

The Edict of Darbar-i Aʿzam was one of the strongest of these attempts to reform the system. The timing of the announcement, significantly, coincided with the shah's decision at last to travel to Europe, as the preamble mentions: "The benefits of such a formal organization are in keeping with His Majesty's new intention for the exalted government of Iran, especially at a time when His Majesty is on the verge of traveling to Europe. It is necessary that in his absence the exalted government should have an official body and a magnificent appearance." The stated objective of the edict was to "follow the example of all civilized nations . . . and to create in the exalted government of Iran a governing body which the French refer to as the *cabinet*." [21]

According to the edict, the *darbar-i a*ᶜ*zam* or sublime court was created to attain two goals: first, to establish the principle of consultation among members of the government—"the soul of the darbar-i aᶜzam is this principle of consultation among the ministers"—to maintain unity of purpose in the government; and, second, to create cabinet responsibility, an idea hitherto nonexistent in the Iranian political tradition. [22]

Malkam Khan, who was serving as Mirza Huseyn Khan's private secretary, may well have been instrumental in writing the edict. Its objectives are similar to those of an organization he proposed in his essay "Daftar-i Tanzīmāt yā Kitābcheh-yi Ghaybī," written for the shah in 1276/1859. In the essay Malkam Khan attributed the weakness of his country and the prevailing chaos and corruption to a lack of ministerial or official responsibility and the failure on the part of ministers to consult with one another. He demonstrated that for these reasons the commands of the sovereign could be ignored or even reversed by his officials. Rather than criticizing established practices, the edict merely defined broadly the relationships between members of the cabinet and each other as well as with the sovereign, and it briefly discussed areas of responsibility.

The sadr-i aᶜzam and nine ministers constituted the darbar-i aᶜzam, which according to the edict was in charge of "the entire administration of the country." Government was divided into nine ministries—war, finance, justice, foreign affairs, interior, stipends, court, commerce, and agriculture. The sadr-i aᶜzam was to be appointed and dismissed by the sovereign, but the other nine ministers were to be appointed and dismissed by the sadr-i aᶜzam subject to the shah's approval.

The edict stated that the sadr-i aᶜzam was to head the darbar-i aᶜzam and to have final responsibility for the cabinet. He had authority to question any minister about the internal affairs of his ministry; and the ministers could communicate with the sovereign only through him, a provision that must have aroused jealousy among many who were accustomed to easy access to the shah, whose favor brought wealth, power, and prestige. These officials considered Mirza Huseyn Khan an intruder. Not only was he a social upstart, the grandson of a masseur, but he was also alienated from them by his European education and years abroad. Denying them access to the shah must have confirmed their mistrust and their fear that by putting into practice what he had learned in Europe he would throw them into the shade. All these considerations contributed to his eventual downfall.

The edict defined the responsibilities of the ministers in general terms only. More specific definitions of function and scope of ministerial activity appeared some months later, on the eve of the shah's departure for Europe.[23] The edict stated only that each minister was to be responsible and autonomous in his own ministry and was not to interfere in the affairs of any other ministry. The ministers were to meet weekly, at an appointed time and place, and to be jointly responsible in session. No minister was permitted to hire, dismiss, promote, or alter the salary of any of his subordinates without permission of the prime minister and knowledge of the cabinet. Salaries were to be determined by the office rather than by the person who held it: "The salary should be determined by rank, and not by those who receive it. The salary is a remuneration for services rendered and is dependent on the rank. Individuals do not determine the rank and salary of an office." Another principle in the edict contrary to prevailing practice stated that promotion was to follow definite procedures and was to be based on merit rather than connections. Each minister, like the prime minister, was required to conduct the affairs of his ministry from an office rather than from his home.

In its structure and the duties of its members, the darbar-i aᶜzam was clearly patterned after a European cabinet or council of ministers. The process of decisionmaking belonged to the whole cabinet; issues were to be determined by majority vote. The internal affairs of each ministry were to be left to its minister, but total responsibility and final authority in all government affairs rested with the prime minister. Mirza Huseyn Khan obviously intended to render the darbar-i aᶜzam an instrument for making policy as well as coordinating government functions; in short, he was developing a competing executive branch of government.

Implementation of the edict would have yet another important result. It would place a restraint on the shah's traditional authority, which was limited by prescriptions of expediency and of the sharᶜ law, such as consideration for a strong governor, a member of the ᶜulama, or a popular ᶜurf practice. According to the edict, the shah was the source of authority of the state, but he could exercise his authority only through delegation. It was his right to appoint and dismiss the sadr-i a'zam, who bore responsibility for executing his commands and wishes; but the sadr-i a'zam appointed and dismissed all other ministers subject to the shah's approval.

The attempt to place partial limits on the sovereign's exercise of arbitrary authority was not intended to change royal absolutism. Still the edict was a significant step in the direction Mirza Huseyn Khan had been advocating, namely, that law and not individual whim should regulate the affairs of government. Before the edict the shah's relationship with his sadr-i a'zam had been nebulous. The sadr-i a'zam had no authority of his own; his power was an extension of the king's authority. While a strong sadr-i a'zam could at times override the will of the sovereign or abuse his authority, he did so at his own peril. Without legal sanction, he was entirely at the mercy of the monarch and an easy target for court intrigue, a situation that was hazardous not only for the sadr-i a'zam but also for the welfare of the state. The two outstanding prime ministers of the Qajar period, Qa'immaqam and Amir Kabir, provide tragic examples of the defect in the Iranian political system before the Edict of the Darbar-i A'zam was enacted. Mirza Huseyn Khan's intent to effect some restraint on the sovereign's unlimited power is revealed in a letter he wrote to Mu'in ul-Mulk, a friend who was of like mind, who had just been appointed Iran's ambassador to Istanbul: "[His Majesty] has delegated the execution of all the affairs of government, and [he] no longer deals with anything personally. He has abandoned those old ways you knew about." [24]

The question is, why did Nasir ed-Din Shah approve a law that limited his own authority, which, according to many contemporaries, he took great pains to preserve?[25] The most simple explanation is that the edict, promulgated shortly before his first European trip, was merely a gesture to placate his European hosts. That may be the reason for the timing, but it surely was not the sole reason for its promulgation. Had the edict been merely a gesture to please liberal European governments, it would not have engendered as much opposition to Mirza Huseyn Khan as it did among the more traditionally oriented political elite of the country.

It is possible, of course, that the shah did not realize the extent to which the edict would curb his authority. Nowhere does it mention the ruler's prerogatives—only that he should exercise his authority through the prime minister. The omission may have been an intentional effort to avoid alarming the shah. Mirza Huseyn Khan may have emphasized to the shah what he could gain from the edict: more effective control over his men. As Dr. Polak observed, the shah was well aware that, despite his unlimited power, he had no actual control over the enforcement of his wishes.[26] Any doubts he had about the shortcomings of his position as despot in relation to his men could have been removed by Malkam Khan's essay on "The Organization of the Army and Administrative Council." In it Malkam argued that despotic power was more apparent than real, and he pointed out that it was to the sovereign's advantage to exchange the mantle of despotic power for one of absolute rule, under which officials would have definite delegated responsibilities for which they could be questioned when at fault. As long as the shah realized that the edict could render his hold more effective, it would have earned his full support.

Since the Edict of the Darbar-i A^{c}zam defined the role of the cabinet only in general terms, the task of extended definition was completed with a second edict that was issued privately on the eve of the shah's departure for Europe on 11 Safar 1290/9 April 1873.[27] The stated purpose of the edict was to create a provisional council to supervise the affairs of government during his absence and that of his prime minister. It revealed the determination of the shah and Mirza Huseyn Khan not to leave the affairs of state to chance. By describing the duties of the members of the Provisional Council, which was to be composed of a regent, a deputy prime minister, and other ministers or their deputies, it further clarifies the prime minister's authority under the Edict of the Darbar-i A^{c}zam and shows how the government was intended to function. Prince Kamran Mirza, the shah's third son, was appointed regent; and Prince Farhād Mīrzā, the shah's uncle, was named deputy prime minister.

Two articles in the second edict deserve particular mention. One (art. 3) stated that all correspondence between the various ministers and governors general had to be carried out with the knowledge and approval of the prime minister. The other (art. 8) discussed the prime minister's responsibilities for civic affairs of the capital, including sanitation and the police. Civic affairs, with the exception of the police, had traditionally been left to private individuals or to the quarters of the city.

Issues pertaining to routine work were to be dealt with by individual ministers, each of whom was required to present the Council of Ministers with a weekly report of events in his domain.

But matters concerning border areas, extortions by governors, delays in the payment of taxes, complaints of battalions against commanders, requests from individuals for tax reductions, and the like should be discussed at the council and decided upon by the members collectively. The council was to meet twice a week. All ministers were equally free to discuss all issues, and a majority vote would determine the decision of the council. In the event of a tie, the vote of the prime minister would be counted twice.

The new edict reveals an attempt by Mirza Huseyn Khan to break the power of the minister of finance by transferring some of his traditional duties to the Ministry of Interior. The Ministry of Interior had been created by Nasir ed-Din Shah in 1276/1858 to control such functions as education, post and telegraph, industry and mines, and commerce and agriculture. Under Mirza Huseyn Khan it had become increasingly involved in provincial affairs, including the assessment and collection of taxes, which had previously been the exclusive domain of the Ministry of Finance. This was an attempt on the part of Mirza Huseyn Khan to reduce the power of the mustowfi ul-mamalik, the minister of finance, and the men working in his office.

These two edicts constituted only one part of the extensive plan Mirza Huseyn Khan devised to regulate the affairs of government by law. Another part consisted of laws designed to reorganize the provincial administration. By defining and sometimes limiting the power of provincial governors, these laws strove to enhance the power of the central government so that it would, indeed, be the highest authority in the land.

It takes only a brief review of center-province relations to reveal how difficult that task would be. The Qajars had reverted to the pre-Safavid practice of assigning princes to be governors general or governors of provinces and townships. In theory the governors were representatives of the monarch in the provinces. In practice most had a good deal of autonomy. They controlled tax collection, conscription, and the judicial system; thus they had a firm basis for controlling the resources of the areas under their rule and for exploiting the local population.

The desire of provincial governors to gain as much independence of action as possible was not limited to Mirza Huseyn Khan's period, but has been a recurrent feature of Iranian history.[28] In the past most rulers and statesmen had attempted to assert central control by a show of force that lasted only as long as a strong leader was in power. In this way Amir Kabir had extended central control to every province, but after he was gone certain governors once again gained ascendancy.

Struggles between the central government and defiant governors had at times led to war; and the main burden in these conflicts, no matter who emerged as victor, fell upon the civilian population. Even worse for the people of a province was the absence of any check against the abuses of an unscrupulous governor. Although the injunctions of the shariᶜa praised justice, it contained no specific laws to punish a transgressing governor. A ruthless governor could always justify his actions and those of his subordinates with al-Ghazali's dictum that an unjust ruler was better than none; for without a ruler there would be chaos and no community to act as the living embodiment of the shariᶜa. This religious justification, and the circumstances that had for centuries legitimized rule by the sword, had caused the ruling classes in Iran and other Muslim lands to feel that as long as they provided protection for the civilian population, they could exploit it to the limit of its endurance.

Mirza Huseyn Khan was one of the few members of the ruling classes to condemn this attitude. A few months before his return to Tehran from Istanbul, he commented in a letter:

> When our governors are appointed to a place, at first they try to rob the government by creating unnecessary expenses. Then they try to reduce the amount of tax they have to pay the government. But they do not pass a penny of what they get out of the government to the people. . . . They leave behind them memories of injustice, of oppression, of exorbitant fines, of their ruining the country, of their destroying the house of the subject and the house of the king; and they take away a personal fortune.[29]

To curb the powers the governors had come to regard as their own, Mirza Huseyn Khan devised laws that would ensure the supremacy of the central government vis-à-vis the provincial administration and would also diminish the power of the governors over the populations in their regions. He wanted to introduce reforms that would outlast him, would strengthen central control, and would give better protection to the people.

As early as 1288/1871, Mirza Huseyn Khan expressed his intention to define and limit the power of the governors. In a circular issued in the shah's name, addressed to Muzaffar ed-Din Mirza, the crown prince and governor of Azerbaijan, it was announced that henceforth the right to pass the death sentence belonged exclusively to the sovereign; all others were forbidden to pass such a sentence. The decree also prohibited inflicting any type of physical punishment on those suspected of crime. The judicial ramifications of this edict have already been discussed.[30] What should be emphasized here is that the edict introduced the concept of the sanctity of human life and established, in principle, the notion of a centralized system of justice in the secular branch of the law. It is difficult to determine how effective the edict was, but I'timad us-Saltaneh, the official historian of the reign of Nasir ed-Din Shah, mentions it as one of Mirza Huseyn Khan's greatest contributions and testifies that it "prevented the despotism of governors."[31]

Shortly after Mirza Huseyn Khan was appointed prime minister, he announced his government's intention to punish severely all governors found guilty of accepting bribes or of extortion. He called bribery "the mother of all evils besetting the country," and he had attacked it since his days in the Ministry of Justice. But in this instance he was not attacking bribery as such but an established practice among the Iranian official class to use their office to enrich themselves.

Mirza Huseyn Khan's policy was expressed in a circular sent to all governors.[32] His opening remarks, reminiscent of the traditional manuals of government, set forth prudence and expediency as guidelines for behavior. He recommends that governors treat their subjects with justice and without extortion, explains that the prosperity of the subjects upon whom the government depends for most of its revenues was, along with good laws, one of the two most important pillars of state. Yet, he adds, many governors blinded by greed have oppressed the population to enrich themselves at cost to the state. Then, adopting his usual didactic tone, he cautions against greed, "which, according to all rational and traditional injunctions, is the worst enemy of the state; and not until greed has been uprooted, can the state be assured of its future greatness."[33] He reminds the governors that:

> The government has assigned from the levies of the province sufficient salary for each of you, to enable you to live honorably. . . . If you are content with what has been assigned to you and you can dispel greed and the tendency to extortion, so much the better for you. Otherwise, it would be better for you to resign from your governorships lest you get caught.[34]

Then, in a tone both direct and menacing, he adds:

The ignoramus might console himself by saying that he has
heard the same thing before, without its ever being put into
practice or any culprit being punished. But let me tell you
that the government will be observing you at all times and
everywhere, and should anything contrary to what has been
mentioned in this circular be committed by you . . . I will not
be lenient, but will inform His Majesty, and demand your
punishment.[35]

The circular contained another ominous note for the governors.
It stated, "The work that remains to be done is defining the limits
between the governors and the subjects."[36] But Mirza Huseyn
Khan was not able to do that work until March 1874, when the
code of the Tanzimat-i Hasaneh was promulgated—a delay caused
by the events following upon the shah's return from Europe.

Mirza Huseyn Khan's circular must have had a mixed reception
among the governors. Some, like Hisām us-Saltaneh, governor of
Khurasan, the shah's uncle, ignored it entirely. The "conqueror
of Herat," Hisam us-Saltaneh was the only military leader considered capable of thwarting Turkoman attacks from the northeast,
and he felt invincible. He disregarded Mirza Huseyn Khan's warning in the circular. Mirza Huseyn Khan acted swiftly. With the
shah's full knowledge and support, he dismissed the prince from
his post. The shah's opinion of the action is clear from his comment
on the letter of dismissal Mirza Huseyn Khan sent to Hisam us-
Saltaneh: "I really enjoyed your letter. This is what I call a sincere
and fair letter, motivated by concern for the state. Former ministers, prompted by greed and the like, would not write such a
letter to the governor of Kashan, let alone the governor of Khurasan, and Hisam us-Saltaneh at that."[37]

The dismissal must have come as a shock to Hisam us-Saltaneh
and other strong governors. Zill us-Sultan, one of the latter group
and the shah's eldest son, reflects their reaction: "In this year
Shihāb ul-Mulk, Huseyn Khan Shāhī Savan, who was one of the
wisest of men, was sent to Khurasan at Mirza Huseyn Khan's
suggestion. Hisam us-Saltaneh, who had been taking away whatever people had, was ignominiously put in prison, fined heavily,
and sent to Tehran in a most humiliating fashion. Huseyn Khan
[Shahi Savan] was appointed governor in his place."[38] The lesson,
as the above passage reveals, was not lost on Zill us-Sultan, who
had accumulated great wealth by similar methods in the province

of Isfahan. When instructed to return to Tehran, he did not resist, even though he had boasted of having an army equal in number and equipment to that of his father. However, neither he nor Hisam us-Saltaneh forgave "the grandson of the *dallāk* [barber and masseur in a public bath]" who had affronted them. Several months later, when Mirza Huseyn Khan left with the shah for Europe, they found an opportunity for revenge.

High government officials and powerful governors were not the only groups to resent Mirza Huseyn Khan's attempts at reform. One edict also hurt a majority of the official class. It came shortly after Mirza Huseyn Khan's appointment as sadr-i aᶜzam, when he launched a thorough investigation of the government payroll that resulted in drastic reductions in the salaries of most government officials, including the most powerful princes. The measure was extremely unpopular, as Iᶜtimad us-Saltaneh makes clear: "He was extremely unbending on cutting the salaries . . . and this very act irritated the people and turned their hearts against him. They all united and set about to ruin him. They did not relax until they had achieved their objective." [39]

Lower-level bureaucrats were probably even harder hit by this measure than the top officials. To make matters worse for the lower echelons, after careful scrutiny of the pension lists, the government stopped payment to the descendants of many pensioners who had long since died. The bitterness of an ordinary official is reflected in a comment by a chronicler of the court—a comment at the end of a laudatory account of Mirza Huseyn Khan's efforts to help the poor during the famine of 1870–71. Although the chronicler admired these charitable acts, he said:

> He cut the salary of some of the government's servants. But he did even worse; whoever died, and their number was great, he crossed his name and said, "When a man dies his salary dies with him, only those who can render the government a service should be entitled to receive anything. . . ." Woe on the people who were considered dutiful servants for many years. They made a name for themselves, and lived for many years on the salary assigned to them by the government; a group of people including wives, children, relatives, and servants had depended on these men for daily bread. But all of a sudden, without any reason or excuse, his allowance is struck off the list, and his dignity is destroyed. This is not the act of a sane man or a person of right belief. No God-fearing man would commit such a deed.[40]

The chronicler, Mīrzā Ibrāhīm Vaqāyiᶜ-Nigār then produced a *khabar*, an oral statement by a Shiᶜi imam, from the Imam ᶜAli, the first Shiᶜi imam, in which it was predicted that the *mahdī* would appear when the world had been filled with injustice by a *zindīq* (heretic) named Mirza Huseyn Khan.[41]

Despite the mounting opposition to reform, *Iran* carried regular reports of ministers and governors appointed by the shah at Mirza Huseyn Khan's suggestion and of cabinet meetings held at specified times, and similar matters, indicating that the changes were being effected. The shah repeatedly expressed pleasure and support in letters of praise written either to Mirza Huseyn Khan privately or publicly in *Iran*.

Mirza Huseyn Khan himself was optimistic about the outcome of his efforts. He revealed this mood to his intimate friend Muᶜīn ul-Mulk in Istanbul. After informing his friend of the shah's cooperation and resolve to rule by delegating authority, he said:

> Taxes from the provinces have been coming regularly, and the salaries of all the people, including the army, the princes, and the *khans*, men of the pen, and the various men working in the bureaus have all been paid. The army has been organized, and there are at present ten battalions in Tehran, and it could be said that very soon they will equal European armies. . . . If God wills, we will continue to improve and restore order [in the affairs of government].[42]

This optimism was shared by a handful of colleagues, one of whom, Hasan-ᶜAlī Khān Garrūsī, minister of public works, wrote to the same Muᶜin ul-Mulk, now an ambassador, "If you have the Bāb-i ᶜĀlī in Istanbul [the office of the prime minister, then held by Midhat Pasha, a well-known reformer], we have formed here a darbar-i aᶜzam and a council of ministers, which will be an increasing source of benefits." [43]

Meanwhile, Malkam Khan, another close friend and colleague, was urging the prime minister to speed the pace of reform. On learning of Midhat Pasha's appointment as grand vizier in August 1872, he tried to arouse Mirza Huseyn Khan's sense of rivalry: "Undoubtedly Midhat Pasha will try to accomplish great things for the Ottoman government, and he will be your rival in this respect, for now the eyes of Europe will carefully watch and compare the actions of the two sadr-i aᶜzams." [44] Eager to save the country from the destruction he thought imminent, and modeling his efforts on those of the Ottomans, another Muslim land in a state of decline, Mirza Huseyn Khan set out to introduce new institutions that were European in spirit if not always in name.

What he and his friends failed to take into account was that the Ottoman effort to emulate the West had begun almost a century earlier, during the reign of Sultan Selim III (1792–1807) and that by the mid-nineteenth century the old order, for better or worse, had been destroyed so completely that a return to the past was impossible. In the meantime, as a result of the reforms of Mahmud II (1808–39), a class of men had already been trained there, among them "a high proportion of men of loyalty, integrity, and responsibility, with a real understanding of the problems and difficulties of their country and a determination to face and overcome these problems." [45]

In contrast, no work similar to that of Mahmud II had been undertaken in Iran; and most Iranians, even those in important government positions, were totally ignorant of Europe and its institutions. The number of men with anything approaching modern training could not have exceeded two hundred fifty,[46] and because the official class was suspicious of modern education, these few were mostly in positions as translators and teachers or served in the armies or in embassies. Few were available to help Mirza Huseyn Khan, who had great difficulty in finding men to carry out his reforms. In the darbar-i aᶜzam, for instance, with the exception of Mirza Huseyn Khan himself and Hasan-ᶜAli Khan Garrusi, the members all belonged to the existing class of officials. Changing their titles was not enough to carry out change effectively. Mirza Huseyn Khan himself did not seem to realize that change could not be effected by royal decree alone.

Another serious obstacle to reform was Iranian society's lack of familiarity with and understanding of Mirza Huseyn Khan's ideas and the reform measures. Consequently they gave rise to a feeling of apprehension and genuine concern for the fate of the existing order. The apprehension of the vast majority about the major changes introduced by Mirza Huseyn Khan was expressed by Prince Farhad Mirza in a letter to the prime minister:

> Your Highness has spent many years abroad. This is good, and it is an indication that you have no personal malice, your actions are not prompted by personal considerations for anyone. But this fact indicates also that you are more accustomed to the ways of the foreigners. . . . If you suddenly try to change all the ways of doing things in Iran, such as the fact that an aged Qajar is receiving a thousand tumans, and that instead

the money should be spent on buying guns for the arsenal, of course this can be done. However, it might cause a great disorder.... If you try to make Iran like Europe overnight, saying, "Why shouldn't our country be like Europe?" this cannot be done, it would require a long time.... It would be beyond the realm of possibility for you to try and change within a period of six months the five-thousand-year-old laws of Iran.[47]

Such expressions of alarm, direct and indirect, were rare; this was the first time, to my knowledge, that anyone communicated such sentiments to the prime minister. Perhaps only the shah's uncle dared to criticize Mirza Huseyn Khan's plans and projects. Since the reforms were carried out in the shah's name, it would have been difficult to oppose them openly. Yet it appears that mere self-interest was not the sole motive of those who opposed Mirza Huseyn Khan; they were genuinely apprehensive about the outcome of his reforms.

Mirza Huseyn Khan appears to have underestimated the extent of the opposition to him and his reforms among members of the ruling class, or he surely would not have arranged to take the shah on an extended tour of Europe at such a sensitive time. He had hurt the interests of powerful governors and officials and had also alienated lower officials. His decision to reinforce his reforms with the shah by taking him to Europe gave the opposition a chance to group forces and attack those reforms in an organized fashion.

The Reuter Concession, signed on 25 Jamādī ul-Avval 1289/25 May 1872, gave the opposing forces an excuse to ask for the dismissal of Mirza Huseyn Khan. The concession granted to Baron Julius de Reuter, a British subject, a seventy-five-year right to exploit all the mines in Iran with the exception of those containing precious stones; to build railways, farm the customs, purchase land wherever the company needed it; and to bring into the country any foreign experts and laborers these activities required.[48]

The reasons for signing the concession will be fully developed in a later chapter. It is sufficient to state here that Mirza Huseyn Khan thought the economic involvement of a powerful European country like England in Iran would act as a safeguard against Russian encroachment from the northeast. He also thought the regeneration of Iran required an extensive and elaborate railway system, which could only be built with European help.

Mirza Huseyn Khan was surely naïve, but his motives grew out of genuine conviction. Those opponents who condemned him for signing the agreement had more complex motives. Personal dislike for Mirza Huseyn Khan and his reforms ran high among them—the concession was just an excuse to bring about his downfall—but the uncertain future also caused a great deal of fear among the opposition.

Among the opposition were important princes, top officials, the shah's favorite wife, and two influential mujtahids. Leading the opposition were three princes—Zill us-Sultan, the shah's eldest son; and Hisam us-Saltaneh and Muʿtamid ud-Dowleh, two of his uncles—each of whom bore a personal grudge against Mirza Huseyn Khan for what they considered humiliating treatment. Personal considerations also appeared uppermost among the motives of high officials. Mirza Yusuf Khan Mustowfi ul-Mamalik, the former minister of finance, had lost his post and his favored position with the shah when Mirza Huseyn Khan had returned to Tehran in December 1870. Nasir ul-Mulk and ʿAlaʾ ud-Dowleh, both members of the council, hated Mirza Huseyn Khan for exposing their misuse of government funds. Although the shah had forgiven them, it was difficult for them afterward to draw anything except their salaries from their offices. Amin ul-Mulk, who had been a party to the activities of the opposition to the concession and to the prime minister, put it this way: "They mentioned many reasons for opposing the concession except the real reason: that it was a real threat to the country's sovereignty. This proved that they had not been motivated by concern for the welfare of the state or by love of their country, but that personal motives had prompted them to create the disturbance." [49]

The involvement of the shah's favorite wife, Anis ud-Dowleh, was clearly personal. She had been chosen to accompany the shah to Europe, but in Moscow the protocol problems that the presence of the shah's consort would raise in St. Petersburg led the prime minister to advise the shah to send her back to Iran. When she reached Tehran, she offered her support and the use of her residence to members of the opposition. [50]

The petition for Mirza Huseyn Khan's dismissal was also signed by two members of the ʿulama, Hājjī Mullā ʿAlī Kanī and Mīrzā Sālih ʿArab. Hajji Mulla ʿAli Kani was by far the most influential member of his class. He owed his influence not to piety or great learning but to the vast wealth he had amassed and to his charismatic power over the people, concerning which the American minister in Tehran gives the following account:

> When he goes abroad he is mounted on a white mule and followed by a single attendant; but the crowd parts before him as though he were a supernatural being. A word from him would hurl the shah from his throne or be the fiat of doom to every Christian and foreigner in the land. The shah stands in his presence; the soldiers deputed to guard the United States legation told me that, although sent there for my protection, they would not hesitate to slaughter us all if so ordered by Hajji Mulla Alee.[51]

Hajji Mulla ʿAli Kani did not openly oppose Mirza Huseyn Khan before this time; he merely indicated disapproval by refusing to meet with him. His refusal to meet with the sadr-i ʿzam was most likely due to the latter's open European manners and Sufi sympathies.[52] Although Mirza Huseyn Khan's attempt to codify the ʿurf or secular law during his days as minister of justice did not come to much, it must have been repugnant to the great mujtahid. However, if Hajji Mulla ʿAli was using the Reuter Concession to get rid of Mirza Huseyn Khan, he advanced sound reasons for disliking it. He said he feared it would open the doors of Iran to untold numbers of Europeans.[53]

Mirza Salih ʿArab owed his prominence to being one of Kani's associates. He, too, was exceedingly popular. Although Mirza Huseyn Khan had helped him during the famine,[54] perhaps at Kani's request he lent his support to the opposition.

What led the opposition to step up its activities against Mirza Huseyn Khan was the knowledge that the shah had been favorably impressed with Europe and that he would allow Mirza Huseyn Khan a free hand in introducing fundamental change. According to an eyewitness:

> The enemies of Mirza Huseyn Khan gathered and said he had penetrated into the shah's mind. Of course, when he returns to Tehran he will introduce change, and the state of the kingdom and people will undergo change. He will cause the regulations of the Europeans to prevail, and he will cause the habits of the people of the West to spread. Then the influence and exchange of the Europeans with Iranians will be increased, and Iran's ancient power will be lost. It is better that we unite and present the consequences of his evil thoughts and deeds to the sovereign.[55]

The added knowledge that the Russian government had expressed dissatisfaction with the signing of the concession to Nasir ed-Din Shah during his visit to St. Petersburg undoubtedly increased the resolve of the opposition to come out openly against Mirza Huseyn Khan.

The activities of the opposition gained momentum as the time for the shah's return approached. A united front was formed to "inform His Majesty of [Mirza Huseyn Khan's] intentions and evil deeds." [56] When the shah landed on September 7, 1872, at Enzeli (now Bandar Pahlavi), a petition requesting the dismissal of the prime minister, signed by Farhad Mirza Muʿtamid ud-Dowleh and other high princes and officials, was handed to him. A large number of princes took refuge in the royal stable at Enzeli and the residence of Anis ud-Dowleh in Tehran, announcing that they would not leave until His Majesty had dismissed Mirza Huseyn Khan. The most vociferous was Hisam us-Saltaneh, the former governor of Khurasan, who declared that "he would rather sacrifice his own life than see the prime minister remain in office." [57]

Taken by surprise, the shah and Mirza Huseyn Khan acted hastily to avoid embarrassment. The prime minister offered his resignation, and the shah accepted it. Two days later the shah tried to reassert his authority by reinstating Mirza Huseyn Khan as sadr-i aʿzam. Having done so, he called in the complainants and threatened that:

> if they continued in their present state of insubordination, he would use his sovereign right and power to inflict summary punishment on every one of them. They all became frightened, admitted their fault, begged for pardon, and swore that they were ready to obey implicitly His Majesty's command. The shah then desired that they go and make it up with the sadr-i ʿzam, which they did. His Highness asked them all to dinner, and swore that he would retain no rancor against them and that the whole affair would be forgotten.[58]

But far from forgetting their grudge against Mirza Huseyn Khan, his opponents resorted to a new technique. They convinced Hajji Mulla ʿAli Kani to publicly express his opinion of the Reuter Concession. On 22 Rajab 1290/16 September 1873 the great mujtahid issued a public proclamation addressed to the shah, in which he advanced sound reasoning for opposing the concession. Recalling the history of the British occupation of India, he argued that a similar fate awaited Iran if the concession was allowed to remain in force. He argued: "With the onrush of Europeans into Iran, no mujtahid would survive. Even if some ʿulama did survive, what guarantee do we have that Mirza Malkam Khan or the company, with all the wealth it can amass, and all the men it can bring into the country, would not surround us with their troops and weapons?" [59] Hajji Mulla ʿAli also condemned the concession for providing a foreign company with the right to purchase land, which could lead to the invasion of the country by Europeans under the pretext of building railways.

News of the proclamation reached the shah at the same time as Mirza Salih ʿArab publicly demanded the death of the prime minister.[60] To further intimidate Mirza Huseyn Khan, rumors were spread through Tehran that the planned railway would pass through the shrine of ʿAbdul ʿAzīm, a highly venerated and popular Shiʿi saint buried near the capital. This sacrilege, the rumors intimated, was part of a plot by the prime minister to convert Iran to Christianity.[61] Nasir ed-Din Shah could no longer ignore the mounting menace that seemed to defy his authority. "If he had any intention of implementing some of his observations in Europe, he kept it to himself and decided to save his throne." [62] For the second time in a week, he accepted the resignation of his prime minister, whom he instructed to remain in Rasht for safety.

This incident ended the close cooperation that had existed between the shah and Mirza Huseyn Khan. Although a month later the latter was once more entrusted with high office, he never again enjoyed the same active, overt support of his sovereign. The shah did not lose interest in reform, neither did he mistrust his minister. The clamor for dismissal of his sadr-i aʿzam had revealed to him the mood of his subjects; and being primarily concerned with preserving his own authority and by nature inclined to an easygoing life, he preferred not to involve himself in anything that might endanger his own position. His attitude toward reform became guarded, and he supported only those measures and projects of Mirza Huseyn Khan that would least hurt the vested interests of his officials and courtiers.

6

POLITICAL REFORM, 1873–80

DURING Mirza Huseyn Khan's first two years as sadr-i aᶜzam, the great power at his disposal enabled him to introduce measures that promised to bring about fundamental change in the political system, and he planned further reforms of equal significance. To ensure the shah's continued support and interest, Mirza Huseyn Khan took him on a trip to Europe, where the results of good laws and order could speak for themselves.

But their absence provided hostile groups with an opportunity to organize. When the shah landed at Enzeli on the Caspian coast, the opposition succeeded in forcing him to dismiss his sadr-i aᶜzam. Although Mirza Huseyn Khan was restored to power within six months, the incident made an impression not only upon him but also upon Nasir ed-Din Shah. The shah became more cautious in his support of Mirza Huseyn Khan and his reforms, and Mirza Huseyn Khan became more circumspect in the pursuit of his objectives.

Upon entering the capital, the shah's first act was to abolish the post of sadr-i aᶜzam and revert to practices prevalent prior to Mirza Huseyn Khan's appointment to office. He appointed new ministers, the most important of whom was Mirza Yusuf Khan Mustowfi ul-Mamalik, who was named minister of the interior, minister of finance, controller of the treasury, president of the Majlis-i Dar ush-Showra, and supervisor of the capital and of the shah's private estates.[1] An official announcement expressed the shah's pleasure that Mirza Yusuf Khan had returned to the capital from retirement in Ashtiyan "to assume those affairs entrusted to him so that he can once more restore them to order."[2] The abolition of the cabinet, one of Mirza Huseyn Khan's major reforms, and the appointment of Mirza Yusuf Khan, who was known for his hostility to the reforms and their initiator, were clear gestures on the part of the shah to reassure the opposition and appease the public at the capital "who thought Mirza Huseyn Khan was going to convert them to Christianity." [3]

After calm was restored and control reestablished, the shah began to chastise the organizers of the disturbance. The first to be punished was Mu'tamid ud-Dowleh, his uncle, who had been brought from his seat of government in Kurdistan to act as deputy prime minister during the absence of Mirza Huseyn Khan. Then another uncle, Hisam us-Saltaneh, was removed from the governorship of Fars. Others who also lost their positions included the minister of war, Nasir ul-Mulk, and the minister of foreign affairs, Mīrzā Saʿid Khan.

Then, in what was more than a mere attempt to assert authority, the shah invited Mirza Huseyn Khan to return to the capital. He had depended heavily on Mirza Huseyn Khan for three years and had great confidence in his abilities. He had remained in constant communication with him and had promised him a high post at the earliest opportunity. He wrote:

> Mushir ud-Dowleh, We are indeed sorry about your absence. . . . I announced to you that by 20 Shaʿban you will be appointed foreign minister. If you really want this post, let me know frankly, otherwise you can stay in Gilan for the time being. Don't say, "It is up to you." My desire is that you should be involved with the affairs of government. But do let me know what you really want.[4]

Shortly afterward the shah discussed his problems with Mirza Huseyn Khan in another letter as though he were a close friend:

> Mushir ud-Dowleh, today is Sunday, 4 Shaʿban, and I felt a need to write to you. Muʿtamid ul-Mulk [Mirza Huseyn Khan's brother] is sending a special messenger, so write the answer immediately. I hope to keep my word and unite you with your family by 20 Shaʿban. I am trying to cope somehow with the affairs of government, which seem most confusing and complicated. I have appointed the ministers and refer most of the important questions to the showra. But I have the control in my own hands, though this at a great physical and mental harm to myself. There is no other way, otherwise the affairs of government will be disrupted. . . .
> There are so many things that could bring about Iran's progress if the necessary funds are allocated to them. . . . With someone with your ardor and love of progress at my side I

could accomplish great things. But it is necessary that you devote yourself to carrying out my plans.[5]

Perhaps still under the influence of what he had observed in Europe, he listed many projects he hoped to carry out for the country with the help of Mirza Huseyn Khan. But he did not mention the most urgent problem, the abrogation of the Reuter Concession.

Although the members of the Majlis-i Showra were consulted, the main burden for this fell on Mirza Huseyn Khan, as is indicated by the shah's letters and the reports of W. T. Thompson to the British Foreign Office. Fortunately for Iran the British government wished to preserve its friendship with the Russian government, whose hostility to such a concession with a British subject had been clearly expressed to the shah in St. Petersburg. The British were therefore willing to remain neutral toward Baron de Reuter and the fate of his concession.[6]

With an assurance of British neutrality from Thompson, Mirza Huseyn Khan prepared the text of an official announcement which stated: "The readers of *Iran* are, of course, informed that formerly the government of Iran had held a contract for the construction of a railway between Rasht and Bushehr. However, since a month has elapsed from the promised date of beginning construction on the line, it has become evident that the said baron is not capable of keeping his word and the terms of the contract. Therefore, the Iranian government regards the contract as nonexistent and has informed Baron Reuter of its decision. It has further announced to his representative in the capital that it considers the contract void."[7] A dispute ensued between the baron and the Iranian government, and the ease with which Iran freed itself of the concession was to a great extent due to the tact and diplomacy of Mirza Huseyn Khan. This becomes evident in a comparison between the handling of this case and the Tobacco Concession, which was similar, seventeen years later. In the latter, in 1890 the Iranian government granted to Major Gerald Talbot, a British citizen, a monopoly to buy, sell, and manufacture tobacco throughout the country for fifty years. Popular opposition forced the government to annul the concession, but it was required to pay Talbot £500,000 as an indemnity.

Mirza Huseyn Khan terminated the Reuter Concession before his official appointment as minister of foreign affairs on 20 Sha[c]ban 1290/17 December 1873. Because of his experience as a dip-

Zill us-Sultan, eldest son of Nasir ed-Din Shah
Source: S. G. W. Benjamin, *Persia and the Persians*
(London: John Murray, 1887)

lomat and his special relationship with Nasir ed-Din Shah, he continued to initiate and determine foreign policy rather than just carry out the shah's will. In fact, the latter's reliance upon him is evident in the correspondence that passed between them. The shah wrote Mirza Huseyn Khan: "You know how ... extremely important these problems are.[8] That is why one hesitates so much and needs so much courage to approve and sign it. What must be done now? You know better. At occasions such as this, I am torn by doubt."[9] Even more revealing is the following passage:

> I am sending the letter I have received from Muʿtamid ud-Dowleh. I had asked Nasir ud-Dowleh to talk him out of it, but I doubt if that has done any good.
>
> You must do something about it and change Muʿtamid ud-Dowleh's mind about wanting to leave Fars. It is not in the interest of the government to have him leave. His son would not be capable of handling that province singlehanded. Tell me what to write Muʿtamid ud-Dowleh.[10]

On the whole, Mirza Huseyn Khan's years as foreign minister were uneventful. During his visit to Britain he tried to secure some form of support from the British government for the territorial integrity of Iran, which seemed increasingly threatened by Russia's advance in Turkestan, Khurasan's neighbor to the north. However, Granville, Britain's foreign secretary, indicated that Iran should be satisfied with the informal understanding reached between Russia and Britain in 1834 and reiterated in 1838, "based on the sincere desire of the two governments to maintain not only the internal tranquility, but also the independence and integrity of Persia."[11] Once convinced that no aid in the form of arms or military instructors would be forthcoming from the British, Mirza Huseyn Khan reverted to Amir Kabir's policy of trying to maintain a balanced attitude in Iran's dealings with the two governments. For the rest of the decade he maintained a guarded attitude toward concession seekers, especially Russian and British, and no concessions were granted.

Although an outline of Iran's dealings with other countries under Mirza Huseyn Khan as foreign minister are beyond the scope of this study, it should be noted here that he did not cease to attempt to bring about change in the political organizations of Iran. And although Nasir ed-Din Shah had lost some of his zeal for reform, he continued to trust Mirza Huseyn Khan and considered him the sole person to carry out any type of reform in Iran. Within a year after he was relieved of his official duties,

Mirza Huseyn Khan was again entrusted with powers similar to those he had had as prime minister. His promotion was made public by a decree that announced the creation of a diumvirate. It stated:

> We have assigned all the civil affairs to his highness the Aqa [Mirza Yusuf Khan Mustowfi ul-Mamalik] and to his highness Mushir ud-Dowleh [Mirza Huseyn Khan] whom we designate *sipahsalar-i aᶜzam* [commander-in-chief of the army]. We entrust him with all the military affairs, without any exception and with great autonomy. The Aqa is not so old yet, and the sipahsalar is still young. They both abound in great virtues. . . . We hope they will lessen our burden from now on, and that they will perform to the best of their abilities the tasks entrusted to them.[12]

The authority granted to Mirza Huseyn Khan by far exceeded that of his rival. He was placed in charge of the provinces and townships of Azerbaijan, Khurasan, Kirman, Kurdistan, Baluchistan, Khuzistan, Luristan, Garrus, Qazvin, and Asad-Ābād. He was minister of foreign affairs, minister of war, commander-in-chief of the army, and minister of trade. Also under his control were the departments of communications, roads, and railways, the mines, passports, post, arsenals, and granaries; and he was also to supervise the affairs of teachers and European instructors and the newly founded factories. The significance of his new appointments was not lost on the British minister. In his report to Lord Granville, he observed that Mirza Huseyn Khan had once again become sadr-i aᶜzam but under a new title.[13]

The most significant reform to be introduced in this period, the Tanzimat-i Hasaneh code, was promulgated in Safar 1291/March 1874. It once again set down regulations for provincial administration and limits to the authority of governors. Mirza Huseyn Khan had signaled his intention to introduce such a code in a "Circular to Governors," which stated that "The work that remains to be done is defining the limits between the governor and the subjects." The fact that the code was proclaimed only six months after the shah's return from Europe strongly suggests that it may have been prepared before the trip. Indeed, it may well be that this edict, which contained forty-seven articles covering all aspects of provincial administration, was prepared simultaneously with the Edict of Darbar-i Aᶜzam and that the two were part of Mirza Huseyn Khan's plan to reorganize the Iranian administration on both the central and provincial levels.

The stated aim of the Tanzimat-i Hasaneh was the reorganization of provincial administrations; but although the curbs on the governors were nowhere mentioned, they were equally important. Implementation of the code would remove the governors' control of tax collection, conscription, and the judicial system, and would transfer responsibility for them to provincial councils set up under code regulations in the capital and all major cities in the provinces and townships.

The authors of the code, the shah and Mirza Huseyn Khan, unfolded their plan cautiously, remembering well their recent experiences. In its preamble the code stated that it was to be implemented in three stages: (1) it would be introduced in the capital and some small townships around it (like Qazvin, Damghan, Qum, and Kashan); (2) the following year it would be extended to some lesser and safe provinces (like Mazandaran and Gilan); and (3) it would be carried out in the rest of the country.[14] Neither the code's preamble nor the official announcement of its promulgation in *Iran* contains any such words or phrases as *reform, progress,* or *practice of advanced nations* as had been the case in the past. In fact, the code gave no indication of the significant changes it would bring about in provincial administration.

It stipulated the creation of a council in Tehran and all provincial capitals and townships to supervise and manage tax collection, recruitment, and the secular courts, functions that had hitherto been controlled by the governors. The provincial councils were subordinated to a central council of Tanzimat-i Hasaneh in Tehran, headed by I'tizād us-Saltaneh, one of the shah's great-uncles, a prince well known for his sympathy for Mirza Huseyn Khan and his reforms.

The creation of these Majlis-i Tanzimat or Tanzimat councils was the most novel aspect of the code. Each council consisted of five members, who were appointed by the Central Council of Tanzimat in Tehran. Each consisted of members drawn from the province's various ministries and departments: a mustowfi or accountant from the revenue department supervised the collection of levies; an official of the war ministry looked after army affairs and conscriptions; an official of the Ministry of Justice was in charge of judicial matters; one official had charge of trade and excise; and another, a secretary, was charged with sending regular reports to the Central Council of Tanzimat in Tehran. The provincial council was an arm of the central government. The code stipulated that its members were to make decisions and carry out their duties collectively. They were to consult with each other on all questions, even those concerning their own departments. Decisions relating to the code were to be made by all the members, not by individuals (art. 25). This provision was obviously a safeguard against the possibility of pressure being exerted on a single member. To further ensure the independence of the council, the code stipulated that a governor's complaint against or dissatisfaction with any council member would not result in his removal from the council, but would instead lead to an investigation of the complaint by the Central Council (art. 9).

Despite such precautions, however, the code still had a major weakness. The lack of an adequate salary for council members left them susceptible to bribery. This weakness did not escape the attention of the British consul in Rasht, who pointed out:

> Eight hundred tumans [£320] is the aggregate amount of salary assigned to these six members of the Tanzimat-i Hasaneh by the Persian Treasury! Will His Majesty the shah or the sipahsalar be surprised to learn, in the course of time, if they have not been informed of it already, that the very council sent out to Gilan to control the executive power has become a hotbed of corruption and extortion, and a source of additional vexation to the people?[15]

Mirza Huseyn Khan's reforms were once again placed in jeopardy by inadequate financing and inadequately trained manpower.

The most important function of the Majlis-i Tanzimat was the collection of taxes. Until then taxes had been collected on the basis of assessment laws prepared at the time of Amir Kabir. Each province was assigned a sum to be collected by the governor. A share of the levies was assigned for provincial expenses; the rest was sent to the central treasury in Tehran. However, at least twice the levy assigned was collected because of "the greed of the governors who demanded from the lieutenant governors a surplus in excess of the taxes. So the lieutenant governors were forced to put pressure on the district managers, and they in turn on the village heads. These officials made a mockery of the assessment; and instead of order, extortion and oppression prevailed." [16] Also, the practice of farming out tax districts in lieu of salary provided corrupt and ruthless officials with another method of oppressing taxpayers, the majority of whom were simple peasants.

The first article of the Tanzimat code specified that twice a year the governor of each township or province was to call to his office all the village heads in his region for an official statement concerning their levies. The levies would be determined by the mustowfi, with the full knowledge of the other members of the Majlis-i Tanzimat. Each tax sheet thus prepared would then be signed by the governor. This same article prohibited the sending of tax collectors to the villages. Instead, the villages were to send their taxes by a messenger of their own choice to the governor's office. It also stipulated that villagers could pay their assessments on a monthly basis to ease the strain somewhat.

The fourth article specified that both the code and the shah's announcement of its promulgation be read in every village mosque in the country. This provision was intended to deny village officials any opportunity to misrepresent its meaning to the people, and to involve the people themselves in the reforms.

These provisions, as well as those dealing with conscription and the judiciary, discussed the authority of the Majlis-i Tanzimat. By omission they also defined the limits of the governor's authority, because he no longer had control of these functions. The governor's role in running the vital affairs of the province was reduced to a minimum.

The duties of the governor were discussed in the appendix to the code. He was to be a consultant to and overseer of the functions of the council of Tanzimat, but he could not take an active part in the decisionmaking process. He was to ensure the prompt payment of tax installments by his people, maintain order in the city, and secure the roads. In short, he was no longer a virtual ruler but a mere functionary of the central government. The change must have shocked most governors, especially the shah's uncles and sons, who were used to a great deal of autonomy in running their provinces.

As the code indicated, it was first implemented in Qazvin, Khamseh, Saveh, and Qum. Weekly reports on the progress of the Tanzimat councils of these towns began to appear in *Iran*. The following passage is typical: "Qum, Saveh, Nihavand: The city of Qum is in order, the people are enjoying prosperity. Huseyn Khan, the deputy governor, is making special effort to keep the city in order. The members of the Majlis-i Tanzimat assemble every day at the majlis and review the affairs of the people." [17]

Such success induced the government to speed up implementation of the second phase of the code. The city of Isfahan was added to those included in this phase of the program. As a precaution the government recalled Zill us-Sultan, the governor of that province, before the code was put into effect there.[18] In addition, Mirza Yusuf Mustowfi ul-Mamalik was appointed to supervise the second phase. By involving Mirza Yusuf, who was known for his opposition to Mirza Huseyn Khan and his reforms, with the execution of the Tanzimat code, the government no doubt hoped to neutralize his opposition and to render the code more acceptable to the public.

For a brief period the Tanzimat code seemed to accomplish its goals of eliminating the governors' source of power and concentrating all power in the hands of the central government. But its success was short-lived. Like the Edict of the Darbar-i Aᶜzam, the Tanzimat-i Hasaneh hardly had a chance. It was abandoned, not as a result of the opposition of governors, but because of the hostility of the ᶜulama.

The ᶜulama's opposition was undoubtedly prompted by two of the code's articles that concerned the judiciary. One stipulated that the verdict of the religious court was to be sanctioned by the Tanzimat council; the other required that all trustees of public vaqfs give to the council an account of their revenues and expenditures. Neither article alone would have led to opposition from the ᶜulama, whose attitude had a basis beyond the code itself in their attitude toward the prime minister.

The ᶜulama had watched Mirza Huseyn Khan's systematic effort to codify the ᶜurf laws and create a new secular court system. Although in theory the ᶜurf courts were controlled by the state and the sharᶜ courts by the religious sector, the line of demarcation between them was not clear; and, in effect, the ᶜulama exercised much control over the secular courts as well. Therefore, it is not surprising that Mirza Huseyn Khan's efforts to reorganize the ᶜurf courts and establish closer governmental control over them was viewed by them with alarm and resentment.

Most of Mirza Huseyn Khan's judicial reforms were carried out during his term as minister of justice, when his conduct in office was exemplary. The ᶜulama could find no reform that impinged upon their formal rights and contradicted the sharᶜ laws, and no basis for open opposition. The success of a handful of ᶜulama in removing Huseyn Khan from office in the dispute over the Reuter Concession had provided the religious with a new self-awareness, a realization that their support of the opposition had been instrumental in the outcome of the conflict. After that they assumed a more active and aggressive role in the political life of Iran.

At times their intervention in the political process did promote the welfare of the country, as was the case in the Tobacco Concession in 1298/1890–91 and the Constitutional Revolution in 1905–11. But, like all such groups, the ʿulama had their own interests to protect; and when those interests did not coincide with the interests of the country, their power could be harmful to the state, as it was in the case of the Tanzimat-i Hasaneh code. The code touched only lightly on the prerogatives of the ʿulama, but they were quick to realize that a steadily centralizing state would eventually tolerate no authority but its own. They could see what was happening to the governors, and they wanted none of that for themselves.

If the leading ʿulama had any doubts about the direction of Mirza Huseyn Khan's reforms, Zill us-Sultan removed them upon his return to the capital from Isfahan. There is no documentary link between Zill us-Sultan and the ʿulama; but soon after his arrival in Tehran the leading ʿulama there began to send instructions to the provincial ʿulama to oppose the code, and those in Isfahan were among the first to express opposition. The prince was surprisingly submissive to the government upon his recall to Tehran. He had made no secret of his intense dislike of Mirza Huseyn Khan and he had tried repeatedly to undo his reforms for that reason. His sudden lack of resistance may well indicate that he was secretly active in inciting the ʿulama to work against the code.[19]

The British consul in Rasht reported that a prominent mujtahid publicly denounced the code and was soon joined by other members of his class.[20] In the face of this active religious opposition, the Tanzimat-i Hasaneh code was quietly abandoned, and the weekly reports in *Iran* suddenly ceased. The situation fell in well with the shah's new cautious attitude toward reform.

Although the setback affected Mirza Huseyn Khan deeply, he was not yet ready to admit defeat. The shah's letters to him and public pronouncements showed that he still enjoyed the shah's confidence, and this support must have sustained him considerably. One contemporary observed: "It seems that Mushir ud-Dowleh is not pessimistic yet. Day after day he continues to encourage the shah to create the Showrā-yi Vuzarā [Council of Ministers]."[21]

This council, which Mirza Huseyn Khan was promoting, was different from the Darbar-i Aʿzam. Indeed, it was meant to replace the latter, but in spirit it was closer to the Majlis-i Maslihat Khaneh of 1275/1858.[22] Its membership would include not only present, but also former, ministers; men who were close to the shah; and important princes. Contemporaries referred to it by various names, including Majlis-i Dar ush-Showra-yi Kubra (the Great Consultative Council), Mashvirat Khaneh-yi Dowlat (the State House of Consultation), Dar ush-Showra, or simply Majlis.

The council was inaugurated by the shah on 15 Ziqaʿdeh 1292/ 14 December 1875. In the inaugural address he stressed the importance of governing by consultation. "Surely," he said, "several minds working together would assess things more exactly and probe into matters more thoroughly than one mind, even if it is a perfect mind." [23] Unlike the Majlis-i Maslihat Khaneh or the Darbar-i Aʿzam, the functions of the Majlis-i Dar ush-Showra-yi Kubra were never clearly defined. It was more limited in scope than either of the other two bodies in that it was never invested with any legislative or executive authority. Judging by the types of issues discussed by the members, it was an advisory body to the shah and no more. A passage in the shah's opening address confirms this: "Whenever we have no specific issue to refer to the council, the members must themselves discuss whatever concerns the welfare of the state and inform us of the result of their parley." [24]

The impact of the shah's European trip and the atmosphere prevailing in the democratic countries he visited is evident in this body, as a royal rescript addressed to Amin ul-Mulk, the shah's secretary, shows. The style of the rescript is purely Mirza Huseyn Khan: "The members of the majlis should feel free to discuss anything they wish. They should also discuss everything without malice or fear." [25] Also clear is the democratic atmosphere that was meant to prevail in the meetings of the council: "For example, if a man from the shoemakers' guild should get up and criticize one of the important ministers, saying, 'I think you have acted on this matter without properly understanding it,' that minister must not take offense. He has no right to feel insulted. What he must do is reply to that criticism, either refuting it or accepting it." [26]

Unfortunately no contemporary source reveals whether a shoemaker or anyone of similar rank ever attended a majlis meeting. Yet, despite our lack of knowledge about public interest and participation in actual sessions, the introduction of the majlis was another important step in creating a Western-inspired institution in the country. The rescript introduced the idea of free discussion into the machinery of government and, perhaps more important, recognized the right of subjects to criticize their rulers—two prin-

ciples that would be of major concern to the leaders of the Constitutional Revolution twenty-five years later.

The members of the majlis, sadly, never took advantage of the
freedom allowed them under the rescript, as Amin ud-Dowleh
makes clear: "When Amin ul-Mulk read the shah's letter, the
ministers looked at each other and began to think. Finally, Mustowfi ul-Mamalik said, 'We must find out who has disturbed His
Majesty's peace of mind and motivated him to raise these questions.' " Then they decided to send the following reply to the shah:

> Your Majesty, you are the most knowledgeable and wise hu-
> man being in the universe. We know that whatever is decided
> by us will be subject to change by your will. Therefore, in the
> present case, if you see fit, maintain the prevailing conditions.
> [The shah had asked the majlis whether they thought any
> reforms were necessary.] But if it is not to your liking, then
> change would be necessary.[27]

The sessions of the majlis, its secretary Amin ul-Mulk recorded,
deteriorated into just another gathering place for top officials to
intrigue and gossip. Ironically, the target of their intrigue was the
founder of the majlis, Mirza Huseyn Khan, and the leader of the
intrigue was Zill us-Sultan, who in his memoirs candidly admitted
having spread malicious rumors about Mirza Huseyn Khan to
further encourage his enemies.[28]

With the number of his enemies steadily increasing, Mirza Huseyn Khan began to feel more and more isolated. His knowledge
of the efforts to turn the shah against him and his extreme sensitivity to criticism, "even when it is false and unfair," [29] are reflected in numerous letters he wrote to the shah during the last
four years of his life. His extreme loneliness is revealed in another
group of letters, written to Nasīr ud-Dowleh, whom he helped
raise from obscurity to high status.[30]

It is not difficult to explain Mirza Huseyn Khan's lack of friends.
Most of his adult years had been spent abroad on a variety of
missions. When he returned to Tehran in 1870, he was a virtual
stranger. His sudden rise to power and his various reform plans
had alienated large numbers of princes and officials as well as
most of the lower-level bureaucrats. He had never been in one
place long enough to train a cadre of efficient administrators to
support him either from conviction or vested interest.

Personal traits also added to his increasing sense of isolation.
This is especially true of his manner of speaking bluntly at a time

when a careful and indirect manner of speech prevailed. I'timad us-Saltaneh, who was a constant attendant on the shah and had charge of the royal printing house, reports that on one occasion Mirza Huseyn Khan approached him and said "I know you are my enemy, and I am your enemy, but would you do this for me?" [31] He attributed this bluntness to arrogance that was a result of his sudden rise to power: "If the shah had not swelled his head so much by suddenly raising him to power, he may have become the state's best servant. But to have made him in the space of one year first the minister of justice, then minister of war, and on top of that sadr-i a'zam, with powers that were tantamount to turning over the sovereignty to him, was surely too much. This is why he went mad with pride." [32] According to another contemporary source, these same traits offended many high-ranking officers of state, who feared him enough to set about plotting his destruction.[33]

Mirza Huseyn Khan's personality was no less difficult for his friends. As the number of his enemies grew, the number of his friends declined. His correspondence with Nasir ud-Dowleh reveals the unusual demands he made upon the time and attention of his friends. Being sensitive he took offense easily, but his suspicious nature made it hard for him to forgive. As a consequence, by the end of the decade he had lost the close friends who, like Malkam Khan, Mustashar ud-Dowleh, or Hasan Khan Garrusi, could have supported him in the face of the growing opposition.

The deterioration of his friendship with Malkam is also revealing. The two men had disagreed over the abrogation of the Reuter Concession. Malkam, who had stayed behind as ambassador to England, had opposed the abrogation and reprimanded Mirza Huseyn Khan for not resisting the pressure of the opposition. His lack of sympathy and the later revelation that he had accepted a gift of £5,000 from Reuter dismayed Mirza Huseyn Khan deeply.[34] The two men were never friends again.

Mirza Huseyn Khan's part in the signing of the Reuter Concession, which he had hoped would transform Iran into a modern country, had ironically also led to the disillusionment of the "younger men and advocates of progress," [35] the students and teachers of Dar ul-Funun, and those with European training. In his memoirs, Hājjī Sayyāh gives this as an important cause of the loss of interest among his supporters. He wrote:

> I met Mirza Huseyn Khan a long time ago, in the Ottoman Empire. I expected him, who was raised by Mirza Taqi Khan [Amir Kabir], to follow in the footsteps of that great man both

in foreign and domestic policies, and to make use of the great confidence and trust the shah has in him to lead Iran to prosperity. But unfortunately, I have heard many things about his term as prime minister. This includes his extreme friendship with England, according to which all rights for building a railway, tramways, and exploitation of the coal, iron, copper mines, the oil, and all the forests, the farming of the customs [renting out of customs revenues] in Iran, were all placed in the hands of the British. Thus he made a great mistake.[36]

He was also without powerful family connections that might have helped to sustain and support him against the opposition. Although he was married to one of the shah's great aunts, ʿIsmat ud-Dowleh, neither he nor his wife had any close relations in high places at the court or in the Majlis-i Dar ush-Showra to come to his aid in time of need. The only other prominent member of his family was his younger brother, Yahya Khan Muʿtamid ul-Mulk, who was married to the shah's sister, ʿIzzat ud-Dowleh, but who was nevertheless unable to bring much influence to bear when he needed it.

With many friends and supporters gone and without powerful family connections, Mirza Huseyn Khan felt his enemies growing more active. He then began to devote his attention and concerns to protecting himself from attack. During the last four years of his life, his interest shifted from introducing reforms to maintaining his power and favored position with the shah. Unflinching commitment to reform gave way to cynicism, especially with regard to the shah, of whom he once said, "Every day that passes and I become more experienced, I realize more fully that the only right attitude a minister must have toward his job is that of Mustowfi ul-Mamalik," [37] referring to a remark of an old colleague: "It is wrong to speak to the shah about what is right or to the best interest [of the country]. If the shah says, 'I want to throw myself down from the top of the roof,' I would answer, 'Whatever Your Majesty wills is of course the right thing.' " [38]

Amin ul-Mulk, the shah's private secretary, also noticed a change in the shah's attitude toward reform. He recorded the new mood:

The shah asked the servants who had access to many circles to bring a weekly report on what they had heard. The man prepared an account of the state of the people in Tehran, the behavior of some of the governors in the provinces, and the dealings of some government officials, and whatever seemed of significance. The shah took the report. After two days he saw the man, bade him to come forth, and said to him, "What was this nonsensical report you prepared?" The man apologized and promised to prepare a better report. The shah responded, "What I meant by various news was not what would disturb my peace of mind, but what would make me happy. Like which woman they took to such and such a party, which homosexual they used in that party, and what they said when they were drunk." [39]

Amin ul-Mulk attributed the change in the shah to the growing influence of Mīrzā Ibrāhīm Amīn us-Sultan, a total illiterate who had risen from a lowly position in the shah's household to become one of his most trusted advisors. Mirza Ibrahim had attracted the shah's attention by chance during one of his trips and, by appearing disinterested in money and position, had risen steadily until the shah appointed him to the Majlis-i Dar ush-Showra.[40]

Nasir ed-Din Shah, who lacked self-confidence, was easily influenced by the company he kept, but his growing dependence on Mirza Ibrahim for advice and comfort does not totally explain his loss of interest in reform and his cooling toward Mirza Huseyn Khan. It may well be that repeated opposition to reform and the realization that success would require a great deal more energy than he could invest had turned him away from reform. Hajji Sayyah, one of his severest critics, has remarked: "Even if Nasir ed-Din Shah had wanted to lay down the foundation for order and progress in Iran, his grandees, who were used to sucking the people's blood, and the mullas who benefited from the state of lawlessness would create a thousand obstacles in his way." [41]

The rise of Mirza Ibrahim in the shah's favor was a setback for Mirza Huseyn Khan. Mirza Ibrahim, who was motivated mainly by his own interests, regarded Mirza Huseyn Khan as a rival and reform as an impediment. He joined the opposition and began to discredit Mirza Huseyn Khan and his ideas in the eyes of the shah. The most unfortunate consequence of this rivalry was the failure of the last major law proposed by Mirza Huseyn Khan, which would have granted immunity of life and property to all Iranians.

On the eve of the shah's second trip to Europe in Rabiᶜ ul-Avval 1295/April 1878, during a visit to the shrine of Shah ᶜAbdul ᶜAzim near Tehran, a soldier threw a stone at the shah's carriage. The shah ordered that the entire group be chained, brought to Tehran, and put to death. A few hours later he was struck by remorse and the realization that his European hosts might react adversely to his action.[42]

This remorse was seized upon by Mirza Huseyn Khan, who, although present at the incident, had not dared interfere because the soldier belonged to a battalion under his own command. Now he stepped forward and said:

> In this trip that Your Majesty has ahead, nothing will remove the ugliness of this cruel and barbarous deed in the eyes of the Europeans except the change in your style of rulership and the institution of justice. Your Majesty must hold a public prayer and write officially to the ambassadors of the various friendly nations at your court that "The government of Iran respects the rights of all its subjects to life and property, the rights of the people will be respected according to the exalted laws of the shari‘at, and no sentence will be issued by any government office without full investigation." [43]

The shah liked the idea and asked Mirza Huseyn Khan and Nasir ul-Mulk, the minister of war, who had supported the proposal, to prepare a text. When the text was completed, the two men gave it to Mirza Ibrahim, who pretended to be in agreement with them, to take to the shah. In presenting the document, however, he told the shah: "These two ministers . . . are planning to overthrow Your Majesty. They thought me ignorant and illiterate, so they took no precautions and spoke openly in my presence. Despite my ignorance I gathered from what they said that their intention is to do away with Your Majesty's omnipotent powers." [44] The shah declined to sign the declaration.

With such a man as his trusted adviser, it is not surprising that the shah found Mirza Huseyn Khan increasingly difficult to tolerate. As the shah's interest in reform diminished, Mirza Huseyn Khan's bitterness grew, and one of its causes must have been personal jealousy over Mirza Ibrahim's rise in the shah's esteem. He began to voice his feelings openly, with a frankness that sometimes verged upon impudence. The following incident, related by ‘Abbas Mirza, the shah's brother, is typical:

> Mirza Huseyn Khan continued to swear at the shah. No matter how hard I tried to change the subject, he went back to swearing at the shah. I kept telling him, "This is not so nice, after all we are indebted to him." He would reply, "You don't know what a bastard he is. He has none of the qualities of his father, may God bless his soul. He has only inherited his . . . mother's qualities. He never tells a word of truth. He does not like anyone, and cannot see anyone happy. He only likes base and low-class people. He is wary of rational men and does not

care to have anything in order, except his hunting site and that his food should be nicely cooked and his fruit ready. He never appreciates anyone, and he will finally kill me and anyone who should try to carry out the laws. He only wants to be surrounded by a few men of low character.[45]

The shah was aware of Mirza Huseyn Khan's impudence. Upon hearing the news of Mirza Huseyn Khan's death, he reportedly remarked, "He was extremely rude to me."[46] Although the shah did not openly react to Mirza Huseyn Khan's insolence, his enemies did. Encouraged by the rift between them, they began to spread malicious rumors about him, a fact that Zill us-Sultan candidly admitted.[47] The most serious charge was that he had embezzled army funds. But, since these accusations were never proved, it is difficult to determine whether they had any foundation or were merely raised to disgrace him in the eyes of the shah.

What is certain, however, is that his enemies turned the Dar ush-Showra into a tribunal to prove him guilty of wrongdoing. It is ironic that after Mirza Huseyn Khan worked so hard to create the Dar ush-Showra, he should have suffered so greatly at the hands of its members. In a letter written during his last year in office, he reveals the agony he suffered in these sessions. He informed the shah that despite ill health he had delivered his message to the Dar ush-Showra. He then requested that he be spared such assignments. He wrote, "I cannot hide from Your Majesty how bitter and difficult, nay, worse than death it is on your humble servant to attend these sessions."[48]

In any event, the shah decided that he could no longer tolerate the presence of a man who had assumed the role of his conscience; and, despite the many assurances he had given him, in Shavval 1297/September 1880 he stripped him of all his powers. He appointed him governor of Qazvin for a short time and a few months later sent him to put down the rebellion of the Kurdish chief Shaykh ʿUbiydullah in Azerbaijan.[49] Then he sent him to Mashhad as chief trustee of the shrine of Imam Riza, the eighth Shiʿi imam, where he died several months later, on 21 Zihajjeh 1298/15 November 1881.

For ten years Mirza Huseyn Khan had been the key figure in the administration of the country. He had tried hard to replace an erratic, informal system of government based upon a sovereign's whim with a rational, efficient system based upon law. He clearly did not succeed. Both the Majlis-i Showra and the Darbar-i A'zam survived his fall from power, but in name only. He regarded his efforts a total failure and died a lonely, embittered man.

Within the context of Iranian history, however, his efforts and ideas seem to have had a positive effect. As a result of his efforts, many of his contemporaries were introduced to new notions of the role of government, its responsibility toward the people, the need for limits to the authority of those in power, the relationship between ruler and ruled, and the need for government by law. Perhaps he was naïve to think Iran could be transformed overnight by good intentions and with the support of a few like-minded friends, but the groundwork he laid was ultimately a foundation upon which others could build.

The spirit that had motivated his reforms penetrated ever more deeply into the national consciousness. Once this spirit gained sufficient force and momentum, it led to the overthrow of the old system in the Constitutional Revolution of 1901–11. This revolution gave reality to many of the ideas Mirza Huseyn Khan was only able to introduce.

7

ECONOMIC REFORM

ECONOMIC REGENERATION was an integral part of the total scheme Mirza Huseyn Khan hoped to effect in Iran. His plan for revival of the country's stagnant economy called for the founding of a bank; the construction of railways, roads, and bridges; a reform of the financial system; the introduction of modern industrial techniques; and the encouragement of trade. However, these aims were neither presented in a cohesive program nor pursued systematically. This, combined with inconsistent support from Nasir ed-Din Shah and active opposition from hostile individuals and groups, explains why many aspects of the program were never even attempted. Still, Mirza Huseyn Khan did succeed in introducing into Iran such important Western economic concepts as systematized banking and modern roads.

When Mirza Huseyn Khan came to power in 1870, Iran's economy was stagnant: a two-year drought had so crippled agriculture that famine prevailed in most parts of the country, and the failure of the silk crop every year since 1864 had reduced production of the country's main crop by three-quarters. [1] A comparison between the trade figures for 1864 and those for 1871 confirms the country's economic plight. In 1864 imports totaled £1,800,000 and exports £600,000, with silk accounting for £502,000 of the exports. Seven years later, however, imports totaled £789,559 and exports £340,790, with silk a mere £119,440 of the exports. [2] The disparity between imports and exports if continued would lead to elimination of the stock of gold and silver and would increase the number of unemployed.

Most of the projects planned by Mirza Huseyn Khan required funds. Yet the antiquated complexities of the revenue system made the acquisition of funds difficult. For this reason reform of the financial system was high on his list of priorities.

Before 1871 Iran's governmental revenues were derived from agriculture, which was taxed both in cash and in kind, and from customs. Total revenue for 1868, for instance, amounted to 4,361,660 tumans (£1,744,664), of which only 536,660 tumans (£214,664) or about one-eighth came from customs.[3] Governors were entrusted with collecting taxes from their provinces. After deducting their own expenses, they handed the balance to *Idāreh-yi Istīfā*, the Revenue Office, in the capital. But most governors, in complicity with the *mustowfī* or revenue official for their province, avoided paying what was due the treasury.

> When appointed, they [the governors] have to account to the central government for the sums specified above; but it often happens that at the end of the year's tenure of office there is a large deficit which they declare they have been unable for some reason or other to collect from their district. A fee is then paid to the financial authorities in Tehran; and the shah is persuaded to remit a large portion of the deficit, which has in reality been received from the peasants and is eventually shared by the defaulter and his protector at court.[4]

A brief sketch of the organization and functions of the Revenue Office may give some perspective on the kinds of obstacles facing Mirza Huseyn Khan as he attempted to reform the financial system. The Revenue Office was organized during the reign of the second Qajar ruler, Fath-ʿAli Shah (1797–1834), on the pattern of a much more elaborate organization that had prevailed under the Safavids. The Revenue Office controlled all matters relating to state revenue and expense, and tax collection was one of its principal functions. Each mustowfi was responsible for the tax revenue of several townships or of one or two provinces. Governors were required to submit an annual account of their revenues and expenditures to the appropriate mustowfi. A certificate attesting to the submission, signed by the local mustowfi, the *mustowfī ul-mamālik* or head of the Revenue Office, and the shah, evidenced that the governor had fulfilled his obligation.[5] Duplicates of the provincial accounts were kept at the central Revenue Office to prevent the possibility of collusion between mustowfis and governors, and to ensure regular and prompt delivery of provincial dues to the central treasury. But most mustowfis did not examine closely the accounts of governors who were willing to share some of the spoils of office with them.[6]

The Revenue Office also supervised government expenditures. It provided funds for official salaries, expenses of the royal household, and activities conducted by the central government, such as

The audience chamber of Nasir ed-Din Shah
Source: S. G. W. Benjamin, *Persia and the Persians* (London: John Murray, 1887)

the Dar ul-Funun. High-ranking officials, important princes, and royal wives received stipends not in cash but in *tuyūls* or revenues of a specific district in a province. Less important officials were paid *barāts,* an annual assignment of revenues from a specific district. Some officials, usually those of lowest rank, received cash from funds in the central treasury. A detailed account of all tuyuls, barats, and salaries, as well as expenses of the royal household, was kept in the Revenue Office, which also supervised the assignment of tuyuls and barats.[7]

Finally, the Revenue Office also managed the allocation of funds for any new expense of the government, such as a military campaign, the shah's trips, and new projects. Over the years a complex system of bookkeeping had evolved, with minutely detailed accounts of all revenues and expenses kept in *sīyāq,* a form of writing similar to shorthand.[8]

Because the work of the Revenue Office was complicated and required years of training, it had become the monopoly of a few who kept the knowledge of their profession within their own families. Mirza Yusuf Khan Mustowfi ul-Mamalik, chief of the Revenue Office, for example, had been elevated to the post in spite of his youth upon the death of his father, who had held the position under two previous Qajar monarchs.[9] By 1870, when Mirza Huseyn Khan came to power, Mirza Yusuf Khan had held the office for many years and had the shah's confidence. When the shah had left for Iraq in that year, he had entrusted the affairs of the kingdom to Mirza Yusuf Khan, who expected to be officially appointed sadr-i a͑zam upon his return.

When the shah returned to the capital with Mirza Huseyn Khan and made public his intentions for change, Mirza Yusuf Khan decided to boycott the court and the newly established Dar ush-Showra to which he had been appointed. "This strategy had worked in the past and many new decisions and organizations had been rendered ineffective in the last fifteen years." [10] But the shah's commitment to reform was now firmer and "this new champion [Mirza Huseyn Khan] could not be intimidated so easily." [11] The shah may indeed have welcomed the opportunity provided by the old minister's behavior. He wrote a letter to Mirza Yusuf Khan "expressing his regrets that his minister had found his duties so overwhelming, accepted his resignation, and advised him to take a long rest in Ashtīyān [the family homestead]." [12] He had no choice but to obey. He had unwittingly helped to promote the goals of his rival. With his departure, Mirza Huseyn Khan had more freedom to pursue his reforms.

Lacking sufficient knowledge of the functions of the Department of Finance or Revenue, Mirza Huseyn Khan made no attempt to introduce elaborate or immediate change. He began by trying to uproot the widespread practice of bribery, which he called "the mother of all evils," by forbidding the acceptance of bribes in the department. He also forbade extortion by the governors and their agents soon after he became prime minister. The edict stated:

> It is obvious that the greatness of every government is dependent upon two factors: order in the affairs of court and other branches of government and the wealth of the subjects. Whenever these two factors are weakened, the greatness of that government will be in danger. What causes these two factors to deteriorate are greed and ill will. Therefore, according to all rational and traditional injunctions, greed is the worst enemy of the state. Not until greed has been uprooted can the state be assured of its greatness.[13]

The edict then warned that any extortion, no matter how small or under what name, would not be overlooked by the government and that the offender would "meet the worst punishment."

In one of the first provisions of the same decree, Mirza Huseyn Khan also sought to encourage the development of uncultivated land and the exploration of mines. It declared: "As a favor to you and as a means of furthering prosperity of the land, the Government grants you a rightful method of increasing your wealth, as much as your talent enables you to do so. You may develop the *khalisijāt* [state lands], you may explore the mines, and build new qanats in those parts of your domain not being utilized by anyone." [14] We do not know whether the governors accepted this challenge; we do know that those who ignored the warning about extortion were severely punished.[15]

The edict must have come as a welcome relief to the famine- and plague-stricken population. Its effectiveness in alleviating the plight of the people is attested by the official historian of Nasir ed-Din Shah's reign and one of Mirza Huseyn Khan's harshest critics:

> This edict brought comfort to the people everywhere. The governors and heads of the telegraph offices were forced to read it in the *jum'eh* [principal] mosques, where everyone could hear it. He [Mirza Huseyn Khan] issued many such edicts, and none of the governors dared disobey. Whenever the governors saw the name Huseyn under a telegraph, they would lose heart and try not to make errors or mistakes.[16]

It appears then that during the two years of Mirza Huseyn Khan's office as prime minister, the people in the towns and villages had a respite from rapacious tax collectors and governors.[17] In addition, a greater proportion of taxes collected during those years reached the central treasury. This was because Mirza Huseyn Khan had placed men whose integrity he could trust in crucial positions in the provinces.

Zill us-Sultan, the shah's eldest son, who had a reputation for embezzling government funds, was a particular challenge for Mirza Huseyn Khan. When he was removed from the governorship of Isfahan and appointed governor of Fars, Mirza Huseyn Khan, at whose suggestion the transfer was made, wrote candidly to the shah: "On the one hand, due to his close connection with the throne, the prince feels he is unaccountable for what he does; on the other hand, he is greatly interested in amassing wealth. Consequently, he will not have pity on the *ra'iyat* [subjects] and no taxes will reach the government's coffer." [18] He therefore recommended that "we send along a wise and efficient steward and make him responsible for taxation." [19] The shah replied: "Concerning the appointment of provincial and township governors either in this year or in the future, as I have told you repeatedly, I will make no demands and express no opinion. Act in the best interest of the country and the government. Decide about the choice of governor and steward for Fars, and send them as soon as possible." [20]

The steward chosen was Zahīr ud-Dowleh, a man known for his honesty and sympathy for reform. Zill us-Sultan, who had already been humiliated by his dismissal from Isfahan, considered the appointment of "a simple man who is completely duped [by Mirza Huseyn Khan]" a further insult, for which he never forgave Mirza Huseyn Khan. He resorted to direct threat to render the plan ineffective and described his efforts in his autobiography:

> I called Zahir ud-Dowleh to my presence and said to him . . . "You are the same Zahir ud-Dowleh and I am the same Zill us-Sultan of a few years ago. Likewise, the old ways must prevail." That miserable man tried hard by different methods to get out of my clutches and to follow the orders of the sadr-i a'zam. But I made it clear to him that if he persisted I would resign and go to Tehran, but he would not be kept in Fars without me. Then I reminded him of the services his ancestors had rendered my ancestors and the favors we had granted them, and I proceeded to talk to him in the manner of the Turkomans and the *īlāts* [tribes] until I won him over.[21]

The regulation and investigation of the government payroll made Mirza Huseyn Khan unpopular among an even wider group than the princes. It caused a major reduction in the salaries of most government officials as well as the highest and most powerful princes. This measure, too, was issued soon after Mirza Huseyn Khan's appointment as prime minister.[22]

While these measures made enemies for Mirza Huseyn Khan, they also enabled him "to increase the revenue and balance the budget, both of which are important steps," as he reported to the shah a year later.[23] And they did provide some temporary relief for the lower classes of the population. Mirza Huseyn Khan was looking for measures that would be more than temporary and would outlast him. He designed regulations that would make it increasingly more difficult for tax collectors to practice their accustomed extortion.

Government revenue, as was mentioned previously, totaled less than two million pounds and derived primarily from land tax. Other sources of taxes were gardens, domestic animals (such as sheep and cows), homes, and shops. Some districts had a poll tax for males over the age of fourteen.[24] However, as John Piggot observed, the main burden of taxation "falls almost entirely on those little able to bear it. The great nobles and wealthy merchants pay nothing into the public exchequer; the taxes are extorted from the peasants, shopkeepers, and artificers."[25]

The people who bore this burden were almost totally at the mercy of the tax collectors. "Almost every transaction of the government is performed through a *mohessil* [tax collector], and every mohessil is a tyrant, an oppressor—in general, a thorough ruffian."[26] The response of the taxpayer was generally "to counterfeit poverty and inability to meet the demands made on him."[27] Those living near the borders took flight into neighboring countries. Majd ul-Mulk, a high official, lamented that, due to the injustices of the system, "Two-thirds of the people of Kurdistan, Khuzistan, and other cities of Iran have gone to the security of Arab Iraq. The injustice of the rules of Iran has been such that they have given preference to the unsuitable climate and poisonous winds of Iraq over the resorts of Iran."[28]

The major difficulty in the system of taxation was a lack of uniform assessment. This lack of uniformity in tax rates and the absence of any regular revisions of the assessments provided ample opportunity for tax collectors to extract what they could from the population, often charging double the amount due.[29] Mirza Huseyn Khan was strongly motivated by a desire to relieve the burden on the taxpayer and a concern to increase the share of the central government in what was collected, for little of the additional revenue extorted by the tax collectors made its way to Tehran.[30]

The funds that did reach the central treasury were sufficient to meet the expenses of the shah and the court, but little was left over for the extensive projects Mirza Huseyn Khan had in mind to improve the quality of life in Iran. Moreover, under the old system the revenues of the central government were under the control of the provincial governors. In correspondence with the shah, Mirza Huseyn Khan constantly repeated the necessity of having an independent source of revenue:

> Until these [army] expenses are regulated in an orderly fashion, none of the affairs of the government can be managed in an orderly manner for the simple reason that the security, order, and strength of the Government, the collection of taxation within the country, the protection of the rights and prestige of the government and its standing abroad, depend on a well-organized army. But the army cannot be organized effectively unless its expenses, be it the ration, the salary, the clothes, the tent, and other needs, reaches it on time. . . . None of these can be created except with money. It has been said of old, and rightly so, that the Army can be organized with gold.
>
> However, even if all these expenses are met by the Government, but not met on time and according to strong regulations, the desired purpose will not be achieved.[31]

Mirza Huseyn Khan used the pages of *Iran* to try to familiarize readers with the benefits of a regular and universal tax system. As an example, he discussed the tax system and its history in Great Britain, pointing out: "Since the people know that the Government has been forced to impose this innovation, they willingly and out of a sense of patriotism and national pride and need of the moment acquiesced to it [paying taxes]." [32]

The removal of Mirza Huseyn Khan from the post of sadr-i aʿzam in September 1873 prevented him from carrying out the extended tax reform he obviously had in mind, and after that he never again had the full support of the shah. However, the Code of the Tanzimat-i Hasaneh, issued in Safar 1291/March 1874, leaves no doubt that he had a master plan in mind at the time he was deposed. Several clauses of the code deal with at least partial tax reform; indeed, the first fifteen of its forty-seven clauses bear on it. The preamble reveals that "Since the purpose of His Imperial Majesty . . . is to spread justice and comfort of the servants and subjects and the prosperity of the province and the country, he has ordered and decided such regulations be devised that would realize his intentions. Therefore, this book has been devised and called *Tanzimat-i Hasaneh* [*The Beneficent Regulations*]."[33]

One of the most important provisions of the code eliminated the post of tax collector by transferring his duties to the village head, the *kadkhudā*. The code did not specify whether new assessments were to be made regularly, but it did leave room for assessment revision.

> Villages that have declined and cannot pay their taxes of necessity must be reassessed to deduce the difference and determine the new assessment. The Government will appoint an assessor and inform the members of the Majlis-i Tanzimat in the province so that those villages which have declined or been newly assigned will be assessed in the same manner as assessors have reassessed some villages.[34]

Another provision prohibited the imposition of any other type of expense on the village under the pretext of taxation. Yet another forbade the offering or accepting of any type of presents in money or in kind by government officials or governors. This was directed at a tradition that prevailed widely even up to the level of the shah. Houtum-Schindler and George Curzon among others have stated that presents offered to Nasir ed-Din Shah were part of the government's revenues.[35] It is not surprising, therefore, that while the code enjoyed widespread support in the towns where it was implemented,[36] it met with hostility among those in power, particularly among the ʿulama and the governors. The code, like so many other measures introduced by Mirza Huseyn Khan, was tried briefly and then put aside.

Still Mirza Huseyn Khan did not give up hope of effecting some kind of financial reform. His attempts to create a permanent, independent budget for the army have already been mentioned.[37] During the shah's second trip to Europe in 1878, he made another major attempt to reform the country's finances. When they were in Vienna, he encouraged the shah to invite a group of Austrians to come to Iran to serve as advisers. Of the twenty-five hired, one—Baron Weiss-Teufenstein—was "to reform the financial administration."[38] The baron met with less success than most of the other Austrians, who were primarily in service to the army. Mirza

Huseyn Khan wrote to the shah: "This Austrian who has come to reform the financial matters has been here for some time, and has received three months pay. Very soon, we will have to pay him for the next three months, and he will demand his pay in cash. . . . Your humble servant does not know what His Majesty has in mind . . . for him and what services he is to perform for the salary he gets." [39]

In reply the shah told Mirza Huseyn Khan to arrange a meeting between the Austrian financial adviser and two members of the Dar ush-Showra "so that they can prepare a draft. If we approve of it, then we shall order that it be put into effect." [40] A second letter from the shah to Mirza Huseyn Khan reveals that nothing was accomplished by the baron: "I have not yet heard what happened as a result of the meeting between the Austrian and those men. It seems they did not pursue the matter even one day. It is surprising. Show this letter to Amin ul-Mulk and Nasir ul-Mulk [the Dar ush-Showra representatives]. Let me know why my order was not carried out. A man [the Austrian financial adviser] has been waiting, and the government's money is being wasted."[41]

The inability of Baron Weiss-Teufenstein to accomplish anything in Iran is readily explained. The aged minister of finance, Mirza Yusuf Khan, had been reinstated after the shah's return from his first European trip. He was not likely to welcome interference in the affairs of his ministry without direct pressure from the shah. Mirza Yusuf Khan, who was extremely arrogant and status conscious, would have considered such interference not only an attack on his personal and professional interests but also a victory for his rival, Mirza Huseyn Khan. The majority of influential princes and high officials also preferred the prevailing system, which allowed them "to get as much as possible out of the peasant and let the wealthy and influential proprietor contribute little or nothing toward the expenses of the State." [42]

Sensing this reluctance toward reform, Nasir ed-Din Shah chose not to exert any pressure, and the baron's elaborate plans were soon forgotten. The shah's handling of the matter typified his ambivalent attitude toward reform after his return from Europe and the deposition of Mirza Huseyn Khan in response to pressure from the nobility. The shah was concerned with his own safety and was not ready to back up his philosophy of reform with action if that might place him in a vulnerable position. In this case he had dealt only indirectly with the minister of finance and the two representatives of the Dar ush-Showra so that it would be easier for him to save face if his wishes were ignored. His desire to spare himself a showdown deprived the country of a chance to establish a more equitable tax system and efficient financial administration.

Another Austrian whom Mirza Huseyn Khan had invited to reform the country's coinage met with more success. Until that time many towns had had their own mints. Despite government efforts to control the manufacture of coins, there was much room for forgery, and coins of all sizes, shapes, and weights were in circulation. This came to an end when the Royal Mint, purchased in Europe and run by European engineers, began to manufacture coins in 1294/1877 and all other mints were closed down.[43]

Mirza Huseyn Khan also attempted to establish a bank, with capital of 5 million tumans (about £2.2 million). Since he liked to encourage the principle of consultation, he invited a group of important officers of state, including cabinet ministers, princes, courtiers, and merchants, to discuss the proposal the government had received from Baron Reuter. To make sure his presence did not inhibit discussion, he said, "I would leave the meeting and entrust your discussion of this matter to your wisdom, piety, love of your government, and sense of honor."[44] However, he suggested that they compare the text of the proposal with the texts of the Ottoman Bank. Malkam Khan, his private secretary, was to present his views for him.

The day-long discussions are highly interesting because they reveal (1) the ignorance of most Iranian political and business leaders toward the economic concepts prevailing in the West and (2), through Malkam Khan, the main points of Mirza Huseyn Khan's program for financial and economic reform. He sought to centralize control of the financial system, to exploit the natural resources of the country, to build projects such as railways and roads, and to help Iranian merchants compete with European traders through expanded trade.

Before opening the discussion, Malkam Khan explained the function of a bank, the significance of money economy, the importance of the circulation of capital for increase of trade and regeneration of the economy, and the need to attract foreign capital to Iran so that major projects like railway construction could be undertaken. One response is typical: "If what you say is true and they will bring gold and silver money, then it [the bank] is very good."[45] Malkam Khan then turned to the proposal received by the government and enumerated the benefits the government and country would gain from such a bank.

The first of these benefits was that the government could regulate its finances more effectively and thus meet its obligations
more promptly. According to Malkam Khan the most important
of these obligations was the payment of salaries to government
officials at home and abroad. If this could be achieved, government
officials could become devoted servants and, consequently, the
efficiency of the government would increase: "It is obvious that
no government can have devoted servants unless those servants
are paid regularly and promptly. Without these, no aspect of
government service can achieve order. It would be impossible to
achieve this without a bank, no matter how rich the government.
Not even a government like England could pay its servants
promptly if it tried to pay its servants from the money it receives
in taxes." [46] What was implied but for obvious reasons was not
elaborated was the fact that having a source of ready cash at its
disposal would free the central government from dependence
upon tax receipts in the provinces and would enable it to deal
more effectively with the provincial governors, who were then
providing most of the government revenues.

The second benefit was that it would make possible the exploitation of the country's rich natural resources, which would in
turn enable the government to construct railways and roads.

> We have much natural wealth—such as mines, forests, roads,
> and rivers, which if exploited in the manner of the Europeans,
> could lead to a thousand benefits. But until today these re-
> sources have remained unused because we do not have any
> capital. And the capital that exists in our country is scattered
> among many people. To undertake these great projects, it is
> essential that we put together and bring all the available capital
> in our country to one place. If there was a place in Tehran
> where we could borrow amounts from one hundred to one
> hundred thousand tumans at a low interest rate, imagine what
> benefits could be attained for all the people and for the pros-
> perity of our land. [47]

A third benefit of the bank would be to make credit available
to Iranian merchants. As a result, the volume of merchandise they
exchanged could be increased and they could compete better with
foreign merchants. "The reason European merchants are ahead
of our merchants and beat them in every instance," the argument
went, "is because they have banks and we do not." [48]

A fourth benefit would be the release of hoarded capital into
circulation, where it would benefit not only its owners but also the

country. This was obviously a special inducement for the immediate audience. "Those present here," Malkam Khan explained,
"certainly have in their possession one *kurūr* [five hundred thousand tumans] in cash that is now lying idle. If there was a bank,
this idle capital would be invested constructively, benefiting both
the owner and the borrower. . . . If there was a bank in Iran, most
of the leading figures in government would have substantial capital. This benefit is obvious to all of you." [49]

Malkam's eloquence did not, however, remove all of the natural
suspicion toward the founding of a private bank with foreign
capital. One fear voiced was that "If such a bank goes bankrupt,
the whole country will be ruined." Another was: "If this is the
case, why can't we form the bank ourselves? We can take out two
kururs [one million tumans] from the treasury and build a bank.
What is wrong with the law and shariʿa of Islam that we have to
follow such and such a monsieur? If [the bank] is necessary, then
we form a bank and issue paper money." [50] Malkam Khan evaded
this question. He more than any other reformer believed that Iran
could be saved only by totally discarding the existing institutions
and adopting others based on European models and methods.
The idea of forming a bank with Iranian capital alone must have
seemed preposterous to him. He remarked sarcastically to Mirza
Huseyn Khan: "We want to reform our financial system on the
knowledge of Nizām ud-Dowleh and the know-how and devotion
of Sanīʿ ud-Dowleh. We do better to go to Karbala." [51]

The meeting ended in hope, and it was decided to send the
proposal to the shah for approval. But the shah, too, had mis-
givings about the benefits of such a bank without a guarantee from
a European government. He must have been relieved when the
bank proposal was abandoned along with the Reuter Concession
of which it was a part.

The discussions about the abortive proposal did at least provide
the business sector of Iran with some knowledge of modern eco-
nomics. In 1296/1879 Hajji Muhammad Hasan Amin uz-Zarb, the
prominent Iranian financier, presented a proposal to the government for a bank formed entirely with Iranian capital. The proposal
met with great public enthusiasm, but it did not meet with the
approval of the court for reasons yet unknown. It was not until
1888 that the first bank, a branch of the London-based New
Oriental Banking Corporation, was opened in Tehran. [52]

The improvement of trade and expansion of industry, as Malkam pointed out, were among the principal objectives of Mirza

Huseyn Khan's government. From the beginning of the nineteenth century, imports had outstripped exports, causing the decline of some towns, such as Shiraz and Isfahan, and of some traditional crafts, especially those associated with the weaving industry. Local craftmen and manufacturers in such industries as weaving were unable to compete with the cheaper mass-produced products of European industry.

Although the Iranian market was able eventually to adjust to these changing circumstances and new crafts such as carpet weaving replaced some dying crafts, the process of decline had not yet been reversed.[53] Except under Muhammad Shah and during the ascent of Amir Kabir, Qajar rulers made no effort to boost native crafts and industry; they and their courtiers led the way in creating a demand for European products.[54] However, indifference to the fate of the moribund crafts was not universal, as the following comment recalls: "With the import of European goods, the treasury is being drained. The chandeliers, wall-hangings, luxury goods, tables, the useless clothes and the great competition among the people has impoverished almost everyone and is causing the resources of this government to leave the country. What is surprising is that no one seems to realize the ugly consequence of these attitudes.[55] Mirza Huseyn Khan shared this concern. While still in Istanbul he had pointed out that the encouragement of craftsmen and manufacturers and the support of trade ranked second among the four elements that determine a nation's progress in the view of the world. Then he recalled a time when

Iran was envied by the world for her crafts and manufactures, Iranian handicrafts were the most prized items exchanged for presents, and Iranians themselves valued what they manufactured above all other goods. Gradually Europeans began to pursue and excel in the making of manufactured goods, while both Iranians and their government began to ignore their own industry and crafts. If the present trend continues, gradually what little remains will also be abandoned, and Iran's trade with the outside will come to a standstill. And they [the Iranians] will become dependent for whatever they need on foreign products. However, with a little effort on the part of the Iranian people, they could easily dispense with foreign goods.[56]

Mirza Huseyn Khan adopted two basic methods for improving trade. First, he tried to encourage and support the merchant class. Second, he attempted to improve the means of communication by planning and constructing roads and railways. His contact with merchants had begun on his first diplomatic mission to Bombay, where he was sent to protect the interest of the Iranian community in India. Most members of the community there were merchants. His closeness to this group continued when he was sent to the Ottoman Empire, through which a great portion of Iran's trade with Europe passed. Mirza Huseyn Khan used his friendship with high Ottoman officials to improve conditions for resident and transient Iranian merchants. His success was so great that even the critical I'timad us-Saltaneh would say: "Mirza Huseyn Khan was so clever and behaved in such a manner with ʿAli Pasha, the sadr-i aʿzam, and the Sheykh ul-Islam that he could do whatever he wished, and most citizens of Farang [Europe] who had to trade with the Ottomans and even the Ottomans would pay five, six, or a thousand pounds to acquire protection from Iran.[57]

The importance Mirza Huseyn Khan attached to the merchants is evidenced by the inclusion of several in the bank proposal discussions. More important, a Majlis-i Showrā-yi Tijārat or Council of Trade was created to meet twice a month in the house of the minister of trade, Nasir ud-Dowleh, who was a close friend of Mirza Huseyn Khan. The official announcement stated that prominent merchants were invited to participate in these meetings "so that they can present their requests to His Majesty, who has issued useful orders for the improvement and expansion of trade." It added: "[Since] merchants are the respected subjects of each government and the principal cause of the prosperity and revenue of each country, it has been decided to inform all the governors to be more considerate of the merchants and to protect their interest so that even the weakest of them does not suffer an injustice."[58]

Mirza Huseyn Khan felt that the most important prerequisite for trade expansion was the construction of means of transport. To him and other advocates of reform, notably Malkam Khan and Mirza Yusuf Khan Mustashar ud-Dowleh, modern transportation, especially railways, seemed a panacea: "It has been proven, and without a doubt, railways and steamboats create jobs even in remote places like Turkestan and the Shāhī Lake. Moreover, the construction of railways in Iran will revolutionize Iran, that is, it will be the most effective means of order, organization, and strength of the country. In a word, Iran will turn into a paradise."[59] This belief is also reflected in a letter sent by Mirza Huseyn Khan from Istanbul to the Foreign Ministry in Iran, in which he

described the construction of railways from Basrah to Iskanda-
roun: "In my opinion, if this plan is implemented, it will not only
revive Anatolia, Iraq, and Arabia, but will also infuse a new spirit
into the Ottoman Government." [60] Later, as sadr-i aʿzam, Mirza
Huseyn Khan created a Favāʾid-i ʿĀmmeh or Ministry of Public
Works to improve transportation in Iran. The new ministry was
responsible for (1) the construction and maintenance of highways
between major cities; (2) the construction of ports, dams, and
bridges; and (3) the construction and maintenance of railways.[61]
Mirza Huseyn Khan chose Hasan-ʿAli Khan Garrusi, who had
spent years as ambassador to France, as head of the new ministry,
no doubt in the hope that the influence of a man well acquainted
with Europe and an advocate of Westernization would guarantee
efficiency. The ministry was founded while discussions on the
Reuter Concession were underway. The new ministry would undoubtedly have been entrusted with the project.

The Reuter Concession has been thoroughly discussed by Rawlinson, Curzon, and Kazemzadeh, but they seem to have overlooked the motives of Mirza Huseyn Khan, the principal agent
for Iran in effecting the concession. The instrument authorized
Baron Julius de Reuter to form a society for the construction and
operation of railways and tramways throughout the kingdom of
Iran for a period of seventy years. It also granted to the baron
the right to exploit Iran's natural resources, including the mines
(with the exception of precious metals), forests, and rivers, for the
same length of time. He was also granted a monopoly for the first
bank in Iran.

The concession's grant of extensive rights to a foreign subject
over the country's economic resources called forth harsh verdicts
on its signers:

> For paltry sums which would not suffice even to maintain the
> Imperial Court, Nasir ed-Din Shah did not hesitate to sell the
> future of generations of his subjects. The pretty phrases about
> benefiting the country by bringing the fruits of European
> progress to Iran and the pretense at concern for the well-
> being of the people made the actions of the corrupt ruler and
> his equally corrupt ministers still more offensive by adding
> hypocrisy to treasonable greed.[62]

Judging by the same standards, one might perforce agree that
both Mirza Huseyn Khan, who had "acquired a taste for innovation, especially the kind that promised to add to his fortune,"

and the shah, "anticipating large profits for himself," were merely motivated by greed.[63]

That the Reuter Concession had many pitfalls is readily established, but to reduce all the motives of its principal agents to greed and corruption is to make the same mistake as that made by most historians of Qajar Iran. Hindsight enables one to see faults easily, and distance turns crisis into child's play. But understanding cannot be reached without placing people and events within proper context, so that history can be seen as a continuous unfolding of a drama with live actors who are motivated by passions, some petty and mean, some pure and unselfish. Mirza Huseyn Khan's involvement with the Reuter Concession needs to be viewed in its contemporary context.

Fortunately, a sufficiently large number of private documents has survived to establish that the principal aim of those who advocated the signing of the concession, notably Mirza Huseyn Khan and Malkam Khan, was to provide the country with a useful system of railways. In an essay written in the late fifties, Malkam Khan urged the shah to construct an efficient system of transport as part of an extensive economic reform. He wrote, "The people of Asia have not yet realized the great benefits the building of roads can have for the strength of the government and prosperity of the country." [64] Although Malkam was banished from Iran shortly afterward, he did manage to convince the shah of the importance of modern transportation. The shah wrote to his ambassador in England, Mushin Khan Mu'in ul-Mulk to ask him to find a suitable firm to entrust with the task. But reputable firms hesitated "to invest" in Iran because they felt the risk was too great and that such a costly project "promised nothing but loss." [65]

When Mirza Huseyn Khan was appointed sadr-i a'zam in 1872, he was intent on transforming Iran into a modern state, even though he realized that political transformation would be hard to achieve within a short time. He decided to use a shortcut to economic transformation, through European assistance. He and Malkam Khan considered the construction of railways vital for economic regeneration, requiring a great amount of European assistance not only in capital but also in technique. Then Baron Julius de Reuter made his proposal.

Mirza Huseyn Khan was aware of the responsibility he was undertaking in working for the concession and of its consequences. He mentioned his apprehensions to Mu'in ul-Mulk, who was his close friend: "I need not remind you, I know you are quite aware, that this [signing of the concession] is not an easy task. It could bring about a good or bad reputation forever. Each problem and question must be scrutinized with great care so that, may God forbid, no mistakes occur and no bad consequences come about for the government [dowlat]." [66] Mirza Huseyn Khan regarded the concession merely as a means of access to the building of much-needed railways. After long deliberations with Reuter, he wrote the shah urging him to approve the proposal: "So far as it was in our ability we [members of the Darbar-i Aᶜzam] have discussed the railway project. Since the numerous advantages of the project and the grave harm the country would suffer if it is delayed are obvious to Your Majesty, it would be imprudent for us to try and repeat these. But what mortal would not realize the advantages of railways, which are as clear as daylight, or would not confess to their miraculous results?" [67]

Reuter demanded in return for his investment seventy years of exploitation of Iran's mines, forests, and barren lands, as well as the right to farm (rent out) the custom revenues. Echoing Malkam's proposal of fifteen years earlier, Mirza Huseyn Khan urged the shah to agree to these demands:

What seems obvious to us all is that to construct railways in Iran, we need fifty kurur (25 million tumans) in cash. It is also obvious that the exalted Government will never be able to afford this amount. It is further obvious that no firm will give us this amount for nothing, and if a firm shows willingness to spend this sum for us, then it will anticipate a handsome profit in addition to what it will have to spend. Now a firm has come forward and is willing to spend fifty kurur for us. What must we offer this firm in return for the fifty kurur?[68]

For once the shah's natural timidity seemed justified. He could not bring himself to agree to the terms. He replied: "I read your translation of the railway contract, which you sent with Muhammad Āqā. As it stands, it contains very bad sections and undertakings, which cannot be accepted under any circumstances. On the whole, it is a very bad contract and its harms exceed by a thousandfold the advantages of the railway. It is not acceptable at all." [69]

Despite these strong objections, Mirza Huseyn Khan did change the shah's mind. He argued that by granting extensive economic interest to a British subject (Reuter), the Iranian government would be able to overcome British reluctance to become involved in Iran's destiny and thereby provide a guarantee of protection in the face of Russian advances in the Transcaucasus. As Malkam Khan wrote to the authorities in the British Foreign Office in 1873, shortly before the shah's arrival in England: "Persia, abandoned to herself, would not be able to do anything at all. Alone she is irrevocably lost. But guided and supported by England, she is not only able to avert immediate dangers, but she will also be in secure enough condition to offer guarantees more seriously than all those to be found elsewhere." [70]

Russia's conquest of the Muslim regions of Central Asia, the khanates of Tashkent and Bukhara, in the previous decade and its renewed activity in the early 1870s to annex the khanate of Khiva justified the fears of Iranian leaders. After the fall of Khiva, the only unconquered region along the northeastern frontier of Khurasan was that inhabited by the Akhal, Tekke, and Yamut Turkomans. Not only was this the homeland of the Qajar tribe; also since time immemorial its inhabitants had been under the suzerainty of the governors of Khurasan. Aware of the country's military weakness and its inability to contain Russian movement southward into Khurasan and eventually into the rest of Iran, Mirza Huseyn Khan sought help from Britain through the Reuter Concession.

Increased British interest in Iran would have had another beneficial effect, Mirza Huseyn Khan felt. While in Istanbul he had witnessed Britain's continuing support of Ottoman reform efforts.[71] He hoped for the exercise of the same benevolent influence in Iran. Although he recognized that British support of Ottoman reforms was motivated by self-interest, he considered their support to be less potentially dangerous than the threat from Russia. Iran had already twice lost territory to Russia, so the British naturally appeared a lesser evil. Mirza Huseyn Khan's actions in the Reuter Concession may have been naïve, but they surely were not dishonest and treasonous as has been charged.

Although his scheme to provide Iran with a railway system that would "create for His Majesty a country and government that has no resemblance to what it is now" [72] died when the Reuter Consession was abrogated, he continued to plead the cause of railways in the press. A long series of articles on the "History of the Invention of Railways" discussed the uses and construction of railways elsewhere and recommended to readers that they contribute to the making of a new Iran by supporting the construction of railroads "now that the government and the people have attained a new stage, and now that the country, due to the encouragement of industry and crafts, and the expansion of trade, and the improvement of agriculture, and the exploitation of mines, and the use of forests, is being renewed, as if a new Iran were being created." [73] The author suggested that they try "to connect the roads to each other at the utmost speed." The author was Baron de Norman, whom Mirza Huseyn Khan had invited to Iran to help set up the first Western-language newspaper in the country. [74]

The discussion generated a good deal of interest in railways. A comprehensive plan was presented to Nasir ed-Din Shah in 1297/1878 by Mirza Yusuf Khan Mustashar ud-Dowleh, a close associate of Mirza Huseyn Khan. The proposal recommended that the railway be built with capital raised within the country, and it demonstrated with figures that such a project was possible and could be extremely profitable. He even got the *fatwā* or religious judgment of a few important mujtahids in Mashhad, where the proposed line was to end, to alleviate the shah's fear of religious opposition. [75]

Several years later, in 1884, the enterprising Iranian capitalist, Hajji Muhammad Hasan Amin uz-Zarb obtained a monopoly for the construction of a railway from Mahmūd-Ābād in Mazandaran to Tehran. He engaged Belgian engineers to carry out the project; but they left, due to a disagreement with Hajji Muhammad Hasan, after only eighteen kilometers had been completed. The road to Āmol was then constructed by Iranian workers. The rest of the line was never completed, but the Mahmud-Abad to Amol portion was used for some time. [76]

Iran was among the last major countries of the Middle East to have a railway. Although railway construction continued to hold high interest, efforts in that direction were stymied by British and Russian attempts to extend their spheres of influence in Iran. [77] Both Britain and Russia opposed the various railway proposals submitted by local and foreign parties on the basis that they might promote the political and trade instruments of the other. [78]

The newly founded Ministry of Public Works had greater success in constructing roads. A road was built from Amol on the Caspian Sea to Larijian, even though the project was hampered by a lack of capital. The road was only 102 kilometers long, but it took five years to complete because it had to pass through the Elburz Mountains. It also required nineteen bridges, several major dams, and fifty-three minor dams. Its construction, under the supervision of an Austrian engineer, Albert Castiger, facilitated the transport of people and goods between the Caspian seashore, Tehran, and the central part of the country.[79] An English traveler in Iran found the road excellent by European standards in 1881.[80]

Mirza Huseyn Khan should also receive credit for the first paved road, six kilometers long, between Tehran and Shah ᶜAbdul ᶜAzīm.[81] New roads were also built within the capital and some old roads around the royal palace were enlarged when the government undertook to enlarge Tehran.[82]

The exploitation of mines and forests was also included in Mirza Huseyn Khan's economic program. It was a central consideration in both the bank proposal and the Reuter Concession. As Mirza Yusuf Khan said: "For how long will so many mines lie idle and hidden underground in Iran, and God's bounty remain unrecognized? The Europeans have realized the value of this bounty and have made a thousand uses of it, like the use of coal, which is as important as railways." [83] Had the country's mines been exploited within the terms of the Reuter Concession, the share of Iran would have been minimal, only 15 percent of the net profits— hardly sufficient to turn Iran into a replica of a European state. But with the abrogation of the concession, Mirza Huseyn Khan abandoned the idea of large-scale exploitation of the mines with European financial and technical assistance. Instead, he adopted a more cautious but realistic attitude.

In 1874 a European mining engineer was hired to survey the country's mineral resources. His services accomplished little, however, as the shah was only interested in gold and silver mines. He was annoyed when the engineer came forward with news of copper mines. The engineer resigned and left Iran in disgust.[84] One possible effect of the mining engineer's visit was an advertisement that announced the government's intention to grant a monopoly to anyone who wished to exploit a mine, "a very profitable business . . . in the interest of the public." [85] Mme Serena, who reported on the visit of the European engineer, also pointed out that the few enterprising Iranians who tried to take advantage of the government's advertisement also failed.

Two years later an article on the country's mineral resources appeared in a newspaper issued soon after Mirza Huseyn Khan was appointed head of the Ministry of War. The article was prepared by an Austrian engineer who pointed out the abundance of oil everywhere. He commented that, whereas extensive use was being made of oil in Baku, it was being totally ignored in Iran.[86]

Another significant factor in the country's economy was the government's effort to cultivate poppy seed, which had begun to be an increasingly important export item: "The Iranians buy little of this product compared to what they send out. Last year the total product in the country was 2,060 boxes. Of this, 1,419 were sent to China and 583 went to London." [87] In addition, as a result of the government's step-up of timber exports from the forests of Mazandaran and Gilan in about 1870, "The value of timber and boxwood exported exceeded £50,000." [88]

One area in which notable progress was made was in the expansion and modernization of the ammunition industry. While accompanying the shah on his second trip to Europe in 1295/1878, Mirza Huseyn Khan arranged for the purchase of a steam-powered cannon foundry, which was set up a year later in Tehran. A visitor to Iran in 1889 testified that the production of this factory met all the country's needs.[89] A second steam-powered factory produced a variety of items, from lamp bases to metal fences. To Mirza Huseyn Khan these factories were not only useful but highly symbolic of the advent of a new era in Iran. They evidenced a small but very definite step toward Europeanization: "These products were equal in excellence to anything made in Europe. No one could believe that such things could be made in Iran." [90]

Mirza Huseyn Khan's plans to regenerate the economy of Iran, like so many of his other plans, were soon crushed for many of the same reasons. His plans were neither persistent nor cohesive. He failed because his enemies feared that success might endear him to the shah and promote his strength, and the shah's failure to sort him completely was another influential factor. Yet in 1884, only a few years after Mirza Huseyn Khan's death, a group of native merchants presented the government with a proposal for a bank built with Iranian capital, the government stepped up efforts to build roads and railways, and several attempts were made to create small factories. It is doubtful whether any of these actions would have been undertaken without the process of inspiration and education that resulted from Mirza Huseyn Khan's activities in the economic sphere during the previous decade.

8

CULTURAL INNOVATION

Mirza Huseyn Khan had been deeply impressed by Europe. European civilization was a paradigm by which he measured the advancement of non-European nations. In comparison with Europe, Iran seemed to him hopelessly backward, not merely in governmental institutions and industrial techniques, but also in behavior and thought. Therefore, when he was invited by Nasir ed-Din Shah to Tehran in the autumn of 1870 to help set up a new order in society, he attempted to bring about total change. His efforts in the political, judicial, military, and economic spheres have already been discussed. What remains to be dealt with here are his attempts to introduce new ways of thought and manners to his countrymen.

The innovations Mirza Huseyn Khan introduced covered a wide range, from installing gaslights in the streets of Tehran to teaching European table manners to the shah and his courtiers. The new thought he disseminated was likewise varied. It sometimes concerned sublime ideas of fatherland and sometimes trivial details like not speaking out of turn during cabinet sessions. Most of these efforts met no serious resistance, and Mirza Huseyn Khan was thus able to familiarize at least a few of his fellow Iranians with new modes of thought and patterns of behavior that were of European origin.

Like most nineteenth-century advocates of reform in Iran, Mirza Huseyn Khan felt an unbounded and uncritical admiration for Europe and its civilization. He had been sent to France while in his late teens and in his brief stay there was dazzled by the apparent glitter of Europe. He did not remain long enough to penetrate beyond this surface to the real sources of its strength and weakness. Consequently he left with a deep conviction of the superiority of

European civilization. His later contact with Europeans, as head of Iran's mission in Bombay, as consul general in Tiflis, and as minister and later ambassador in Istanbul, confirmed and reinforced his beliefs that placed Europeans in the lead in every field. His reports to the Foriegn Ministry and correspondence with friends reveal that by *civilization* he meant *European civilization*. He thought only Europeans were civilized, and anyone who wished to become civilized had to emulate them. He remarked, for example, that the aim of the Majlis-i ʿĀlī-yi Tanzīmāt or Supreme Council of Tanzimat in the Ottoman Empire was "to make the country a part of the civilized world." [1]

He thought his country's backwardness was due primarily to its being outside the orbit of European civilization. Its only salvation was to be found in an attempt to join the league of European nations. What particularly grieved him was that most of his countrymen were not even aware of the advances of Europe and their own backwardness. He told the foreign minister:

> The reason for my sadness is that, not only have we made no effort in this direction [to carry out European-style reforms], but we do not even believe there is anything wrong with our state or that our affairs need improvement. To the contrary, we believe that we have reached the highest degree of progress and have nothing to worry about.[2]

Throughout his long stay abroad, he had tried to acquaint Iranian leaders at home, especially the shah, with the achievements of European civilization, in the hope that this would create in them a desire to emulate the Europeans. He used his reports to the Foreign Ministry to this end; and, when he returned to Tehran, he used numerous articles in various newspapers to reach a much larger group of people.

His efforts to acquaint the shah with Europe extended beyond his many letters from Istanbul. He encouraged the shah to visit Europe, because he thought that by seeing Europe for himself, Nasir ed-Din Shah would become more anxious to carry out wide-scale reforms in Iran. He was pleased to be able to report in 1867 that Sultan Abdulaziz (1861–76) had decided to attend the Paris Exposition. Mirza Huseyn Khan reflected on the opportunity it would provide the sultan to meet other heads of state who would also be in attendance. Conscious of the shah's parsimony, he wrote: "I asked Fu'ad Pasha whether this trip of the sultan to Europe will not cost the treasury heavily. He said, 'I can assure you that the cost of the trip to Egypt was greater.' " [3] Then he explained why such a trip was necessary. "In this day and age the situation has become such that one must assert one's presence and keep up with one's peers. If one shows negligence once, one can fall fifty years behind in one's affairs." [4]

When Nasir ed-Din Shah showed a desire to make a pilgrimage to the shrine of Imam Huseyn, the third Shiʿite Imam, in Karbala, Mirza Huseyn Khan tried to divert his interest to Europe. The shah was interested, but he insisted, "I prefer that my first trip outside the country be to the shrine of the saints, which will do me good both for this world and the next." [5]

Finally in 1290/1873, when Mirza Huseyn Khan was already sadr-i aʿzam, he convinced the shah and several officers of state to go to Europe. A newspaper article marked by the prime minister's unmistakable style tried to conciliate the public to the idea of the sovereign visiting the lands of the "infidel *farangīs*." The author appealed to the readers' religious pride and sentiment, demonstrating that the policy of isolation and ignorance of European developments had hurt the majority of Muslim and Asian states. Not only was the adoption of such an attitude harmful to Iran, it was also contrary to Islam, which had instructed Muslims to pursue knowledge and to travel. This great damage to Islam would be rectified by His Majesty's decision to meet with European kings. Even more significant, the visit would

> enable His Majesty to lead the country to the path of European progress and bestow upon the people those advantages of which the peoples of the East had been deprived for so long. His Majesty will be able to witness personally all those beneficial means used by European governments to ensure the welfare of their people and to protect their rights and prosperity. Observing these means, which are the basis of Europe's fantastic advancement, will assist His Majesty to provide immediate solutions for the prosperity of his own people. [6]

This naïve belief that a trip to Europe would spur the shah to reform and convert his retinue into lasting advocates of European-style civilization is reflected in his correspondence with the shah:

> The benefits and significance of Your Majesty's trip have not become apparent to our wise men. It is apparent that Your Majesty's decision is not prompted by a desire for diversion, but will constitute a great road to Iran's progress. On this trip Iran's sovereign will not be alone; with him will go all of Iran's government, to investigate the world for the purpose of saving

Gateway and avenue leading to the palace
Source: Century Magazine, December 1885. Historical Pictures
Service, Chicago

this land. If Your Majesty's purposes are accomplished on this trip, no doubt its consequence will be even greater than what Nadir accomplished from his venture to India.

After Your Majesty's return, all false doubts will disappear and all that has been neglected for a long time will change. Those people who, unintentionally, have been obstructing the cause of progress and sometimes knowingly have regarded the principles of progress as contradictory to the shariʿat, will more than anyone support Your Majesty's exalted intention [to reform the country]. . . . Then [following the trip] we can claim that Iran has entered the company of civilized states. In short, today Iran's future depends on this trip to Europe, and without a doubt it will bring about a thousand major benefits for Iran; nay, it will be the means of saving this land.[7]

The same letter also reveals Mirza Huseyn Khan's ignorance of the undercurrent of hostility he and his reforms had engendered in his colleagues. The shah and his retinue—thirty princes and officials, the sadr-i aʿzam, and the shah's favorite wife, Anis ud-Dowleh, had no sooner left for Europe on Monday, 14 Rabiʿ ul-Avval 1290/10 May 1873 than a coalition formed to remove Mirza Huseyn Khan from power.[8] Among the leaders of the coalition were Hisam us-Saltaneh, ʿImād ud-Dowleh, and Amin ul-Mulk, whom Mirza Huseyn Khan had taken to Europe to be enlightened; they kept abreast of activities in Iran by telegraph and through couriers.[9] Organizing their efforts around the Reuter Concession and rumors that it would threaten Islam, the coalition stirred up the populace in the capital against Mirza Huseyn Khan, who was chiefly responsible for it. Then, as a result, rather than have his own authority undermined by opposition to the sadr-i aʿzam, Nasir ed-Din Shah dismissed him a few days after landing at Enzeli in 14 Rajab 1290/9 September 1873.[10]

After the shah became fully aware of the intrigues of the opposition upon his return to Tehran, he communicated his knowledge to Mirza Huseyn Khan, who had remained in Rasht in fear for his life. "Mushir ud-Dowleh," the shah wrote, "We are sorry not to have you with us. It seems that they [the opposition] have deceived the people." [11] Soon afterward, calm was restored and Mirza Huseyn Khan was invited back to the capital. In due time most of the members of the coalition were punished. But, despite repeated promises to support reform programs, Nasir ed-Din Shah never recovered his former zeal for sweeping change. In the words of Amin ul-Mulk, his private secretary: "The shah was so dismayed by these affairs that even if he had any intentions of making use of what he had seen in Europe, he did not reveal it, he merely concentrated on protecting his throne." [12] Thus the two projects in which Mirza Huseyn Khan had placed so much hope for the transformation of Iran—the Reuter Concession and the shah's trip to Europe—became instead the primary tools used to destroy much of what he had planned.

Mirza Huseyn Khan found it somewhat easier to enlighten the people than to reform the country. He considered it tremendously important that the public be made aware of developments both inside and outside the country. In a letter from Istanbul to the Foreign Ministry, he said:

> The degree of a nation's progress and its ability [to become civilized], in the view of the outside world [the Europeans], is measured by four things. The first is the existence of a well-ordered press, which abounds in information on national and foreign news. . . . It is a pity that the only newspaper printed in the capital of the August Government [Tehran] has completely failed in its main task by not providing its readers with information about what is happening in the world, a knowledge that is essential for a nation's progress. This newspaper has also failed in its duty toward the outside world, which treats it with ridicule. The Iranian government began printing a newspaper in 1267/1851, yet during this period the Iranian nation [millat] has remained ignorant of the important events in the world. The newspaper has also not mentioned a word about the great developments that have occurred in Europe, let alone given the readers any information about regular occurrences, unless such occurrence is amusing and has nothing to do with real news.[13]

On another occasion, referring to the role of the Ottoman press in disseminating information about the efforts of the government to the public, he tried to draw the attention of his colleagues to the importance of good newspapers: "How good it would have been if this praiseworthy practice were followed by the Exalted Government of Iran, and the leaders of the Exalted State tried to inform the public of all their services and the progress the Exalted State has made as a result of their efforts. [It would be good] if new and beneficial regulations were implemented to inform both the people inside the country and the foreigners of these new rules in order to inspire confidence [in the state]." [14]

Mirza Huseyn Khan found few of his colleagues interested in serious newspapers. The only newspaper printed in Tehran at that time was *Rūznāmeh-yi Dowlat-i ʿAlīyeh-yi Irān*. First published in 1267/1851, when Amir Kabir was in power, it changed both its name and character after Amir's death. Its main features were accounts of the shah's hunting expeditions and court appointments, which were accompanied by elaborate drawings of the shah hunting or portraits of high dignitaries of state.[15] Not until Mirza Huseyn Khan came to Tehran in 1287/1870 to assume the post of minister of justice was he able to put into effect his recommendations for a more responsible press. His first newspaper, *Rūznāmeh-yi ʿAdlīyeh,* was published twice weekly by the Ministry of Justice to inform the public of new regulations instituted by the ministry. It was abandoned in 1288/1871 for a more general publication, *Iran,* which also replaced the official newspaper, *Ruznameh-yi Dowlat-i ʿAliyeh-yi Iran.*

During the ten years Mirza Huseyn Khan was in power, he exercised close control over the publication of *Iran.* This is obvious from the numerous articles in almost every issue reflecting his views, explaining and justifying his reforms, and describing similar steps taken by other governments. Patriotism, compulsory education in European countries, Westernization in Japan, the history and purpose of taxation in Britain, the wars of Napoleon III, Russia's intentions toward the Ottoman Empire, the education of women in Egypt, and a variety of reforms in the Ottoman Empire were all discussed in its pages. To generate more interest among readers, *Iran* also urged them to use it as a platform to express their views about the government. Among the letters printed were some that indicate the readers welcomed this suggestion.[16]

It would be difficult to state with any accuracy the circulation of newspapers at that time or the impact they had on readers. Mirza Huseyn Khan made subscriptions mandatory for all high-ranking officials inside and outside the capital. Moreover, the announcements in *Iran* indicate that it was sold in the Tehran bazaar. Therefore, it would be safe to assert that the the literate public of the time was familiar with the ideas expressed in these newspapers. Mirza Huseyn Khan's ideas did spread. The governors of Kashan and Isfahan both expressed regrets to at least one British traveler that their country had no railway, an issue that was much discussed in the newspaper.[17] This is particularly interesting, since the governor of Isfahan, Zill us-Sultan, had opposed railway construction only two years earlier.

Mirza Huseyn Khan felt strongly enough about newspapers to also undertake a French-language newspaper after the shah's first European trip in 1290/1873. On that trip he had purchased a modern printing press from Istanbul to print Persian, Arabic, and Latin books. He had also hired a Belgian engineer, Baron de Norman, who knew about both railways and printing.[18] With the baron's help Mirza Huseyn Khan published the French newspaper *La Patrie* to inform the outside world about Iran: "Persia has until this day been without a serious medium that could effectively make her known and in necessity defend her abroad." [19]

The newspaper's statement of purpose is typical of Mirza Huseyn Khan:

> As for internal affairs, we shall speak of them with complete Independence; we have no party and do not wish to have any; we present ourselves free of any commitment and without any official tie. We want to serve the country by shedding light on its true needs. We shall support progress any time it manifests itself, we shall not fail to encourage, but we shall never be vile flatterers, and we shall not bow to power; we shall defend every just cause and blame every reprehensible act.
>
> We shall support the power that for us represents the law, but if its proceedings are contrary to the law, we shall blame it so much more severely. We shall never occupy ourselves with private affairs, nor with personalities; we shall not only be neutral in this regard but also completely blind; we shall criticize the proceedings that are harmful to the general interest of the country.
>
> War then on abuse and on those who commit them. Respect for religion, respect for the sovereign. Progress, justice, and equity: there is our motto, there is our program.[20]

All these ideas had already been stated by Mirza Huseyn Khan but never before so vehemently. The shah must have known of the content of the paper before it was published. There must have been considerable opposition to it from high-ranking statesmen, for there was never a second issue.

Two other weekly newspapers founded under Mirza Huseyn Khan's direction after his return from Europe fared better. They were *Rūznāmeh-yi Nizāmī*, first published 29 Ziqaʿdeh 1293/16 December 1876, and *Rūznameh-yi ʿIlmīyeh va Adabīyeh,* issued two months later. They were concerned with military and scientific affairs respectively, but they also gave a fair share of general knowledge about developments in the outside world, particularly Europe. Two years later the two newspapers merged under the name *Mirrīkh*, with the following stated purpose: "This *Mirrīkh* newspaper will contain the official news concerning the armies of the Exalted Government of Iran, the translation of official telegrams from other states, a comprehensive account of the sciences prevalent in Europe, and some material concerning civilization, and the rights of man." [21]

Although *Mirrikh* was discontinued when Mirza Huseyn Khan was removed from the Ministry of War in Shavval 1297/September 1880, it had during its brief existence tried to propagate very definite ideals. As minister of war Mirza Hyn Khan had exercised close control over it. One article, entitled *"Bashar"* or "Mankind" typifies the style and content associated with him. It dealt with the importance of the pursuit of knowledge, a pursuit which it claimed enabled man, saved him from himself, ensured his happiness, and was, in short, "the source of his distinction, prosperity, and superiority." [22] In the course of its discussion the author introduced another even more important idea that was less familiar to his readers, namely, that the worth of an individual should be determined by achievement and not by birth:

> Our ancestors divided men into three groups: the nobility and aristocracy, the subjects and the poor, and the slaves. The civilized world today, which is at the dawn of the progress of science, no longer agrees with that classification. Today honor is achieved through merit and not birth. Whoever possesses the right religion, the correct conviction, and perfect knowledge is sovereign and excellent.[23]

The same principle was expressed in a circular sent several years earlier to the governors. It had reminded them that all subjects were to be regarded as equal by the sovereign.[24] Another unprecedented idea was its tacit rejection of the Qur'anic account of man's descent from Adam and Eve: "As a result of the admixture of numerous stories and tales, we cannot know with certainty the state of the world of creation and its development to this day. But we can be certain that there was a time when mankind did not know about writing and, consequently, was more ignorant." [25]

The author considered the discovery of writing to be the most significant event in man's history. But what had enabled man to take this momentous step forward, he asserted, "was the avoidance of injustice, the application of justice, and the recognition of his rights." [26] three principles constantly advocated by Mirza Huseyn Khan. Although the invention of writing had enabled man to institute laws, the article pointed out, "Even after the invention of writing many tribes and nations committed injustice out of sheer ignorance." [27] The greatest safeguard against ignorance, which bred many other evils besides injustice, was knowledge, man's road to salvation. The article concluded:

Every branch of the affairs of the world, be it management of the affairs of cities or of the affairs of home, the education of morals, the improvement of science, the avoidance of harms, the attainment of benefits, the improvement of trade, the progress of agriculture, the improvement of the affairs of state and the nation, the improvement of the affairs of the military, even the preservation of the species and the preservation of health, all can be attained by knowledge.[28]

With such beliefs it was natural that Mirza Huseyn Khan should emphasize the importance of education, the means to knowledge. A report from Istanbul makes clear the emphasis he placed on education as one of the principal bases for improving the state:

What Iran needs more than anything else today are men with experience and know-how. What Your Excellency [Mirza Saʿid Khan, the foreign minister] has heard about the progress of the British, Russian, and French governments, or that they acquire such amount of taxes and have so many soldiers and subjects, all these have come from the work and wisdom of men with foresight and experience. Good soil and good climate without good administrators yield no results. For example, if so and so, who is appointed to the governorship of such and such township [in Iran], be familiar with his real duties as governor and the rights of the subjects and if he has any understanding of his own state and the state of his own government, such a governor will not be bothered by the government, the people in his district will be comfortable, the country will become prosperous, and he will acquire a good name. But a governor cannot know about his duties without education, a knowledge of world affairs, and study of the history of all states, so that he can learn from these pursuits the ways of those governments that have attained progress, have become important nations, have built great cities, and have transformed themselves into much better nations. In short, individuals can with prudence transform a small nation into a strong and great nation; similarly, it is possible for individuals to destroy a great nation by sheer carelessness.[29]

To encourage the leaders of his country to pay more attention to education, Mirza Huseyn Khan sent from Istanbul elaborate reports about the efforts of Ottoman authorities to improve the quality of education there and introduce European methods into their schools. In one dispatch he described the opening of a *lycée*, a French-style secondary school, in which five hundred students would learn French language and literature, Greek, Latin, law, and political science. He pointed out again the importance of modern education for the advancement of the state: "What is certain is that the existence of schools such as this will spread knowledge among the people and make them educated. Consequently, the government will soon have at its disposal a number of well-trained and efficient men." [30]

Mirza Huseyn Khan also believed in the importance of education for women; he wrote in glowing terms of Ottoman efforts in this area. The first Ottoman school for this purpose, he wrote, enrolled one hundred women between the ages of fifteen and thirty-five, and would teach them ethics, history, geometry, management, and French. The curriculum reflected a government aim "that young girls also be provided with the opportunity to reap the results of knowledge, as do boys, who are urged by the government to pursue the study of various fields." [31] Although he was more progressive than most of his Iranian contemporaries in his attitude toward women's education, he was yet a product of his environment. In the same dispatch he noted that in his next meeting with ᶜAli Pasha, head of the Ottoman government, he would point out some of the risks involved in the enterprise: "When a woman learns French, studies literature, and acquires a knowledge of manners, it would no longer be possible to keep her in veil. Once Muslim women participate in public unveiled, a great injury will be done to Islam. And nothing will remain of Islam." [32]

When Mirza Huseyn Khan sent this report to Iran, the country had only one modern school where sciences and languages were taught, the Dar ul-Funun. Most Iranian children were taught at *maktabs*, the traditional primary schools, where children between the ages of seven and twelve could learn Persian, a little Arabic (enough to enable them to read the Qurᶜan), and some arithmetic. These schools received no state aid and were supported by a small tuition from the parents and by vaqf properties or religious endowments. Maktabs were numerous—even villages of fifty families might have one—but the quality of education was not satisfactory. Most families of substance therefore hired private tutors for their children. [33]

After completing education at a maktab, a student could enter a *madriseh* or school of higher education to prepare for a religious, legal, or teaching vocation. These establishments, which were to be found in almost every town, were attached to mosques and were supported by vaqf grants. There the students learned Arabic and Persian literature, interpretation of the Qur'an, logic, and philosophy, the shari'a, and *fiqh* or the discipline of elucidating the shari'a.

Dar ul-Funun, which was modeled after the French polytechnic school, was founded in 1851 by Amir Kabir to teach military and modern sciences. Several mission schools teaching modern science and languages also existed in Tehran, Tabriz, and Isfahan; but they were attended almost exclusively by children of minorities, especially Armenians, and had little influence on the mainstream of Iranian life.

Soon after Mirza Huseyn Khan returned to Tehran, he discovered that Dar ul-Funun had been declining steadily. The school had begun with about one hundred fifty students and sixteen teachers, twelve of the latter European and four Iranian.[34] Although Nasir ed-Din Shah had been at first greatly interested in the school, he had become disenchanted with it when some of its teachers and students became involved with the Faramushkhaneh, a secret society of purported republican sentiments that was banned in 1858.[35] In an attempt to revive the shah's interest, Mirza Huseyn Khan gave him a lengthy report on the deteriorating conditions there:

> Although they knew I was coming and tried to put on their best appearance, the truth is that I was deeply disappointed by that visit. The only European teacher is M. Richards, the Englishman; the rest of the teachers came from among the students. The total number of students is supposed to be one hundred fifty, but I only found seventy-nine, which includes the teachers and their assistants. They tried to make lame excuses for those who were supposedly absent. What is needed today to order the affairs of government are individuals with new thinking, and such individuals can only be produced with the help of education.[36]

Nasir ed-Din Shah responded favorably, ordering his sadr-i a'-zam to do what was needed to improve conditions at the school. A change for the better was soon noticeable, and an article described its new state. "Today the school has about two hundred fifty students who pursue a European education in various fields, such as mathematics, engineering, military science, medicine, natural science, and foreign languages. Some of the teachers are European, and some are Iranians who have studied in Europe."[37]

The military hospital that had been founded to serve the needs of the new model army[38] was attached to Dar ul-Funun so that medical students could use it for study. An Austrian physician, Dr. Bigmez, who had been hired to head the hospital, also taught medicine at the school.[39] "At the death of the European professor who taught the course, it was abandoned entirely." [40]

In addition to improving and expanding Dar ul-Funun, Mirza Huseyn Khan founded two other schools. The first was a military academy that taught only military subjects.[41] Of more significance, however, was the founding of the second school, which was Iran's first public school. It was named Mushīrīyyeh in honor of its founder. Its enrollment was seventy, and its curriculum consisted of European languages, sicence, geography, history, and mathematics. Iʿtimad us-Saltaneh, its first principal, reported that "Many of those serving His Majesty at court are graduates of this school." [42]

Contemporary newspapers reflect Mirza Huseyn Khan's interest in advancing education in Iran. One article that appeared when his power was at its zenith told of the duty of government to supervise the education of children. The style and phraseology indicate that the author was writing under Mirza Huseyn Khan's direction. He said:

> It is the duty of every government to pass laws and regulations that would oblige the parents and relatives of youngsters to entrust the children, according to specific regulations, to schools where capable teachers could educate them in human virtues. So that these children could benefit the state and the people [dowlat va millat]. The advantages of this have become so evident to other countries and states that there is absolutely no room for doubt. It has become obvious that this is the principal cause of the progress of the state and the people.[43]

The article criticized traditional maktab education, under which children were instructed by "unqualified and poor teachers." It pointed to the efforts of other governments, especially Egypt, the Ottoman Empire, and Japan, to improve their educational systems.[44]

Mirza Huseyn Khan also laid the groundwork for a school of religious sciences modeled after the Al-Azhar in Cairo, the school was named Madriseh-yi Nāsirī in honor of the shah. Its library, as described by Iʿtimad us-Saltaneh, was outstanding, the best in Iran due in large part to the many expensive books bought and bequeathed to it by Mirza Huseyn Khan.[45] The name of the school and the mosque to which it was attached were later changed to Sipahsalar to honor Mirza Huseyn Khan.

If Mirza Huseyn Khan's authority had not been challenged, he would certainly have been able to accomplish a good deal more in creating modern schools. The several modern public schools founded in Tehran, Tabriz, and Isfahan in the decade after his death all seem to have been founded on the model of the Maktab-i Mushiriyyeh.

Mirza Huseyn Khan also used the press to propagate his theories on nationalism among the literate public. The idea was central to his thought; it supported his concern for preserving the country's prestige, his desire to restore its past glory, his awareness of his responsibilities in office, his effort to end corruption in government, and his disappointment with the attitude of most members of the Iranian ruling class. Throughout his career he tried to kindle this sentiment in the hearts of his colleagues and anyone he could reach.

The task was not entirely formidable. Discernible far back in Iran's history and culture are the basic features of nationalism, a common language, and a sense of historical and territorial continuity. National consciousness can easily be recognized in the *Shāhnāmeh* of Firdowsi (933–1021 A.D.).

In the early nineteenth century, Iran's loss of territory to Russia after defeat in two wars stirred the national consciousness of some Iranian leaders. This is obvious in the reply of Qa'immaqam, Muhammad Shah's prime minister, to the demands of the British minister, who wanted the same privileges for his government as were granted to Russia in 1828 by the Treaty of Turkmanchay:

> This type of trade would lead to the annihilation of this poor and weak country and would result in the division of Iran between the two fierce lions, who have their claws struck in her corpse. . . . As it is, Iran's chances of survival under the claws of only one lion [Russia] are quite slim. Her chances would be even slimmer if two lions make an attempt to tear her apart. Iran would not be able to withstand that, and, no doubt, she would give out under their pressure.[46]

Another statesman, Amir Kabir, had a deeper understanding of nationalism and how it affected the life of the nation. His words to Colonel Sheil, the British minister to the court of Nasir ed-Din Shah, makes this clear:

No trace of nationalism or love of country is left among the Iranians. The hold of religion, which up till now fulfilled the role of nationalism, is on the wane. The government's authority does not extend far. Every one seems to be eager for change. Meanwhile, the Iranians have been demonstrating great eagerness to befriend foreign powers. . . . Under these circumstances and considering Britain's strength in comparison with Iran, how could I agree to a request that would enhance British power but would result in weakening Iran?[47]

Amir Kabir's lament for the loss of commitment among his colleagues was well-founded; yet most Iranians identified strongly with their country (sarzamīn-i Irān) and took great pride in being Iranian. Travelers to mid-nineteenth-century Iran often remarked on this:

By the way in which Persians in other lands talk of their own country one would imagine that Persia was the most charming region of the world. Its climate, its water, its fruits, its houses, its gardens, its horses, the shooting it affords, its scenery, its women are all subjects of the most unqualified praise on the part of the Persian in Europe or India. In the midst of evidences of European splendor and luxury he boasts how superior in every respect is his native land; and while partaking in European society and dissipation, he longs to drink once more at the fountainhead of the wine of Sheeraz, and to listen once more to the recitation of the odes of Hafiz.[48]

The Iranians' pride in their country could be found inside as well as outside the country, even in the remotest villages:

I was amused by overhearing a conversation between him, Chiragh Ali, and Seyyid Ali, as I sat in my room with closed doors. The subject of debate was the nations of Farangistan [Europe]. Seyyid Ali dilated on the power of England, as evinced by the conquest and government of India. The bold Bakhtiari considered that a trifle. Seyyid Ali attempted to explain. "It is well known," said the kadkhoda, "that no empire can compare in extent and power with that of Persia." This was accepted as proof conclusive and was followed by the silent sucking of qalyāns.[49]

Iran's contact with Europe increased considerably during the reign of Nasir ed-Din Shah. One consequence was that new elements were introduced into the formation and evolution of Iranian nationalism. By the end of the decade that had witnessed Amir's death in 1851, hundreds of educated residents in all walks of life had joined the Faramushkhaneh, a secret society with a strong nationalist sentiment founded by Malkam Khan, who was a vocal advocate of nationalism in the country.

Malkam was not alone in propagating nationalist ideas. He was aided by Mirza Yusuf Khan Mustashar ud-Dowleh, Mirza Fath-ʿAli Akhundzadeh, and Mirza Huseyn Khan. These men came to know and cooperate with each other; nationalism was their creed. They all had intimate knowledge of Europe and the currents of thought there. Their strong attachment to their own country naturally made them susceptible to the doctrine of nationalism that was so prevalent in nineteenth-century Europe. Each man tried in his own way to evoke a national spirit among his countrymen, hoping to create a strong national state. Nationalism motivated their commitment to reform Iran and transform it into an image of Europe. Nationalism also prompted their great distress over the widespread corruption in government and the deterioration of economic and political conditions in Iran. While at Istanbul, Mirza Huseyn Khan made an explicit statement of this position to the Iranian foreign minister:

I wish to see that the Exalted Government is also similar to what can be seen among other nations, and that the name of our country enters the pages of history in a manner similar to those other nations, that the talent and greatness the Almighty has bestowed on His Majesty is witnessed by all nations, and that the name of the Iranian government and nation is mentioned with respect and associated with greatness. Since I do not feel I am getting closer to achieving any of these ends, I get despondent and despair, knowing that I am seeking the impossible.

I have enough sense to realize that what I wish for my country cannot happen overnight and must be attained over a long period. But what makes me despair is that not only have we not even begun, but we also do not realize that there are defects in our system that need to be corrected. On the contrary, we imagine that we have achieved the highest degree of perfection and that there is nothing left for us to do.

You might say to me, "Why have you taken it upon yourself to be so concerned about the affairs of the Government and to be so distressed by it? Why do others not feel the same distress or waste their precious life on these useless thoughts?" I would reply that you yourself probably feel the same way and that you have realized the malaise we feel is induced by our despair. But you, due to prudence, prefer to remain silent.

In my opinion, unless a man is willing to sacrifice himself, unless he puts the welfare of the majority before his own well-being, and unless he talks and writes about topics that are normally left unsaid, he has not fulfilled his devotion to the state and his love of his country and its people.[50]

This theme of patriotism, concern for the welfare of Iran, and pain at the indifference of most Iranian statesmen runs throughout Mirza Huseyn Khan's writings, not only in this period, but also later, after he had assumed higher offices in Tehran. Throughout his long career he tried to teach the meaning of patriotism to his colleagues. Not even those least interested, like Mirza Sa'id Khan Ansari to whom the above message was addressed, escaped his proselytizing.

Terms like *patriotism, concern for the welfare of the state and nation*, and *Iran's greatness* abounded in the circulars and official reports of any office headed by Mirza Huseyn Khan and all publications over which he had control. A typical example is an article entitled "Vatan" or "Fatherland," which opened with a familiar discussion. *Vatan* is a territorial entity in which one is born and one's blood relations live; its inhabitants are like members of a single family or tribe. The article suggested that vatan members are likewise united by a common bond of language, a distinctive feature also of European nationalism. The vatan member's greatest duty is to love his fatherland and devote himself to its service: "Conscientious men and the seekers of honor must devote their strength, knowledge, and skill to the maintenance of their country's prestige and the increase of its glory and worth. . . . Whoever possesses the love of his fatherland and holds these as truth is the embodiment of the good, and whoever denies this is nothing." [51]

Not all ideas the newspapers tried to promote were lofty, but advantage was taken of every opportunity to teach Western concepts. A typical announcement concerned the decision of the sadr-i a'zam to work according to a definite schedule. Mirza Huseyn Khan took advantage of the occasion to explain the importance of order in the affairs of government, the value of time—of which few people in Iran and elsewhere in Asia were aware—and to remind them that "His Majesty has decided that the affairs of the country are to be based on new regulations and the country's prosperity to be on a firm foundation." [52] His long introduction is characteristically didactic in tone:

The Almighty God has bestowed all manners of benefits on the people of Iran, but for several reasons we have not ap-

preciated these favors and have not taken advantage of one-
thousandth of them. We have neglected to make use of our
mines, our resources, our underground treasures, our personal and inherent talents. But what we have neglected above
all is our time and our life, which, due to faulty education,
have been wasted in all Eastern countries.[53]

To convince his readers fully, he pointed out that His Majesty was
in total agreement with him that:

The manners of rulership in these countries has been such
that nothing has been done without too much delay. But the
people of Iran can testify to the many damages and evils they
have suffered from this major defect. On the other hand, we
know that one of the main causes of the advancement of
foreign [European] countries is that they have realized the
value of time and have devised as efficient methods to make
use of it as they have of their other sources of wealth.[54]

After this elaborate opening, the prime minister announced his
schedule and set specific times for anyone who wished to see him
about any particular business. "No one is allowed to come to the
prime minister's office unless he has official business." [55] Friends
and personal callers were enjoined to come only at times set aside
for them: "Any thinking person can realize that abiding by these
regulations is much more beneficial for the public. Anyone who
does not follow these rules or acts contrary to them will have
delayed his own business." [56]

A schedule was a decided departure from the usual manner of
doing business adopted by grandees of the realm. Most officials
were always ready for visits, whether business or friendly, and
encouraged a crowd to gather around them, since this was regarded as a sign of prestige; however, Mirza Huseyn Khan's announcement apparently caused no adverse reactions. Perhaps the
language in which it was couched made objection difficult.

This attempt to set himself a schedule was only one of many
minor regulations he instituted to render the government appa-
ratus more efficient, formal, and seemingly modern. Yet, though
they were obviously of European origins, their introduction caused
little stir, and most survived his fall from power in 1880. These
minor regulations caused little opposition for a number of reasons.

First, most of these minor reforms affected only the class connected with the court and government, in the capital particularly.
Among these reforms were the aforementioned scheduling regulation and the change in style of dress.

Second, few of these innovations challenged any fundamental beliefs of this class or endangered vested group interests. Hence, any opposition was from individuals and was motivated by personal reasons or from small groups of minor officials whose interests were not vital to the ongoing pursuits of the ruling class as a whole.

Third, unlike their colleagues in the Ottoman Empire and neighboring Muslim lands, the official class in Iran had a flexible attitude toward change and innovation. The Ottoman reforms had at first met even more serious opposition than that which faced the reforms in Iran. To understand the pliant attitude of Iranian officialdom, we must remember Iran's geographical location. This location at the crossroads of Asia, Europe, and Africa was the main source of prosperity of the Iranian highlands before the discovery of the sea routes in the fifteenth century; but it also left the region an easy prey to ambitious conquerors. Its terrain was so vast and diverse that any conqueror who wished to rule the region had to rely upon the assistance of native officials. So in spite of the changing fortunes of ruling dynasties, this official class had survived almost unscathed; they were virtually indispensable no matter who was in power.

To be sure, members of the official class occasionally paid tolls; but they usually lost position or life for personal reasons rather than for principle or misplaced loyalties. The sudden rise and fall of dynasties made it hazardous to put faith in the fortune of any ruler. Instead, prompted by self-preservation, the members of the class reserved most of their allegiance for their own class and, to accommodate the realities of their situation, learned to be increasingly flexible toward change.

Class preservation and flexibility thus became the guiding principles of Iranian officialdom and can be traced back in Iranian history to the rise of Islam. A source of weakness as well as strength, this instinct for class preservation enabled the majority of Iranian officials to accept the rule of a group as alien and destructive as the Mongols. It also underlies the preservation of Iranian culture and civilization, which are said to have lasted for twenty-five hundred years. Adherence to these two principles may also explain why the imposition of Shiʿism by Shah Ismaʿil, the first Safavid ruler (1501–24), produced no leader of resistance of the stature of Thomas More, which in a country the size of Iran could have caused political fragmentation and disaster. This may also account for the lack of fanaticism among the Iranians that has been noted by travelers in Iran during the nineteenth century[57] and for the success Mirza Huseyn Khan had in introducing the many minor innovations and reforms that were accepted even by officials who had personal objections to him.

A fourth reason for the lack of opposition to the minor reforms was the sense of rivalry the Iranians bore to the Ottomans, as well as the knowledge that they were well on their way to adopting European methods. It has already been shown to what extent Mirza Huseyn Khan, who was himself deeply under Ottoman influence, tried to use this feeling of rivalry to interest his colleagues in reform. That the use of this method by Mirza Huseyn Khan was effective is borne out by the statement of a contemporary that reveals its author's envy rather than the success or failure of the Ottoman reforms. "If they [the Ottomans] seem to have made any inroads [into civilization], this is because the capital of the country is in the heart of Europe, and the rays of civilization fall on it from every side. So whatever they appear to have accomplished is from the outside." [58]

Fifth, time was ripe for these reforms. Although firsthand knowledge of Europe and Europeans was very limited, European superiority was established for most members of the official class. They were willing, therefore, and sometimes even eager, to emulate European ways, so long as there was no damage to their interests. The great demand for European luxury items among the wealthy class in Iran indicated a trend: "The government is losing much money due to the importation of European goods. . . . The craze for chandeliers, wall-hangings, decorative objects, tables, and useless clothes has reduced many to poverty, but they do not realize the ugliness of their deeds." [59]

Thus Mirza Huseyn Khan's reform of manners and procedures, from clothing to discussions at high level meetings, met with relative acceptance. The change in clothing style was introduced before the shah's first trip to Europe. This trip undoubtedly furnished the incentive to replace the traditional garb, which included a hat a foot tall, with clothing that would be less conspicuous in Europe. The style chosen was like that worn in the Ottoman Empire, a suit with tunic-style jacket and narrow pants, and a felt cap. Only the prime minister's chief rival, Mirza Yusuf Khan Mustowfi ul-Mamalik, opposed the decree that required all government officials to dress in the new style. His defiance was clearly the expression of a clash of personalities rather than a clash of tastes. The new style remained after its initiator was gone.[60]

Another custom introduced specifically in conjunction with the trip was European table manners. Mirza Huseyn Khan held several sessions in which he instructed the grandees in the use of cutlery: "He organized banquets, where he undertook the task of coaching the retinue that was to accompany His Majesty. For a week, while the courtiers learned how to eat in the European style, the Shahynshah (King of Kings) watched them from behind a partition with small holes. The women of the harem could also comfortably watch this spectacle, which was new to them." [61]

Among other unchallenged changes were the use of tables and chairs at cabinet meetings[62] and the erection of a special building for the meetings.[63] An attempt was also made to reduce ceremonials that interfered with efficiency. Of these changes, two are particularly worthy of note. The first came in the form of an official announcement that discouraged the use of long-winded honorifics in official correspondence. It stated: "The exaggerated use of these terms has been such that often the main point has become forgotten and lost. . . . At this time, it has become apparent that this practice is damaging to civilization." [64] The second, which followed shortly afterward also as an announcement, was designed to save time and simplify the life of high officials. Mirza Huseyn Khan announced his intention to dispense with the custom that required dignitaries "to ride with a host of attendants walking at their sides, as well as ahead of and behind them." [65] Henceforth he would ride to his office accompanied only by two grooms,[66] and other officials were instructed to do likewise. Although most officials welcomed this instruction, "which did away with a useless and costly custom," the attendants lamented that "The son of Mirza Nabi Khan has cut off people's livelihood." [67]

In keeping with the practices of "advanced" nations, the government began to publish an almanac containing information about:

> . . . the history of the world; the history of the Qajar dynasty; the administration of the realm; the names of the princes and their biographies; Iran's military capabilities; the population of the capital; the names of the ʿulama; the governors of provinces and the population of each province; the names of the rulers of other countries, their religion, their revenues and expenses, their armies, their national debts, their navies, their mines and products, their trade, their coinage; and, finally, a map of the world; and a map of Iran.[68]

I'timad us-Saltaneh, who was appointed the editor of this ambitious project, assures us that the almanac began regular publication the following year.[69]

Western music played by a military band was also introduced at this time. A French instructor was hired to teach the band members. The band played primarily at official ceremonies of the Ministry of War, and it also performed privately, as on the occasion of a benefit given under the direction of the prime minister to help the needy in Tehran. Although Mirza Huseyn Khan did not himself attend the concert, he sent a contribution; but most of the dignitaries and many of the Europeans in the capital participated.[70]

Far more significant was the creation of a modern postal system in the country. Prior to this time, mail delivery had been handled by private individuals who farmed or rented the postal service for a particular area from the government. During the shah's stay in Vienna in 1873, Mirza Huseyn Khan hired an official of the Austrian Post Office to organize the Iranian postal system along European lines. The new postal delivery system was first tried out in the capital; then it was extended to the rest of the country. Within a year regular service was established between Tehran and most of the other important cities.[71] Even by contemporary European standards, the service was efficient. It was admired by all: "In Karman post-office . . . I watched the distribution of letters and was rather impressed with the business-like character of the performance." [72] By 1877 Iran had joined the International Postal Union, and weekly service linked Tehran with major European cities like London, Paris, and Berlin.[73]

Another important step in improving the country's communication system both within its own borders and with the outside world was the expansion of the telegraph system. The first line, constructed in 1859, connected Tehran with Sultaniyeh one hundred sixty miles to the northwest. In the following year the line was continued to Tabriz, and in 1863 it was connected to Julfa in Azerbaijan on the Russian border.[74]

A few years later, the British government, in an attempt to establish direct communications with India, provided Iran with a direct link to Europe in exchange for permission to pass the line through its territory. The service, which linked Bombay, Tehran, Istanbul, Baghdad, and Europe on the one hand and Tabriz, Julfa, Tehran, and Russia on the other, was "very inefficient, and messages between England and India took several days and sometimes weeks to reach their destination." [75] The situation improved noticeably in 1872, when the Iranian government under Mirza Huseyn Khan's direction signed a new agreement with the British government that added a third wire from Julfa on the Russian border to Bushihr on the Persian Gulf. A. Houtum-Schindler, who served the Iranian government in various capacities during the last quarter of the nineteenth century,[76] has stated that after 1873 the telegraph service "may be considered one of the finest and most efficient lines in the world." [77]

Of equal importance was the construction of telegraph lines between towns such as Kirman, Kashan, Yazd, Isfahan, Mashhad, and some towns on the Caspian coast, connecting them with Tehran.[78] Whereas the Indo-European lines were mainly for communication with the outside world, the new lines improved internal communication and extended central control over the provinces.

The city of Tehran benefited greatly from Mirza Huseyn Khan's endeavors to bring Iran closer to Europe. Tehran had been chosen as the capital by the first Qajar ruler, Agha Muhammad Khan, because it was close to Asterabad, the seat of the Qajar tribe. Since then little had been done to improve its small-town appearance. Before the expansion of Tehran in 1870–72, it was "contracted, filthy, shabby, and what the French so well denominated as *morne* [dreary]." [79] After having experienced the splendor of Istanbul, it is not surprising that Mirza Huseyn Khan should have sought to improve the capital to reflect the prestige of Iran. As soon as he arrived, he began to develop a city worthy of being the capital of the Protected Kingdoms of Iran. This process of development and expansion took two years:

Tehran was suddenly bidden to burst its bonds and enlarge its quarters. The old walls and towers were for the most part pulled down, the ditch was filled, a large slice of surrounding plain was taken in, and, at the distance of a full mile from the old enclosure, a new rampart was constructed upon Vauban's system, copied from the fortification of Paris before the German war. A good deal of money sent out from England by the Persian Famine Relief Fund in 1871 was spent in the hire of labour for the excavation of the new ditch, which has a very steep outer profile, and for the erection of the lofty sloping rampart beyond. There is no masonry work upon these new fortifications; they are not defended by a single gun; they describe an octagonal figure about eleven miles in circuit; and, I imagine, from the point of view of the military engineer, are wholly useless for defence. Their main practical service consists in facilitating the collection of the town *octroi* [tax]. Nevertheless, Tehran can now boast that it is eleven miles round, that it has European fortifications, and twelve gates, while its interior features have developed in a corresponding ratio.[80]

During this decade, too, European engineers hired by Mirza Huseyn Khan built several roads in the capital to replace the narrow winding alleys that had previously existed. One of these roads connected the suburb of Qulhak, six miles north of Tehran, to the shrine of Shah ᶜAbdul ᶜAzim, six miles south of the capital. Four smaller roads were built around the *ark* or residence of the shah, and each of these was connected with minor streets to the city's twelve gates.[81] North of the shah's residence was built a large square, Miydān-i Tūpkhāneh, which was open to the public when it was not being used for military drill.[82] Most of the streets around the ark and those running north were bordered with poplars. To meet the increased demand for water, new qanats were constructed. An American missionary who visited Tehran several times during this decade and witnessed the improvements wrote: "These changes, with the growth of shade trees, the opening of parks and gardens, have had a favorable effect upon the climate and have reduced the average temperature of the summer by several degrees. Tehran is now the most cleanly and healthful city in Persia." [83]

Gas and electric lights were introduced into the capital in the second part of the decade. Mme Serena reported, on her 1878 visit to Tehran, that "In the last two years, the gaslight and the electric light have been introduced." [84] The lighting of the main streets around the ark, the Tupkhaneh Square, and the royal palaces was another improvement initiated by Mirza Huseyn Khan.

In final testimony of Mirza Huseyn Khan's great interest in improving Tehran are the Baharistan Palace and the Sipahsalar Mosque, both of which he built. He did not live to see their completion, but the former was regarded as magnificent enough to be chosen in 1905 to house the Parliament, and the latter is equal in size and grandeur to the Safavid mosques in Isfahan. The mosque has been called a tribute to Mirza Huseyn Khan: "The very best medal to indicate his distinction is the one he provided for himself. That is the building of a madriseh and mosque in Tehran which is known as the Madriseh-yi Nasiri. Never before has anything so strong and grand been built in Iran." [85]

The name of the school and mosque were later changed from Nasiri to Sipahsalar in honor of their founder.

The decade of the seventies witnessed the successful implementation of many minor reforms, most of which survived Mirza Huseyn Khan's fall. Some, like the modern postal system and expanded telegraph system, widened Iran's contact with the outside world. The shah's visits to Europe were of equal importance. Although they did not result in a total transformation of Iran as Mirza Huseyn Khan had hoped, they did reveal to Nasir ed-Din Shah and his entourage the great gap that separated Iran from the European nations. Thus they paved the way for the smaller reforms proposed by the prime minister. To be sure, Mirza Huseyn Khan's ten years of effort did not succeed in implementing any real fundamental change in the country, but his minor reforms did arrest and even somewhat reverse the nation's process of decay. One critic commented: "Truly . . . Mirza Huseyn Khan Sipahsalar . . . was one of the great sadrs [prime ministers] of this government. He was very efficient and capable. He introduced some European industries and techniques, such as the gaslight [and] steam-powered mills. . . . He also introduced more relaxed customs, such as riding with two horses [a small retinue] in Iran." [86]

Mirza Huseyn Khan's contributions in the realm of ideas was also great. With the help of various publications, a small but select segment of the population—the political elite—were introduced to new ideas like duty to fatherland; a government that placed welfare of state and nation first; the threat that backwardness posed to a country's security; the advancement of other nations, especially neighbors; the importance of modern education; and the necessity for government supervision of education. Although the newspapers published under Mirza Huseyn Khan were short-lived, the ideas they introduced did not die; they lay dormant in wait for a more appropriate time. Then an ever-increasing, highly vocal group took them as guidelines for the creation of a new order in society, which found its realization in the Constitutional Revolution.

9

CONCLUSION

THE APPOINTMENT of Mirza Huseyn Khan as minister of justice in December 1870 signaled the beginning of a decade of persistent attempts on his part to revive and modernize Iran. His efforts set into motion new forces within the country's political, economic, military, and judicial institutions, and introduced new modes of thought and behavior into Iran. But his endeavors fell short of accomplishing the hoped-for transformation of the country into a state "worthy of the respect of European nations." In fact, one of his contemporaries had him lament in a fictional trial, "Truly, with my *sidārat* [prime ministership] Iran's troubles began; . . . until that time she had been like a maiden whose honor no stranger had soiled." [1] This view from the opposition gives one insight into the resistance with which his efforts were met. Other factors that also impeded the success of his reform program will be examined here, and the significance of his efforts for subsequent reform movements in Iran will be evaluated.

In 1880, almost a decade after he assumed power, Mirza Huseyn Khan lamented the failure of his extensive efforts to modernize Iran. In a letter to the shah, he said: "My efforts to protect government funds, to preserve the honor of the state, and to maintain the prestige of kingship, as Your Majesty witnessed, made many enemies for me. . . . I am a man with no progeny. . . . Therefore, I resolved to be remembered by commendable works and good laws and regulations. But they assembled and succeeded in destroying my work." [2] These remarks, addressed to the shah, blame him as well for the failure of the projects. In a tirade directed to the shah's brother ʿAbbas Mirza, in which Mirza Huseyn Khan berated the shah for opposing any type of reform and for being a menace to anyone who advocated such ideas, he concluded: "He does not appreciate anyone's service. Finally he will kill me and any man of principle who has a grain of goodness in him." [3]

The shah's loss of interest and the mounting opposition of colleagues undoubtedly were factors detrimental to the success of Mirza Huseyn Khan's reforms; but even if he had succeeded in overcoming these obstacles, factors of which he did not seem to be aware would probably have rendered the total accomplishment of his projects difficult. Most notable among these were (1) the realities of the situation in Iran to which the reforms did not conform; (2) the lack of resources, both in manpower and money, needed to realize the reforms; and (3) the inadequate executive power to enforce the measures.

Mirza Huseyn Khan had been away from Iran for so many years that he could no longer perceive the realities of Iranian society and its actual needs. While his twenty-seven-year stay outside the country enabled him to realize more clearly than any other member of the ruling class the state of decadence into which the country had fallen, his absence had also weakened his perception of the real extent to which change was possible in Iran.

The fact that twelve of the twenty-seven years abroad had been spent in the neighboring Ottoman Empire was also significant. Those twelve years coincided with the activities of two energetic Ottoman reformers, ʿAli and Fuʾad Pasha, with both of whom Mirza Huseyn Khan had had occasional discussions. As his dispatches from Istanbul reveal, his observations and discussions with the Ottoman leaders influenced his own ideas for reform. But his ideas conformed better to the realities of the Ottoman Empire than to the realities of Iran.

In the Ottoman Empire, Mahmud II had prepared the way for the men of the Tanzimat by demolishing most of what was obstructive in the old order. The groundwork laid by 1871 had rendered any return to the past impossible; "only one path lay before Turkey, that of modernization or Westernization." [4] No similar groundwork had been laid in Iran; and, as Gobineau observed, Iranian society had hardly been touched by European ideas. Consequently, despite the great need for reform so rightly perceived by Mirza Huseyn Khan, only those reforms would succeed that were prompted by the immediate needs of the society and were compatible with its ethical and spiritual values.

The importance of this point is clearly demonstrated by the fate of the Babi movement and the Faramushkhaneh. The Babi movement, an offshoot of Shiʿism, strongly advocated social reform. In the mid-1840s it attracted a large following from among all segments of society, especially the urban middle class, because its message could be easily grasped. Despite severe government reprisals in the early 1850s, the movement did not die; it merely went underground. The Faramushkhaneh, Malkam's secret society founded in 1856, too, met with great initial success. Its more than two hundred members, who were drawn from the upper and upper-middle classes, vowed to carry out its platform, which was inspired by European liberal thought. Yet after it was disbanded by royal decree in 1858, no more was heard of it. It is therefore not surprising that Mirza Huseyn Khan's reform projects, which were conceived in the Ottoman Empire, influenced by currents of thoughts in Europe, and filled with foreign words like *cabinet* and *tanzimat,* should have failed to have an immediate impact upon his contemporaries.

What was unfortunate for Mirza Huseyn Khan and the reforms he contemplated or attempted was his own faulty vision of the gulf that separated him and his ideas from the country and his countrymen. This was poignantly emphasized in a letter written to him by the shah's uncle, Farhad Mirza Mu'tamid ud-Dowleh, who reminded him that five thousand years of thinking could not be changed overnight. The prince expressed the fear that Mirza Huseyn Khan's reforms, even if unsuccessful, might disrupt the existing order in society. We do not know how Mirza Huseyn Khan responded, but the prince's fears were probably groundless, since Mirza Huseyn Khan had only a handful of men on his side. Furthermore, neither he nor the prince realized that fundamental change could not come from legislation alone; men had first to be trained and educated in the new ways.

That Mirza Huseyn Khan was more content to pass legislation than to train people to implement it has been pointed out by several of his contemporaries, among them Mirza Fath-'Ali Akhundzadeh. The two men met when Mirza Huseyn Khan was traveling with the shah through Tiflis in 1873. In reply to Akhundzadeh's remark, "You have at last attained your goal and become sadr-i a'zam," Mirza Huseyn Khan replied: "No, I have not attained my goal. My goal was not only to become sadr-i a'zam; I must also do something. But I have not done anything yet." His friend responded: "Whose help are you going to use? You have to find the men first. Those men in Iran, they look like men, but they have no blood running through their veins; they need new blood. This new blood is the new alphabet, and the teaching of

The Baharistan Palace, Tehran
Courtesy of Asghar Muhajir

European knowledge." [5] He had touched upon a fundamental point crucial to the outcome of Mirza Huseyn Khan's reforms: the need for men who understood and agreed with his goals and believed in the necessity of carrying them out. But Mirza Huseyn Khan, as his friend pointed out, had few men of this type at hand and, perhaps, had not even thought of the need for them.

The fate of the Tanzimat-i Hasaneh code puts this problem in clear perspective. The aim of the code was to establish adequate control by the central government over the judicial, military, and financial affairs of the provinces. To implement this control throughout a country divided into two hundred districts would probably have required one thousand qualified officials. Considering that the total number of men exposed to modern education could not have been more than two hundred fifty, the code would have had little chance of success, even if ʿulama opposition had not led to its abrogation.

Another of Mirza Huseyn Khan's problems revealed by the Tanzimat-i Hasaneh code is the financing of his projects. As the British consul in Rashat noted in 1875, the low salary of the members of the Tanzimat councils would have forced them into bribery, which Mirza Huseyn Khan had stated was "the mother of all evils prevailing in Iran." Funds were also needed to modernize the army; to build roads, dams, and canals; to pay officials of the new ministries; and to pay foreign instructors. But Iran's economy was declining, and its treasury was sinking fast.

The signing of the Reuter Concession and the efforts to reform the system of taxation suggest that Mirza Huseyn Khan did have some awareness of the need for funds to implement his projects; but he does not seem to have perceived the degree to which the success of his reforms hinged upon adequate financing. Therefore, he did not resort to any measures to increase the government's revenues other than to assert close control over the collection of taxes, which, while it did improve the state of the treasury, was certainly not enough to finance his elaborate plans.

His apparent indifference to such problems as financing raised charges of superficiality. Amin ud-Dowleh, his severest critic, said, "Because he [Mirza Huseyn Khan] did not lay the foundation of correcting the expenses of the *divān* [government] on sound principles and resorted to the use of words and superficiality, the younger generation and those who believed in progress lost faith in him." [6] The impression of superficiality was, perhaps, not entirely his fault. His projects had to be approved by the shah before

they could be implemented; and the shah, who was at best indecisive, had grown even more hesitant to arouse any opposition.
As a result, the reforms proposed often underwent changes between the time of presentation and the time of implementation.
Unlike Mahmud II or Muhammad ᶜAli, Mirza Huseyn Khan was
an agent and not a principal; he did not have sufficient authority
to override opposition by the sanction of his office. The fate of
the Tanzimat code confirms this. The code might have endured
in a reduced form if the shah had not suddenly withdrawn his
support.

Another factor that may have made success elude him was his
personal traits. Chief among these was his inability to sustain
friendships. Without the support of a specific group in society and
sufficient resources, and with the inconsistency of the shah's attitude toward reform, the support of loyal friends could have been
invaluable, both in keeping him in power and in promoting his
reforms. But Mirza Huseyn Khan was either unaware of the usefulness of such support or was incapable of eliciting such loyalty.
During his ten years in office, he managed to alienate all his
friends; and in his last year it appeared that "His Highness has
never attempted to form a party for himself at the court, nor has
he taken any pains to secure for himself the support of any of
the other officials or influential people in Tehran." [7]

This failure to retain friends was due in large part to the extreme
sensitivity and great demands made on his friends that are so
clearly demonstrated in his correspondence with Nasir ud-Dowleh.
Because he expected too much of his friends, took offense but
did not forgive easily, and considered the slightest negative word
a rejection, he made friendship difficult. He made and lost friendships with Akhundzadeh, Malkam Khan, Mustashar ud-Dowleh,
and Nasir ud-Dowleh, all of whom could have been of great support. He paid dearly for his inability to keep friends. As the British
consul pointed out in reports to his superiors in the Foreign Office,
Mirza Huseyn Khan was completely ignorant of the mounting
intrigues among his colleagues at court that brought about his
final dismissal in 1880. [8]

Other personal traits that helped make matters worse for him
were an offensive manner and a quickness to use abusive language.
These traits did a great deal to alienate potential followers and
turn others into enemies, as the shah's younger brother ᶜAbbas
Mirza has pointed out. [9] Zill us-Sultan and Amin ud-Dowleh,
among others, have illustrated the harm done to Mirza Huseyn
Khan's reforms by the hostility of influential contemporaries. The

sabotage of his plan to retrieve Herat by those who disliked him is a clear example.[10]

Mirza Huseyn Khan's dealings with people, those he liked as well as those he disliked, reflect his inner nature. His response was more emotional and impulsive than rational; he was quick to lose his temper and sometimes even broke into tears. He seems to have lacked flexibility and mature judgment. His sensitivity, combined with great intelligence, had been useful to him as an ambassador, as he made astute observations about what was occurring around him and critically appraised his country's situation among other nations. But when he left his observation tower to assume an active role in the affairs of his country, these virtues proved more an impediment than a help. As a man of action he needed to be resilient in the face of pressure and flexible in his dealings with people; instead he brought a theoretical, even elitist, attitude to problems that needed a pragmatic approach.

Considering all the personal and political obstacles, it is remarkable that he accomplished anything at all. Yet Iran did change. Although the gap between the goals Mirza Huseyn Khan set for himself and the actual improvements made was great, Iran in 1880 was unmistakably different from Iran in 1870. Edward Stack, who traveled widely in Iran in 1882 meeting citizens of high and low station, said:

> But even as it is, in spite of niggardliness, misgovernment, and famine, the progress made by Persia within the last ten years is unmistakable. The roads are safer than they have ever been; a postal service has been established from Karman to Isfahan, from Tehran to Mashhad eastward and to the Caspian northward, and in Arabistan; the cultivation of the poppy has greatly increased; the trade of Karman, Yazd, and Isfahan has gone on growing; Seistan and Western Biluchistan have been reduced to order; the capital has been greatly improved, and new roads have been made connecting it with the Caspian. Possibly a railway will be made some day, from Tehran to Qazvin, though it is said that one of the princes has been cutting into the young embankment for clay wherewith to bake bricks for his country house. If peaceable government continues as at present, the natural tendency to the accumulation of wealth, with its concomitant advantage, may be trusted to overcome all drawbacks and defects in Persia as in most countries of the world. [11]

The changes that took place within those ten years were the result of Mirza Huseyn Khan's utter commitment to reform. They were also an indication that Iranian society, as Gobineau observed, was open and, given sufficient time, welcomed change. At the time of Stack's visit, many projects that Mirza Huseyn Khan had promoted without success were suddenly gaining appreciation and being discussed. Two governors who apologized to Stack for the absence of railways are a reminder of this; but there are also other indications. In the mid-1880s an Iranian merchant proposed a bank with Iranian capital and met with great success. Recalling Malkam's long exposition on the meaning and function of a bank just a decade earlier gives testimony to the fact that Mirza Huseyn Khan's efforts had not been wasted.

Although Mirza Huseyn Khan did not accomplish his goals within his own lifetime, he did raise the consciousness of his countrymen or at least of those of his countrymen who could read newspapers. He made them aware of their country's weaknesses and of what needed to be done to prevent its further decline. With the help of newspapers he enlarged the vision of readers to an awareness of the outside world. A comparison between the two-page weekly newspaper published in 1869, with its accounts of the shah's hunting trips, and the twice-weekly, eight-page *Iran* published under Mirza Huseyn Khan's supervision reveals why his ideas spread so widely. Perhaps their novelty prevented immediate appreciation, but they were in time understood and accepted.

Even more significant than open manifestation of change was the degree to which Mirza Huseyn Khan's ideas about the duties of government toward the people were infused—again, perhaps without full comprehension—into the ranks of the members of Iran's ruling elite. A few months after Mirza Huseyn Khan's fall from grace and shortly after his death in 1881, when Nasir ed-Din Shah addressed the members of the Dar ush-Showra-yi Kubra to announce the formation of a new cabinet, he expressed a hope that they would strive to improve the welfare of the nation.[12] His language was unmistakably reminiscent of Mirza Huseyn Khan. Later, when these ideas became once more widely discussed and written about, he again characteristically had a change of heart as he began to fear his own security might be threatened. He turned against reform and tried to pass stringent laws to prohibit the further spread of such ideas. But the die had been cast and could no longer be altered.

The young generation, who had watched in silence as Mirza Huseyn Khan struggled to reform Iran, had become acquainted with the underlying principles of his reforms. They had been shown the way to create a better society. Such ideas as justice, regulation by law in the affairs of government, and the right of every citizen to security of person and property were no longer mere ideals for discussion by intellectuals like Malkam Khan or applicable only to distant European countries. They could be used as guiding principles in the affairs of Iran itself.

Over the next twenty-five years, Mirza Huseyn Khan's principles gradually came to be regarded as the standards for Iranian policy. The Constitutional Revolution of 1905–11 was waged in an effort to realize those standards. Perhaps the greatest tribute to Mirza Huseyn Khan's role in laying the foundations for the efforts of the next generation was their choice of his residence, the Baharistan Palace, as the home of the new Iranian Parliament.

APPENDIX: THE SOURCES

THIS WORK is based mainly on Persian sources, especially primary documents. Several reasons account for this decision; among them are the abundance of primary source material—such as Mirza Huseyn Khan's mostly unpublished correspondence—official reports, and texts of decrees issued in the decade of the 1870s. This vast supply is augmented by a rich collection of contemporary accounts left by men who participated in the events of the decade, such as I'timad us-Saltaneh, and by the newspapers printed during this period, particularly *Iran*, which presents an eyewitness account of many of these events.

Contemporary Western sources, travel accounts, and diplomatic dispatches have been used sparingly, either to clarify an obscure or controversial point, or to substantiate a dubious proposition. The stereotyped attitude of most Westerners who visited Iran during this period was one reason why I made an effort to rely primarily on Persian source material. More important was my conviction that the quality of life, the hopes, the aspirations, and the problems of the Iranians living during this decade might be captured more easily by making use of the ample contemporary Persian sources.

The nature of the material used in this work has required careful selection and interpretation. In what follows, I shall try to evaluate the merits of the sources used in this work under four headings, in order of usefulness.

Persian Documentary Sources

Many of the state documents and items of correspondence of the men of affairs in Iran prior to the nineteenth century have been destroyed. Several reasons could be mentioned to account for the loss of this valuable source material: the repeated invasion of foreign armies—the Arabs, Mongols, and Afghans—and the numerous internecine wars. Also, when a new dynasty established itself, it would, in an effort to be the sole object of the people's loyalties, attempt to eradicate the memory of its predecessors, including documents. Bureaucrats, too, played a role in the destruction of state documents. Committed to serving the new dynasty, they would destroy the papers of their old masters, not only to please the new, but also to erase traces of their own former roles. Finally, the informality of government and the fact that many high officials discharged their duties from their homes meant that many valuable state papers remained in private hands and were treated as private possessions when the officials left office or died. Descendants of the officials did not always treat the documents carefully, either. Even today stories are told in Tehran of important documents turning up in obscure corners of the bazaars.[1]

Nevertheless, the great proportion of documents from the post-Qajar period survive, partly because the period is so close to our own. A more important reason is the increased familiarity of Iranian scholars with modern methods of historical research and their awareness of the value of primary documents for the study of the past. The founding of archives in the Iranian Ministry of Foreign Affairs, the Library of the Iranian Parliament, the Royal Library, the National Library, and many private collections are an indication of this awareness of the significance of documents among Iranians.

Similarly, for the period of Mirza Huseyn Khan, 1870 to 1880, an ample supply of documentary material still exists. There is his own correspondence with other major figures of the decade, especially Nasir ed-Din Shah; the correspondence of others, such as the shah, Zill us-Sultan, Farhad Mirza Mu'tamid ud-Dowleh, Mirza Musa Vazir-Lashkar, and others; and the texts of decrees issued, as well as accounts in newspapers of the time.

THE REPORTS AND CORRESPONDENCE OF MIRZA HUSEYN KHAN

Mirza Huseyn Khan (1243/1827–1298/1881) was a copious writer. He sent elaborate dispatches from Istanbul; and, later, when he returned to Tehran, he wrote to the shah almost every day, informing him on all state matters, no matter how minute. He also wrote to subordinates and friends. These reports and correspondence form the backbone of this study; they reveal a great deal about the man's ideas, personality, daily routine, hopes, ambitions, fears, and relationships with others, especially the shah. Although the earliest of these documents date to 1859, most were written between 1870 and 1881.

Mirza Huseyn Khan had an easy writing style that was almost conversational. He seems to have been uninhibited in expressing his thoughts and intentions. The answers he received, particularly from the shah, are almost equally revealing. Most of these documents are privately owned and still unpublished. They can be found in:

1. The Farhad Collection, belonging to Mahmud Farhad-Mu'tamid, a descendant of Prince Farhad Mirza Mu'tamid ud-Dowleh, the shah's uncle. The collection contains about 600 pieces of correspondence, most of them written by Mirza Huseyn Khan to Nasir ed-Din Shah, usually with the shah's response written in the margin. Thirty-three of the letters were exchanged between Mirza Huseyn Khan and Mirza Musa Vazir-Lashkar, chief financial official at the Ministry of War.

2. The Majlis Collection, which contains about 50 documents, most of them exchanged by Mirza Huseyn Khan and the shah, and a few others written to Mirza Huseyn Khan by others, for example, Malkam Khan.

3. The Ghani Collection of 844 documents pertaining to the Qajar period, which includes about 100 documents from the period of Mirza Huseyn Khan. One group of 55 letters written by Mirza Huseyn Khan during the last two years of his life to Nasir ud-Dowleh reveals some special aspects of his character.

4. The archives of the Ministry of Foreign Affairs in Tehran, which contains a collection of documents that clarify the period spent by Mirza Huseyn Khan as ambassador to the Ottoman court. These documents, dating from before 1871, may be found in various files, including 11, 16, and 44.

5. Published collections of documents, the most important of which are those edited by Ibrahim Safa'i. Although Safa'i does not always reveal the source of his documents and does not in every case provide a critical appraisal of the document or its provenance, he nevertheless provides the student of Qajar history with an important additional source. Relevant to this work are his *Asnād-i Nowyāfteh*, *Barghā-yi Tārīkh-i Irān*, and *Asnād-i Barguzīdeh*, which contain 74 letters written to or by Mirza Huseyn Khan.

Other works that fall short of their stated aim as historical studies of the period but have value because of the documents they contain pertaining to the 1870s are Mahmud Farhad-Mu'tamid's *Sipahsālār-i A'zam* and *Tārīkh-i Ravābit-i Sīyāsī-yi Irān va Usmānī*, Ibrahim Teymuri's *'Asr-i Bīkhabarī*, and Khan Malik Sasani's *Sīyāsatgarān-i Dowreh-yi Qājār*.

TEXTS OF DECREES ISSUED 1870–80

The texts of decrees issued in this period appear in various contemporary newspapers, especially *Iran*. They are recorded also in other works of the period, especially the two official chronicles by I'timad us-Saltaneh, *Mir'āt ul-Buldān* and *Tārīkh-i Muntazam-i Nāsirī*. These documents, which are usually lengthy, provide a great deal of information about the nature of the reforms implemented, the method by which they were carried out, and the reasons why they were introduced.

Contemporary Persian Sources

During the second half of the nineteenth century, an increasing number of Iranians began to be educated in the West. One outcome of this education was the introduction of a new style and new forms of writing into Iran. The earlier formal and precious style gave way to more informal prose that was closer to the spoken language. New literary forms, such as the autobiography, diary, and interpretative history became popular. The newspapers of the seventies played an important role in disseminating this new style of writing. As a consequence, these new forms joined the older chronicle to provide us with a better perspective of the period.

NEWSPAPER ACCOUNTS

The only newspaper published in Tehran before 1870 was *Rūznāmeh-yi Dowlat-i 'Alīyeh-yi Irān, The Gazette of the Exalted Government of Iran*. Its four pages were exclusively devoted to court happenings, such as appointments, news of the shah's travels, and brief biographies of important princes and high officials. In the 1870s, under Mirza Huseyn Khan, the *Gazette* was replaced by *Iran*, which had eight to twelve pages and appeared twice a week. Several other newspapers were also published: *Rūznāmeh-yi 'Adlīyeh, The Justice Gazette; Rūznāmeh-yi Nizāmi, The Military Gazette; Rūznāmeh-yi 'Ilmī, The Scientific Gazette;* and *Mirrīkh, Mars*. All these newspapers carried articles about government activities both in the capital and provinces. Many pages are devoted to expounding the aims of the government and the philosophy underlying the reforms being attempted, thus giving a good view of conditions that prevailed in Iran at the time. The Milli and Majlis libraries have complete collections. The Khurumi Collection in Tehran is also extensive.

CONTEMPORARY ACCOUNTS IN CHRONICLES, BIOGRAPHIES, MEMOIRS, TRAVEL ACCOUNTS, AND SOCIAL CRITICISM

The fact that most of the authors of the following works participated in the events of the period increases the value of these sources for history.

1. Muhammad Hasan Khan, I'timad us-Saltaneh, and his works. I'timad us-Saltaneh (1259/1843–1313/1895), who was known earlier in his career as Sanī' ud-Dowleh, was one of a long line of government officials. His father had occupied high posts, including governor and minister, in the reign of Nasir ed-Din Shah. I'timad us-Saltaneh was among the first group of students to enter Dar ul-Funun College in 1852. On completing his education, he entered government service in Tehran; in 1863 he joined the staff of the Iranian embassy in Paris, where he improved his knowledge of French. When he returned to Tehran in 1867, he was appointed private servitor and translator to the shah, a post he held until his death in 1313/1895. He also held many other posts during his career. He was a member of the Dar ush-Showra-yi Kubra, the Highest Consultative Council; head of the Office of Government Publications, including the official newspapers and chronicles of the reign of Nasir ed-Din Shah; and minister of publications and translations.

In addition to being in daily contact with the shah and intimately involved with the affairs of government at the highest level, I'timad us-Saltaneh had great literary ability; his works are as enjoyable as they are informative. But he was not completely objective in reporting events that concerned those he disliked or envied. Due to a dispute over land, Mirza Huseyn Khan was one of the men he personally disliked. Yet, despite the ill feeling he bore Mirza Huseyn Khan, the diversity of material us-Saltaneh has left enables us to arrive at a relatively full description of the man and his period.

It is important to note that the works dealing with Mirza Huseyn Khan were written after his death, so we can assume that any favorable statements are not merely flattery. Occasionally the author, captivated by nostalgia, remembers Mirza Huseyn Khan and his time with great regret; but on the whole he makes no secret of his dislike of the man and disapproval of his reforms. I'timad us-Saltaneh's critical attitude lends credence to the favorable picture of Mirza Huseyn Khan that emerges from his works.

The works of I'timad us-Saltaneh are of two kinds: those he wrote as the official historian of the reign, including *Al-Ma'āsir-u val 'Āsār, Mir'āt ul-Buldān* and *Tārīkh-i Muntazam-i Nāsirī,* and *Sadr ut-Tavārīkh;* and works not intended for publication but published posthumously, including *Khalseh yā Khābnāmeh-yi I'timād us-Saltaneh (The Books of Dreams of I'timād us-Saltaneh)* and *Rūznāmeh-yi Khātirāt I'timād us-Saltaneh (The Diary of I'timād us-Saltaneh).*

Of the official chronicles, *Mir'āt ul-Buldān,* published in four volumes in 1295/1877, is the most valuable for this study. The first and last volumes are geographical dictionaries of the towns in Iran during the reign of Nasir ed-Din Shah. Much of the material in these two volumes is derived from older works like *Mu'jam al-Buldān* of Yāqūt Hamavi, a nineteenth century geographer, but the section on Tehran contains much new information, especially about the growth of the city under Nasir ed-Din Shah.

The second and third volumes, written in chronicle style, record the events of the reign of Nasir ed-Din Shah year by year until 1292/1875. Their value lies in their detail, with the full texts of all edicts and official pronouncements of the shah and other high officials. But their status as official chronicles severely limits their author's freedom to explain the significance of the facts underlying the events they record.

The three volumes of *Tārīkh-i Muntazam-i Nāsirī* continue the account of the reign of Nasir ed-Din Shah in similar style up to the year 1300/1886

Al-Ma'āsir val-Āsār, published in 1306/1886 on the occasion of the fortieth year of the shah's reign, lists the names of all the royal princes, wives, high officials, and ʿulama of the period of Nasir ed-Din Shah; it also summarizes all important events, such as wars and travels of the shah, decrees, and reforms initiated in those years. Mirza Huseyn Khan's share in introducing reforms and technological innovations like gaslight and steam-powered cannon foundries is reported in this particularly useful reference work.

A similar work is *Kitāb-i Sālnāmeh-yi Dowlat-i ʿAlīyeh-yi Irān, The Year Book of the Exalted Government of Iran.* This almanac, published in 1292/1875, summarizes all the important events of world history beginning in the year 6212 before the Hijra, "the date of the birth of the Prophet Adam." It includes dates of important discoveries and inventions. In recounting the history of Iran, the almanac records the accounts of both the Muslim historians and the Greeks. A full list of all offices and officials of the court and government is included.

Sadr ut-Tavārīkh, a biography of eleven Qajar prime ministers, was prepared by Iʿtimad us-Saltaneh for Mirza ʿAli Khan Amin us-Sultan, the last prime minister to Nasir ed-Din Shah. The section dealing with Mirza Huseyn Khan provides some insights into his character and personality. The book also contains long descriptions of court intrigues, their organizers, members, and motivations, leaving no doubt that most participants were impelled more by personal considerations than by concern for the welfare of the state. This work was published recently in Tehran.

Khalseh ya Khābnāmeh-yi Iʿtimād us-Saltaneh, The Book of Dreams, also deals with several Qajar prime ministers, including Mirza Huseyn Khan. But the author's attacks on these men are so venomous that the book was probably not meant for publication. The narrative takes the form of a dream in which the author as a judge calls each prime minister to account for his acts and life. Only in this work does Iʿtimad us-Saltaneh openly reveal his dislike of Mirza Huseyn Khan. His presentation of the latter's life is an unflattering view through a keyhole, which adds no substantial insight to the overall picture.

Rūznāmeh-yi Khātirāt-i Iʿtimād us-Saltaneh is a diary begun in the year of Mirza Huseyn Khan's death. The frank language used, including disparaging remarks made about Nasir ed-Din Shah and his courtiers, leaves little doubt that this work, also, was not intended for publication. Surprisingly, here the author has many kind words for Mirza Huseyn Khan, whom he prefers above all the men who then surrounded the shah. His description of the circumstances of Mirza Huseyn Khan's death provides another revelation—the shah's great annoyance with him and the possibility that he might have been poisoned by order of the shah. The diary also gives some clues on general attitudes toward reforms prevailing at the court.

2. *Khātirāt-i Sīyāsī* by Amin ud-Dowleh. Mirza ʿAli Khan Amin ud-Dowleh (1260/1322–1844/1904–5) also belonged to a family with a long tradition of service to the Qajar dynasty. Amin ud-Dowleh had a traditional education; at the age of eighteen he was chosen by the shah as his private secretary because of his beautiful

handwriting. A shrewd and intelligent man, he used his favored position to good advantage and later rose to high posts, including membership in the Dar ush-Showra-yi Kubra and ministership. He became prime minister during the reign of Muzaffar ed-Din Shah.

His proximity to the shah and his natural intelligence render Amin ud-Dowleh an astute observer and his work one of the important sources for the study of this period. However, it is marred by apparent jealousy and dislike of Mirza Huseyn Khan, indicated by the omission of many of the reforms the latter initiated. The omission may have been prompted by Amin ud-Dowleh's desire to appear to be the only serious advocate of reform before the constitutional movement. Yet, despite his partiality, he gives a revealing account of his colleagues and their reasons for opposing reform.

3. *Tārīkh-i Sarguzasht-i Mas'ūdī* by Mas'ud Mirza Zill us-Sultan. Zill us-Sultan (1266/1850–1336/1918) was Nasir ed-Din Shah's eldest son. This work, in which the prince recollects important incidents of his life, reveals the attitude of one of the most powerful Qajar princes toward Mirza Huseyn Khan's reforms. Zill us-Sultan's animosity was apparently motivated primarily by the attempt of the prime minister to create a strong central government. The ambitious prince felt that while Mirza Huseyn Khan was in power, he could not extend his own control beyond the province of Isfahan. Zill us-Sultan's intrigues, in cooperation with other courtiers, are described fully in his memoirs.

4. *Sharh-i Hāl-i 'Abbās Mīrzā Mulk-Ārā* by 'Abbas Mirza Mulk-Ara. 'Abbas Mirza, the shah's younger brother, was born in 1255/1840. This account, which is his memoir, provides a useful source for social conditions and political practices of the period. The prince returned to Iran in 1294/1878 after twenty-six years of exile in Baghdad and Istanbul. His long residence in the Ottoman Empire, where government officials were more public spirited than in Iran, made the corruption in his own country extremely distressing to him. The prevailing ethics of Iranian officials and the chaotic and haphazard functioning of the Iranian administration are the focus of forceful comments and vivid descriptions by 'Abbas Mirza.

5. *Khāṭirāt-i Hājjī Sayyāh* by Mīrzā Muhammad 'Ali Mahallatī [Hajji Sayyah]. Mirza Muhammad 'Ali (1252/1835–1344/1925), better known as Hajji Sayyah was born in 1252/1835 and raised in Mahallat. After a disappointment in love, he decided to leave

his birthplace in 1282/1865. He traveled eventually to Europe and the United States. He returned to Iran in 1295/1876 and spent some time touring the country. *Khatirat-i Hajji Sayyah* recorded his observations on the state of the country. His descriptions of small-town life are elaborate and vivid. He gives many examples of the exploitation of the people by the ruling class, especially the governors. His work is a useful source of information on social conditions in Iran in the seventies.

6. *Safarnameh-yi Khūzistan* by Hājjī Mīrzā ʿAbdul Ghaffār Najm ul-Mulk. Najm ul-Mulk was an engineer sent by the shah on an inspection tour of the irrigation conditions in Khuzistan in 1298/1880, the year of Mirza Huseyn Khan's death. Upon his return to the capital, he prepared a lengthy report for the shah, describing not only the conditions of rivers and dams in the province but the social and economic predicament of its residents as well. His report, *Safarnameh-yi Khuzistan,* published in 1341S/1961, points up the great political influence of the Bakhtiyari tribe in the province, which the tribe virtually controlled.

7. *Risāleh-yi Majdiyeh* by Mīrzā Muhammad Khān Majd ul-Mulk. Mirza Muhammad Khan Majd ul-Mulk (1224/1806–1298/1881) belonged to a prominent family of court officials that had produced two prime ministers. He occupied high positions, including ministerships, during the reigns of Muhammad Shah (1835–48) and Nasir ed-Din Shah. The *Risaleh-yi Majdiyeh,* written in 1287/1870, is a critique of conditions prevailing in Iran on the eve of Mirza Huseyn Khan's coming to power; therefore, it is of great interest for the present work. Although it was not published until 1321S/1942, according to the distinguished scholar Saʿīd Nafīcī, many handwritten copies of it circulated among courtly circles, and most men of the time read the book.

8. *Risāleh-yi Usūl-i Tamaddun* by Mīrzā Malkam Khān (1249/1833–34—1326/1908). Malkam Khan's involvement in Iranian politics covers almost half a century. His impact on the course of reform in Iran, though not consistent, has been profound. His essays written in the late 1850s, published in this volume, had a direct bearing on the reforms reviewed in this study and on other reforms undertaken in the nineteenth century. Malkam is the only nineteenth-century statesman about whom several studies have appeared.

9. *Yik Kalimeh* by Mīrzā Yūsuf Khān Mustashār ud-Dowleh. Mirza Yusuf Khan (b. ?–d. 1313/1895–96) came from a family of prominent merchants. He joined the service of the Iranian

Ministry of Foreign Affairs and spent some thirteen years in Russia, Tiflis, and St. Petersburg, and four years (1283/1866–1287/1880) as Iranian charge d'affaires in Paris. In 1880 he was invited back by Mirza Huseyn Khan to serve as assistant minister of justice, a post he held for two years.

Yik Kalimeh was written in Paris in 1287/1870. It is a treatise on the importance of European progress, which the author attributes to the fact that all affairs of government are regulated by law rather than an individual. This work reveals the thought of one of Mirza Huseyn Khan's intimate friends and associates. It is significant as the first treatise in which an attempt is made to reconcile European concepts of government with the *Sharīʿa*.

NEAR CONTEMPORARY WORKS

Four younger contemporaries of Mirza Huseyn Khan have also written relevant works, which illuminate administrative practices, political conditions, the fate of many of Mirza Huseyn Khan's reforms, and the opinions and attitudes of those who lived between 1881 and the Constitutional Revolution in 1905–11.

1. *Sharh-i Hāl-i Man, ya Tarīkh-i Sīyas-ī va ʿIjtimāʿī-yi Qājāriyyeh* was written by ʿAbdullāh Mustowfī (1294/1877–1369/1949), whose family supplied the dynasty with many high officials from the beginning of the nineteenth century. His narrative of the history of the family before he was born reveals much about the Qajar administration. Equally illuminating are his descriptions of his education and early years of work as a mustowfi or accountant in the *Idāreh-yi Istīfā*, the Department of Finance. Though marginal to our topic, this work is generally useful for any study of the period of Muzaffar ed-Din Shah, Nasir ed-Din Shah's successor.

2. *Khātirāt va Khatarāt* by Mihdī Qulī Khān Hidāyat (1280/1864–1375/1955) covers approximately the same period and content as did Mustowfi. The early part of the work describes the last years of Nasir ed-Din Shah. Both Mustowfi and Hidayat are typical of the top layer of Iranian officialdom. Their main preoccupation was to guard their expertise and privileges, and their loyalty could be transferred from one man or dynasty to another without compunction. This explains why both men could hold high posts in the reigns of Muzaffar ed-Din Shah, who signed the constitutional decree, Muhammad ʿAli Shah, who tried to abrogate the constitution, and Reza Shah, who overthrew the Qajar dynasty. Their bureaucratic mentality accounts more than any other factor for

their silence about the activities of advocates of reform and constitution, whose numbers were on the rise in the ten years before the Constitutional Revolution.

3. Mīrzā Yahyā Dowlatābādī (1279/1862–1359/1940), author of *Hayāt-i Yahyā*, is entirely different. Born into one of the most prominent ʿulama families of Isfahan, he was too young to witness the various reforms of Mirza Huseyn Khan, but he spent most of his adult life advocating the same type of change. Mirza Yahya founded the first modern elementary school in Tehran in 1315/ 1897. He was also active in the constitutional movement. The first volume of his memoirs is of particular interest to the present study as it details the increasing dissatisfaction among the ʿulama, lesser officials, and merchants with the conditions of life in Iran, and their search for a solution to the problems of their country.

4. Another work for special consideration is *Tārīkh-i Bīdārī-yi Irānīan, History of the Awakening of the Iranian Nation*, by the prominent historian of the Constitutional Revolution, Muhammad Nazim ul-Islām Kirmānī (1280/1863–1337/1918). He was born in Kirman in 1280/1863 and received a traditional religious education. He came to Tehran two decades after the death of Mirza Huseyn Khan and joined the advocates of reform. A prominent member of the Constitutional Revolution, he wrote perhaps the only account by a participant of the events shortly after they occurred. Although his book describes events preceding the revolution, its main significance for this study is a brief biography of Mirza Huseyn Khan describing him as one of the first exponents of constitutionalism in Iran. Though the assertion remains unsubstantiated, it reveals the appreciation of constitutionalists for Mirza Huseyn Khan and his reforms.

Secondary Sources in Persian

Most works written about the Qajar period by modern Iranian historians suffer from several shortcomings that render them unsuitable as sources. Most present-day Iranians, appalled by their country's weakness in the nineteenth century, simply blame everything on the venality and corruption of the Qajar rulers and their courtiers, and on the evil machinations of the all-powerful British government. Consequently, they fail to understand the complex nature of the chain of events and circumstances that led to the country's decline. The following unsubstantiated statement is typical of the general attitude:

In general, the one hundred fifty years of Qajar reign has
been the cause of many misfortunes for the people of this
country. . . . In this period, the Iranian nation rapidly sank
toward decline and corruption; and, especially in the fifty-
year period of Nasir ed-Din Shah's reign, as a result of the
rivalry between Britain and Czarist Russia to increase their
influence in Iran and the ignorance, love of bribery, moral
degradation rampant among Nasir ed-Din Shah's courtiers,
and the decadence of the country's administration, Iran could
have easily disappeared from the map had it not been protected by some fortunate events in the world.[2]

The same author, describing the evils wrought by the British in
Iran, states: "At any rate, the British have been coveting Iran for
the last three hundred fifty years, and they have resorted to every
inhuman and immoral act in order to destroy Iran's political and
economic freedom." [3]

Another shortcoming of much historical writing in Iran today
is the unfamiliarity of many so-called historians with the methods
of historical research. Therefore, despite the abundance of primary source material, little attempt is made to analyze or collate
these materials. The value of most of the works is further reduced
by the failure to cite sources. This general attitude toward the
Qajar period also applies to the period here under study. Moreover, although a few treatments exist, this period has not been
fully studied.

Despite this disappointing situation, optimism is warranted by
the writings of a few scholars, whose works will be discussed here.

The dean of this new approach to historical writing is Fereydoun
Adamiyat. His *Amīr Kabīr va Irān* is a scholarly, thoroughly doc-
umented, study of the life and career of Amir Kabir, prime minister from 1263/1848 to 1267/1852 and the outstanding statesman
of the thirteenth/nineteenth century. As background for this period, the work is indispensable. His *Fikr-i Āzādī va Muqaddameh-yi
Nihzat-i Mashrūtīyat dar Irān, The Idea of Liberty and the Beginnings
of the Constitutional Movement in Iran,* is equally valuable. It deals
with some aspects of the intellectual history of nineteenth-century
Iran. The section on Mirza Huseyn Khan expounds his political
thought and his views on reform. A third Adamiyat work, *Andīsheh-
hā-yi Mīrzā Fath-ʿAlī Akhundzādeh, The Thought of Mirza Fath-ʿAli
Akhundzadeh,* is a monograph on an Iranian intellectual who lived
in Caucasia and whose thought, eloquently expressed in numerous
works, influenced many Iranians; one of these was Mirza Huseyn

Khan. The relationship between Akhundzadeh and Mirza Huseyn Khan is discussed. A more recent work by Dr. Adamiyat, *Andīsheh-yi Taraqqī vā Hukūmati-i Qānūn ʿAsr-i Sipahsālār*, is a detailed study of this period. It offers stimulating interpretations of the events and the actors, particularly Mirza Huseyn Khan.

Another work devoted to the career of Mirza Huseyn Khan is Mahmud Farhad-Muʿtamid's *Sipahsālār-i Aʿzam*. However, the study covers only the first three years of Mirza Huseyn Khan's career, and it lacks coherent organization and systematic exposition of the career and the reforms. The value of this work and *Tārīkh-i Ravābit-i Sīyāsī-yi Irān va Usmānī*, another of his works, which is a study of Irano-Ottoman relations in the period under study, lies in the numerous primary documents therein presented.

Mention should also be made of Mihdi Bamdad's five-volume biographical dictionary, *Tārīkh-i Rijāl-i Irān dar Qurūn-i 12, 13, va 14 Hijri, The History of Men of Affairs in Iran during the 12/18, 13/19, and 14/20 Centuries*. Despite its shortcomings—it is neither systematically written nor well-documented—it offers information, especially in the first four volumes, on most of the important men who served during the Qajar period, including their ascendants and descendants.

Two other works, the *ʿAsr-i Bīkhabarī yā Tārīkh-i Imtīyāzāt dar Irān, The Age of Ignorance or the History of Concessions in Iran*, by Ibrahim Teymuri, and *Sīyāsatgarān-i Dowreh-yi Qājār, The Politicians of the Qajar Period*, in two volumes, by Khan Malik Sasani, were also useful, primarily for the numerous documents they discuss.

The works of Ibrahim Safa'i, as mentioned earlier, point to a most useful trend in historical studies in Iran. They are simple collections of documents, mostly related to the Qajar period. Since most of these are still in private hands, Safa'i is greatly facilitating the work of historians and ensuring the safety of the text in the face of possible negligence on the part of those who own the original documents.

Western Sources

The decade of the 1870s suffers from a dearth of source material in Western languages, and reasons are not far to seek. Although Iran shared borders with the Russian Empire to the north and the British Empire to the East, for most Europeans, as George Curzon said, the name of the country breathed "only a sense of utter remoteness or a memory of strange vicissitudes and of a moribund romance."

The two European powers pursued a passive policy toward Iran for most of this decade. Russia, having extended control in the ten years previous over large areas of land in the Trans-Caspian region, was content to solidify her hold there. Britain, on the other hand, was concerned only with the role Iran could play if Russia attacked India. Therefore, Britain, with repeated assurances from Russia that Russia was no longer interested in annexing new territories, felt secure about the Iranian borders and India. British policy toward Iran throughout most of the seventies was characterized, therefore, by what Sir H. Rawlinson termed "the reign of inactivity." The two sides, in short, were content to leave Iran alone, as long as the other did not gain any new advantage from the country; neither was much concerned with internal developments in Iran. Their lack of interest carried over to those who wrote about Iran in that decade and to later historians who wrote about the period in Iranian history.

The sources in Western languages, then, consist mainly of travel accounts and diplomatic dispatches, with some more recent additions. Each category presents problems of interpretation that will be discussed separately.

CONTEMPORARY ACCOUNTS

Most of the available material is in English. It consists mainly of travel accounts and dispatches of British diplomats in Tehran and other parts of Iran to the Foreign Office in London.

1. Travel accounts. Most travel accounts are marred by two shortcomings: (1) the patronizing attitude of their authors, many of them civil servants or officers serving in India, toward non-Europeans; and (2) the briefness of their travels in Iran. Both of these shortcomings limit the value of these sources to the historian, the first because of their biased observations about a culture very different from their own, the second because of their limited view of the internal developments within Iran. Typical is R. B. M. Binning's two-volume *Journal of Two Years in Persia,* which discusses those aspects of life in Iran that prove his point about the inferiority of "Asiatic natives" and describes chiefly what seems to its author quaint or grotesque.

Although most of the travel accounts are not adequate for the study of political institutions or cultural conditions, they do provide an ample description of Iranian cities, towns, and daily life. Of particular interest are the books of three authors who visited Iran respectively at the beginning, middle, and end of the decade under study. William Brittlebank came to Iran in 1872 at the height of the famine. In *Persia during the Famine* he supplies many vivid and horrifying scenes of the current suffering. Arthur Arnold, who went to Iran in 1875 and traveled widely throughout the country, describes at length in *Through Persia by Caravan* many of the places he visited. His account of Tehran and of the opinion of Mirza Huseyn Khan held by the foreign residents there is particularly relevant. Edward Stack, who visited Iran in 1881, reveals in *Six Months' Travel in Persia* a country noticeably changed from the one visited by Arnold. The change is particularly in the awareness of some members of the ruling class of the need for better government and better means of communication.

An exception to the rule concerning the limited value of the travel account is that left by Mme Carla Serena, who visited Iran in the autumn of 1878 and lived there for nine months, mainly in Tehran. Because of her friendship with members of the ruling class, she was able to observe at close hand many high officials and their wives, and to learn a great deal about the customs and manners of the time. Among those she met was Mirza Huseyn Khan, and her account of the meeting supplies helpful information about his character. Her account, *Hommes et choses en Perse*, also gives important information about the lives of Iranian women and the diplomatic corps in Iran.

Two other works that date from before and after the decade of this study but deserve mention are Dr. J. E. Polak, *Persien*, and George Curzon, *Persia and the Persian Question*. Dr. Polak arrived in Iran shortly after the death of Amir Kabir to serve as physician to Nasir ed-Din Shah. His work contains one of the most complete accounts of the shah's life and character, with some astute observations thereon. He also offers meticulous information about a variety of aspects of Iranian life and culture during the 1850s. Curzon's book, published in 1892, provides a great deal of relevant factual information about Iran. Curzon, who later became viceroy of India and foreign secretary, was a journalist at the time of his visit. He believed that Great Britain needed to pursue a more active policy toward Iran. He went to Iran in 1889 to gather information to support his position, and he spent six months traveling around the country. His two-volume work offers innumer-

able statistics about the political, administrative, military, and commercial condition of Iran, much of it information that is not
available elsewhere. In addition to his own observations, Curzon
has made use of sources collected by General A. Houtum-Schindler, an Austrian who served the Iranian government in various
high positions for many years. Curzon's work is of particular value
in assessing the degree of success of many of Mirza Huseyn Khan's
reforms.

Another category of sources consists of works written by people
who had lived in Iran for a considerable time. These authors
naturally have a better understanding of the Iranian people, their
culture, and their institutions.

The most useful of these is *Persia and the Persians* by S. G. W.
Benjamin. Benjamin, the first head of the American legation, arrived in Tehran in 1882, the year after Mirza Huseyn Khan's
dismissal from office and death. Benjamin was mainly concerned
with introducing his fellow Americans to a country and people
he had come to know intimately in three years of residence there.
He relates not only his travels in Iran but also his experiences with
the people; he emphasizes what he admires about them. The
differences are explained by him without condemnation. Equally
significant are his brief but informative accounts of Iran's political
and administrative condition immediately after Mirza Huseyn
Khan's death.

Dr. C. J. Wills's description of his experiences in Iran between
1866 and 1881 in his book, *In the Land of the Lion and Sun, or
Modern Persia*, has two shortcomings: a sense of superiority over
the Iranians, and a clear lack of interest in the country's political
conditions. But the book is an invaluable source of information
on the social history of Iranian towns, particularly Isfahan, where
he spent most of his time. Wills, who was a novelist, shows particular skill in portraying character, especially that of Zill us-Sultan,
the governor of Isfahan.

2. Diplomatic dispatches. The dispatches of the British Foreign
Office used here consist of reports and letters of members of the
British legation in Tehran and the consular staff in other parts
of the country. These documents, F.O. 60/324–442, cover the ten-
year period from 1870 to 1880. They have been used only as
supplementary material, to check details of events mentioned in
Persian sources or to supply additional information on situations
that are not adequately presented in Persian sources. They were
valuable in checking such controversial events as Mirza Huseyn

Khan's removal from the post of sadr-i aᶜzam in 1873 and the government's abrupt decision to abandon the Tanzimat-i Hasaneh code in 1875.

SECONDARY WORKS

The decade of the 1870s and the career of Mirza Huseyn Khan have been largely ignored by present-day Western historians. If Mirza Huseyn Khan and his period are mentioned at all, it is merely in conjunction with and as a footnote to the Reuter Concession. This oversight is due primarily to the fact that most historians writing about Iran have relied heavily on sources in Western languages, particularly English, either because of the difficulty getting hold of Persian sources or because of a lack of knowledge of Persian.

One example of this inadequate treatment accorded the period is Peter Avery's *Modern Iran,* which devotes less than three of its 527 pages to cover the entire period. However, Avery is one of the few authors who attempts more than a mere chronology of political events. He is aware of the importance of physical and climactic conditions in the country and the influence these have exerted on its social and political organizations through the various stages of its history. He also pays considerable attention to economic, social, and psychological factors in determining political and historical development.

Adequate scholarship and use of Persian sources, while the exception, does exist. One example is Hamid Algar's *Religion and State in Iran 1785–1906,* in which some of the reforms of Mirza Huseyn Khan are briefly mentioned in dealing with the latter's relationship with the ᶜulama. But, although Algar's work does make use of many Persian sources, it does not add much to what is known about Mirza Huseyn Khan. Its focus is on the opposition of the ᶜulama that resulted in the abrogation of the Reuter Concession and the dismissal of Mirza Huseyn Khan from the post of sadr-i aᶜzam. But Algar makes no mention of other important conflicts between the ᶜulama and Mirza Huseyn Khan over reform. The abandonment of the Tanzimat-i Hasaneh code, for example, was to an even greater extent due to this opposition. Neither does Algar fully explore the reasons underlying the ᶜulama's opposition.

Another commendable work is Firuz Kazemzadeh's *Russia and Britain in Persia, 1864–1914* about the Russo-British rivalry in Iran, an exhaustive study that meets the highest scholarly standards. Yet, even this work leaves unanswered many of the important issues it raises. Most important of these is why Iranian statesmen accepted, or worse, cooperated with these two superpowers. Kazemzadeh's answer that most of these men were corrupt and venal to the core is not enough. Had he taken into consideration the condition of the country at the time, the concern that Iran might be next to fall victim to Russian imperialist expansion, and Iran's economic and political decline, he would not have so readily condemned the attitude adopted by Iranian statesmen in their dealings with the two powers.

Two general works that were extremely helpful were Ann Lambton's *Landlords and Peasants in Persia* and Charles Issawi's *The Economic History of Iran, 1800-1914.* Although neither deals specifically with the period 1870–80, the authors supply a wealth of material for any student of Qajar Iran. This is particularly true of the Issawi work, which presents many reports, articles, and documents, hitherto unpublished, on the economic condition of Iran under Qajar rule.

Another work, not of the same magnitude but still useful, is Marvin L. Entner's monograph on *Russo-Persian Commercial Relations, 1828–1914.* Although Entner does not use Persian sources, his work supplies much detailed information drawn from Russian archives about an important aspect of that country's relations with Iran.

A study by Shaul Bakhas, *Iran: Monarchy, Bureaucracy, and Reform under the Qajars, 1858–1896,* which limits its scope to the course of administrative reform, was published while this study was in preparation for publication.

BIBLIOGRAPHY

Primary Sources

Archives

Majlis Library. Tehran, Iran.
Ministry of Foreign Affairs. Tehran, Iran
Senate Library. Tehran, Iran.
Public Record Office. F.O. 60/324–F.O. 60/442. London, England.

Collections

Farhād Collection. Tehran, Iran. Letters exchanged by Mīrzā Huseyn Khān, Nāsir ed-Dīn Shah, Farhad Mīrzā Muʿtamid ud-Dowleh, Mīrzā Mūsā Vazir Lashkar, and others.
Fereydoun Adamiyat Collection. Tehran, Iran. Letters by Mīrzā Huseyn Khān, Malkam Khān, Mīrzā Yūsuf Khān Mustashār ud-Dowleh, and others.
Ghanī Collection. Sterling Library, Yale University, New Haven, Connecticut. Manuscript Group 235. Letters by Mīrzā Huseyn Khān, Nāsir ed-Dīn Shah, Hasan ʿAlī Khān Garrūsī, and others.
Hisām ud-Dīn Khurumī Collection. Tehran, Iran. One of the most complete collections of nineteenth-century newspapers.

Manuscripts

Ansārī-yi Kāshanī, Taqī Khān. "Jānivarnāmeh." 1287/1870. Majlis Library. Tehran, Iran.
"Kitābcheh-yi Tanzīmāt Hasaneh-yi Dowlat-i ʿAlīyēh va Mahrūsēh-yi Irān." 1292/1875. Senate Library. Tehran, Iran.
Muhammad Hasan Khan Iʿtimad us-Saltaneh. "Sadr ut-Tavārīkh," Adamiyat Collection. Tehran, Iran.
Qaraguzlū, Muhsin Khān. "ʿĀdāt ul-Mulūk," Adamiyat Collection. Tehran, Iran.

Newspapers

Irān. Millī Library. Tehran, Iran.
Mirrīkh. Khurumī Collection. Tehran, Iran.
Rūznāmeh-yi Dowlat-i ʿAlīyeh-yi Irān. Millī Library. Tehran, Iran.
Rūznāmeh-yi ʿIlmīyeh va Adabīyeh. Khurumī Collection. Tehran, Iran.
Rūznāmeh-yi Nīzāmī. Khurumī Collection. Tehran, Iran.
Vaqāyiʿ-i ʿAdlīyeh. Khurumī Collection. Tehran, Iran.
Vaqayiʿ-i Ittifāqīyyeh. Adamiyat Collection. Tehran, Iran.

Publications

Amīn ud-Dowleh, ʿAlī. *Khātirāt-i Sīyāsī-yi Amīn ud-Dowleh.* Edited by H. Farmānfarmāʾīyān. Tehran: Kitābha-yi Irān, 1341/1962.
Arnold, Arthur. *Through Persia by Caravan.* New York: Harper & Brothers, 1877.
ʿAzd ud-Dowleh, Ahmad. *Tārīkh-i ʿAzudī.* Edited by H. Kūhī-Kirmānī. Tehran, n.d.
Bassett, James. *Persia, the Land of the Imams: A Narrative of Travels and Residence, 1871–1886.* New York: Charles Scribner's Sons, 1886.
Benjamin, S. G. W. *Persia and the Persians.* Boston: Ticknor & Co., 1887.
Curzon, George N. *Persia and the Persian Question.* 2 vols. London: Longmans, Green & Co., 1892.
Frazer, James B. *Narrative of a Journey into Khorasan in the Years 1821 and 1822.* London, 1825.
Gobineau, M. le Comte de. *Les religions et philosophies dans l'Asie centrale.* Paris: Ernest Leroux, 1900.
Hidāyat, Mīhdīqulī. *Khātirāt va Khatarāt.* Tehran: Zavvar, 1344/1965.
Iʿtizād us-Saltaneh, ʿAlīqulī Mīrzā. *Fitneh-yi Bāb.* Edited by ʿAbdul Huseyn Navāʾī. Tehran, 1333/1954.
Lisān ul-Mulk Sipihr. *Nāsikh ut-Tavārikh-i Salātin-i Qājārīyeh.* Edited by Muhammad Bāqir Bihbūdī. 4 vols. Tehran: Islamiyeh, 1344/1965.
Malkam Khān. *Risāleh-yi Usūl-i Tamaddum.* Edited by Muhīt-i Tabātabāʾī. Tehran, 1325/1946.
Majd ul-Mulk, Muhammad Khān. *Risāleh-yi Majdīyeh.* Tehran, 1321/1940.
Muhammad Hasan Khān Iʿtimād us-Saltaneh. *Al-Maʾāsir-u val Āsār.* Tehran, 1307/1888.
—————. *Khalseh yā Khābnāmeh-yi Iʿtimād us-Saltaneh.* Tehran, 1348/1969.
————— Saniʿ ud-Dowleh. *Mirʾāt ul-Buldān.* 4 vols. Tehran, 1295/1878.

————. *Rūznāmeh-yi Khāṭirāt-i Iʿtimād us-Salṭaneh.* Edited by Iraj Afshar. Tehran, 1345/1966.

———— *Sadr ut-Tavārīkh.* Tehran, 1349/1970.

————. *Tārīkh-i Muntazam-i Nāṣirī.* 3 vols. Tehran, 1300/1882.

Mūlk Ārā, ʿAbbās Mīrzā. *Sharh-i Ḥāl-i ʿAbbās Mīrzā Mūlk Ārā.* Tehran, 1325/1946.

Mushīr ud-Dowleh, Jaʿfar Khān. *Risāleh-yi Tahqīqāt-i Sarhaddīyeh.* Edited by Muhammad Mushīrī. Tehran: Bunyād-i Farhang-i Irān, 1348/1969.

Mustashār ud-Dowleh, Yūsuf Khān. *Yik Kalimeh.* Tehran, 1287/1870.

Mustowfī, Abdullāh. *Sharh-i Zindigānī-yi Man yā Tārīkh-i Ijtimāʿī va Idārī-yi Dowreh-yi Qājārīyeh.* 2 vols. Tehran, 1321sh/1942–43.

Najm ul-Mulk, Hājjī Abdil Ghaffār. *Safarnāmeh-yi Khūzistān.* Tehran, 1341/1963.

Piggot, John. *Persia Ancient and Modern.* London: Henry S. King & Co., 1874.

Polak, Dr. J. E. *Persien, das Land und Seine Bewohner.* 2 vols. Leipzig: J. U. Brodhaus, 1865.

Sayyāh, Hājjī. *Khāṭirāt-i Hājjī Sayyāh.* Edited by Hamīd Sayyāh. Tehran, 1346/1967.

Serena, Carla. *Hommes et choses en Perse.* Paris, 1883.

Sheil, Mary Lawrence. *Glimpses of Life and Manners in Persia.* London: John Murray, 1856.

Stack, Edward. *Six Months in Persia.* 2 vols. London: Sampson, Low, Marston, Searle, & Rivington, 1882.

Watson, R. G. *A History of Persia.* London: Smith, Elder & Co., 1866.

Wills, C. J. *Persia as It Is.* London: Sampson, Low, Marston, Searle & Rivington, 1886.

Zill us-Sulṭān, Masʿūd Mīrzā. *Tārīkh-i Sarguzasht-i Masʿūdī.* Tehran, 1325/1907.

Secondary Sources

Adamiyat, Fereydoun. *Amīr Kabīr va Īrān.* 3d ed. Tehran: Khārazmī, 1348/1969.

———— *Andīsheh-hā-yi Mīrzā Fath-ʿAlī Akhundzādeh.* Tehran: Khārazmī, 1349/1971.

————. *Fikr-i Āzādī va Muqaddameh-yi Nihzat-i Mashrūtīyat dar Īrān.* Tehran: Sukhan, 1340/1951.

Akhundzādeh, Fath-ʿAli. *Alifbā-yi Jadīd va Maktūbāt.* Edited by H. Muhammadzādeh and H. Araslī. Baku, 1963.

————. *Tamsīlāt.* Translated by J. Qarajidāghī. Tehran: Andīsheh Publishing Co., 1349S/1970.

Algar, Hamid. *Mīrzā Malkum Khān*. Berkeley: University of California Press, 1973.
——————. *Religion and State in Iran 1785–1906*. Berkeley: University of California Press, 1969.
Bahrier, Julian. *Economic Development in Iran, 1900–1970*. London: Oxford University Press, 1971.
Bāmdād, Mihdi. *Tārīkh-i Rijāl-i Irān dar Qurūn-i 12, 13, va 14 Hijrī*. 5 vols. Tehran, 1347–50/1968–73. Vol. 2.
Bowen-Jones, H. "Agriculture." In *Cambridge History of Iran*. 5 vols. Cambridge: Cambridge University Press, 1968. Vol. 1.
Bulliet, R. W. *The Patricians of Nishapur*. Cambridge, Mass.: Harvard University Press, 1972.
Dāmghānī, Muhammad Taqī. "Sad Sāl-i Pīsh az Īn." *Huqūq-i Mardum* (Fall 1345S/Fall 1966).
Davison, Roderic H. *Reform in the Ottoman Empire, 1856–1876*. Princeton University Press, 1963.
English, Paul. *City and Village in Iran*. Madison: University of Wisconsin Press, 1966.
Farhād-Muʿtamid, Mahmūd. *Sipahsālār-i Aʿzam*. Tehran: ʿIlmī, 1325/1946.
——————. *Tārīkh-i Ravābit-i Sīyāsī-yi Irān va Usmānī*. Tehran, 1327/1948.
Farmanfarmayan, Hafiz. "The Forces of Modernization in Nineteenth Century Iran." In W. R. Polk and R. Chambers, *Beginnings of Modernization in the Middle East*. Chicago: University of Chicago Press, 1968.
Ghūrīyānus, I. *Qīyām-i Shaykh Ubidullāh Shimzīnī dar ʿAhd-i Nāsir ed-Dīn Shāh*. Tehran: Danish, 1336/1957.
Hambly, Gavin. "An Introduction to the Economic Organization of Early Qajar Iran." *Iran* 2 (1964).
Heffening, W. "Wakf." In *Encyclopedia of Islam*. 1st ed. 1913–38. Vol. 4.
Houtum-Schindler, A. "Persia." In *Encyclopaedia Britannica*. 10th ed. Vol. 31.
Iqbāl, ʿAbbās. "Tārīkh-i Rūznāmehnigāri dar Irān." *Yādigār* (Isfand 1323S/February-March 1945):6–17.
Issawi, Charles. *The Economic History of Iran 1800–1914*. Chicago: University of Chicago Press, 1971.
Kazemzadeh, Firuz. "The Origins and Early Development of the Cossack Brigade." *American Slavic and East European Review* 15 (October 1956):351–63.
——————. *Russia and Britain in Persia, 1864–1915*. New Haven: Yale University Press, 1968.
Lambton, Ann K. S. *Landlord and Peasant in Persia*. London: Oxford University Press, 1953.

——————. "Persian Society under the Qajars." *Journal of the Royal Central Asian Society* (April 1961).

——————. "Persian Trade under the Early Qajars." In D. S. Richards, ed., *Islam and the Trade of Asia*. Oxford: Oxford University Press, 1970.

Lewis, Bernard. *The Emergence of Modern Turkey*. 2d ed. London: Oxford University Press, 1968.

Minorsky, V. "Tiyul." In *Encyclopedia of Islam*. 1st ed. Vol. 4.

Muhtasham, M. "Ta'sīs-i Bānk." *Majalleh-yi Bānk-i Sipah* (Autumn 1341S/1962).

Norman, Baron de. "Avvalīn Risāleh-yi Rāh Āhan dar Irān." *Majalleh-yi Bānk-i Sipah* 10–13 (Summer 1342S/1963).

Pigoulevskaya, H. V., et al. *Tārīkh-i Irān az Dowreh-yi: Bāstān tā Sadeh-yi Hijdahum*. Translated by Karīm Kishāvarz. 2 vols. Tehran: Tehran University, 1346/1967. Vol. 1.

Polk, W. R., and Chambers, R. *Beginnings of Modernization in the Middle East*. Chicago: University of Chicago Press, 1968.

Richards, D. S., ed. *Islam and the Trade of Asia*. Oxford: Oxford University Press, 1970.

Sāsānī, Khān Malik. *Sīyāsatgarān-i Dowreh-yi Qājār*. 2 vols. Tehran: Tahūrī, 1337–45S/1958–66.

——————. *Yādbūhā-yi Safar-i Islāmbul*. Tehran, n.d.

Spuler, Bertold. "Central Asia: The Last Centuries of Independence." In F. R. C. Bagley, trans. and ed., *The Muslim World: A Historical Survey*. Leiden, 1969.

Teymūrī, Ibrāhīm. *ʿAsr-i Bīkhabarī yā Tārīkh-i Imtīyāzāt dar Īrān*. Tehran, 1325/1954.

Wulf, H. E. "The Qanats of Iran." *Scientific American* 218 (1968):94–105.

Sources Consulted But Not Cited

Adamiyat, Fereydoun. *Andīshey-yi Taraqqī va Hukūmat-i Qānūn ʿAsr-i Sipahsālār*. Tehran: Kharazmi, 1351/1972.

Avery, Peter. *Modern Iran*. New York: Frederick A. Praeger, 1965.

Bakhash, S. "The Evolution of Qajar Bureaucracy 1779–1879." *Middle Eastern Studies* 7 (May 1971).

Bakhash, Shaul. *Iran: Monarchy, Bureaucracy, and Reform under the Qajars, 1858–1896*. London: Ithaca Press, 1979.

Banani, Amin. *Modernization in Iran*. Stanford: Stanford University Press, 1961.

Bidulph, C. E. *Four Months in Persia: With a Visit to Trans Caspia*. London: Kegan Paul, Trench, Trubner, & Co., 1892.

Binder, L. "The Cabinet System of Iran: A Case Study in Institutional Adaptation." *Middle East Journal* 16 (1962).

Binning, R. *A Journal of Two Years Travel in Persia and Ceylon.* 2 vols. London: W. H. Allen Co., 1857.

Brittlebank, W. *Persia during the Famine.* London: Basil Montagu, Pickering, 1873.

Browne, Edward G. *A Year amongst the Persians.* 3rd ed. London: Adam & Charles Black, 1950.

——————. *The Press and Poetry of Modern Iran.* Cambridge: Cambridge University Press, 1914.

Browne, Edward G. "The Persian Constitutional Movement." *Proceedings of the Persian Academy, 1917–1918.*

Entner, Marvin L. *Russo-Persian Commercial Relations, 1828–1914.* Gainesville, Fla.: University of Florida Press, 1965.

Fasā'ī, Hasan. *Tārīkh-i Fārsnāmeh-yi Nāsirī.* 2 vols. Tehran: Sanā'ī, n.d. Vol. 1 published in English as *History of Persia under the Qajars.* Translated by H. Busse. New York and London: The University Press, 1972.

Feuvrier, Dr. M. *Tròis ans à la cour de Perse.* Paris: F. Juven, n.d.

"Gūsheh-'ī za Tārīkh-i Bānkdarī dar Irān." *Majalleh-yi Bānk-i Sipah.* Khurdad 1341-Azar 1341/May-November, 1962.

Hurewitz, J. C. *Diplomacy in the Near and Middle East.* 2 vols. Princeton, N. J.: D. Van Nostrand & Co., 1956. Vol. 1.

Iqbāl, ʿAbbās. "Avvalīn Rūznāmeh-yi Chāpī dar Irān." *Yādigār.* Aban 1323/October 1944.

——————. "Kitāb-i Hājī Bābā va Dāstān-i Nakhustīn Muhass ilīn-i Irānī dar Farang." *Yādigār.* Dey 1323/December 1944.

——————. "Mulāqat-i du Irānī bā Hirshāl." *Yādigār.* Mihr 1323/ September 1944.

Isfahani, K., and Rowshan, Q. *Majmūʿ eh-yi Asnād va Madārik-i Farrukh Khān Amīn ud-Dowleh.* 3 vols. Tehran: Tehran University Press, 1346–50/1967–71.

Issawi, Charles. *The Economic History of the Middle East, 1800–1914.* Chicago: University of Chicago Press, 1966.

Iʿtizad us-Saltaneh, ʿAlīqūlī Mīrzā. *Fulk us-Saʿādeh.* Tehran, 1278/ 1861.

Jahāngīr, Mīrzā. *Tārīkh Now.* Edited by ʿAbbās Iqbāl. Tehran: ʿIlmī, 1327/1948.

Jamālzādeh, Seyyid Muhammad ʿAlī. *Ganj-i Shāyigān.* Berlin: Kaveh, 1335/1917–18.

Kātīrā'ī, Mahmūd. *Frāmāsunrī dar Irān.* Tehran: Iqbāl, 1347/1968.

Keddie, Nikki K. "The Iranian Power Structure and Social Change 1800–1969: An Overview." *International Journal of Middle Eastern Studies* 2 (1971).

Kitāb-i Sālnāmeh-yi Dowlat-i ʿAlīyeh-yi Irān. Tehran: 1292/1875.

Kramer, J. H. "Tanzimat." In *Encyclopedia of Islam.* 1st ed. Vol. 4.

Khurmujī, Muhammad Jaʿfar, *Haqāyiq ul-Akhbār-i Nāsirī*. Tehran: Zvvār Publishing Co., 1344/1965.

Malcolm, John. *Sketches of Persia*. London: John Murray, 1845.

Martin, Bradford G. *German-Russian Diplomatic Relations, 1873–1912*. The Hague: Mouton & Co., 1959.

Muʿayyir ul-Mamālik. *Yādāshthāʾī az Zindigānī-yi Nāsir ed-Dīn Shāh*. Tehran: ʿIlmī, n.d.

Nāsir ed-Dīn Shah. *Safarnāmeh-yi Farang*. Tehran, 1291/1874.

Nāzim ul-Islam Kirmanī, Muhammad. *Tārīkh-i Bīdarīy-i Irānnīyān*. 2nd ed. ¯ehran: Ibn Sīnā, n.d.

Rosen, Fri⌣ ⌐rich. *Oriental Memories of a German Diplomatist*. New York: E. P. Dutton & Co., 1930.

Rushdiyyeh, H. "Sipahsālār va Masjid-i Sipasālār." *Armaghān*, 1331/ 1952.

Safāʾī, Ibrāhīm. *Asnād-i Barguzīdeh*, Tehran, 1350S/1972.

————. *Asnād-i Nowyāfteh*. Tehran, 1349/1870.

————. *Asnād-i Sīyāsī-yi Dowreh-yi Qājār*. Tehran: n.d.

————. *Barghā-yi Tārīkh-i Irān*. Tehran, 1350S/1971.

Sāsānī, Khan Malik. *Dast-i Pinhān-i Sīyāsat-i Inglīs dar Irān*. Tehran: Ispand, n.d.

Serena, Carla. *Une européenne en Perse*. Paris: Maurice Dreyfuss, 1890.

Shamīm, ʿAlī Asghar. *Irān dar Dowreh-yi Saltanat-i Qājār*. Tehran: Ibn Sīnā, 1342/1964.

Shīrāzī, Mīrzā Sālih. *Safarnāmeh*. Edited by Ismaʿīl Rāʾīn. Tehran: Rowzan, 1347/1968.

Siassi, Ali Akbar. *La Perse au contact de l'Occident*. Paris: Ernest Leroux, 1931.

Sihāb, Abulqasīm. *Tārīkh-i Madriseh-yi ʿAlī-yi Sipahsālār*. Tehran: 1329/1950.

Story, Graham. *Reuter's Century*. London: Max Parrish, 1951.

Sykes, P. *A History of Persia*. 2 vols. London: Macmillan & Co., 1915.

Upton, Joseph. *The History of Modern Iran*. Cambridge, Mass.: Harvard University Press, 1965.

Wills, C. J. *The Land of the Lion and the Sun*. London, 1891.

NOTES

PREFACE

1. Ann Lambton, "Persian Society under the Qajars," *Journal of the Royal Central Asian Society,* April 1961, p. 123.

2. Brief attention has been paid to the period by Hamid Algar, particularly in *Religion and State in Iran, 1785–1906* (Berkeley: University of California Press, 1966); and by Firuz Kazemzadeh in *Russia and Britain in Persia, 1864–1915* (New Haven: Yale University Press, 1968), in relation to the events surrounding the Reuter Concession in 1873.

CHAPTER 1

1. Charles Issawi, *The Economic History of Iran 1800–1914* (Chicago: University of Chicago Press, 1971), pp. 1–3.

2. H. Bowen-Jones, "Agriculture," in *Cambridge History of Iran,* 5 vols. (Cambridge: Cambridge University Press, 1968), 1:566. The figures are for the 1950s.

3. For a thorough study of qanat irrigation, see H. E. Wulf, "The Qanats of Iran," *Scientific American* 218 (1968):94–105.

4. A. Houtum-Schindler, in *Encyclopaedia Britannica,* 10th ed., s.v. "Persia," 31:616.

5. Paul English, *City and Village in Iran* (Madison: University of Wisconsin Press, 1966), p. 3.

6. The emergence of this kind of symbiosis has been illustrated by English in his study of the city of Kirman, ibid.

7. H. V. Pigoulevskaya, et al., *Tārīkh-i Irān az Dowreh-yi: Bāstān tā Sadeh-yi Hijdahum,* trans. Karīm Kishāvarz, 2 vols. (Tehran: Tehran University, 1346/1967), 1:279. For a modern, scholarly discussion of the social history of Nishapur, see R. W. Bulliet, *The Patricians of Nishapur* (Cambridge, Mass.: Harvard University Press, 1972). The intro. and ch. 1 contain valuable information about the city in medieval times.

8. See ch. 7 for further discussion.

9. Issawi, *Economic History,* p. 70.

10. Gavin Hambly, "An Introduction to the Economic Organization of Early Qajar Iran," *Iran* 11 (1964):72.

11. John Piggot, *Persia Ancient and Modern* (London: Henry S. King & Co., 1874), p. 221.

12. Issawi, *Economic History*, p. 112.

13. Ibid.

14. James B. Fraser, *Narrative of a Journey into Khorasan in the Years 1821 and 1822* (London, 1825), p. 222.

15. A. K. S. Lambton, "Persian Trade under the Early Qajars," in D. S. Richards, ed., *Islam and the Trade of Asia* (Oxford: Oxford University Press, 1970), p. 237.

16. Issawi, *Economic History*, p. 114.

17. Ibid., p. 365.

18. Ibid., pp. 50–51.

19. Ḥājjī Abdil Ghaffār Najm ul-Mulk, *Safarnāmeh-yi Khūzistān* (Tehran, 1341/ 1963), p. 26.

20. Issawi, *Economic History*, p. 28; *Encyclopaedia Britannica*, 10th ed., s.v. "Persia," 31:617.

21. Issawi, *Economic History*, p. 28.

22. Piggot, *Persia*, p. 304.

23. Najm ul-Mulk, *Safarnāmeh*, p. 61.

24. W. Heffening, in *Encyclopedia of Islam*, 1st ed. (1913–38), vol. 4, s.v. "Wakf."

25. Julian Bahrier, *Economic Development in Iran, 1900–1970* (London: Oxford University Press, 1971), p. 12.

26. *Encyclopaedia Britannica*, 10th ed., s.v. "Persia," 31:618–19.

27. Piggot, *Persia*, p. 303.

28. Issawi, *Economic History*, pp. 103–4.

29. Ibid., p. 43.

30. Ibid., p. 36.

31. The descendants of Āqā Muhsin Āshtīyanī are an example. He was a *mustowfī* or revenue officer with considerable land in Ashtian during the second half of the eighteenth century. Among his descendants were one *sadr-i aʿzam*, several ministers and high officials of the finance bureau. See Mahmūd Farhād-Muʿtamid, *Sipahsālār-i Aʿzam* (Tehran: ʿIlmī, 1325/1946), appendix.

32. This title of *chief minister* was later changed to *prime minister.*

33. Hamid Algar, *Religion and State in Iran 1785–1906* (Berkeley: University of California Press, 1969), gives a comprehensive account of the ʿulama and their relationship to the Qajars.

34. For a thorough discussion of Amir Kabir's policy toward the ʿulama, see Fereydoun Adamiyat, *Amīr Kabīr va Irān*, 3d ed. (Tehran: Kharazmi, 1348/1969), pp. 417–28.

35. In Islamic society, *ʿurf* laws were derived from the traditions and practices of a community; they differed from one locality or region to another. Sharʿ laws derived from the religious teachings of the five major schools of law (the Shīʿī, Hafanfī, Shafiʿī, Hanbalī, and Mālikī). The sharʿ laws were more uniform and followed the lines set down by each school.

36. The *imam-i jumeʿh*, the leader of the Friday prayer, was selected by the government from among the leading religious leaders in a town. Often members of the same family succeeded each other in this position.

37. Masʿūd Mīrzā Zill us-Sultān, *Tārīkh-i Sarguzasht-i Masʿūdī* (Tehran, 1325/ 1907), p. 250.

38. Algar, *Religion and State*, pp. 60–61.

39. Ann Lambton, "Persian Society under the Qajars," *Journal of the Royal Central Asian Society* (April 1961), p. 165.

40. R. G. Watson, *A History of Persia* (London: Smith, Elder & Co., 1866), p. 24.

41. Ibid., p. 6

42. Najm ul-Mulk, *Safarnāmeh*, p. 55.

43. Ibid., p. 47.

44. In his private correspondence with the shah, Mīrzā Huseyn Khān refers to "the Shah's ears" at cabinet meetings. See also ʿAlī Amīn ud-Dowleh, *Khāṭirāt-i Sīyāsī-yi Amīn ud-Dowleh,* ed. H. Farmānfarmāʾīyān (Tehran: Kitābha-yi Irān, 1341/1962), p. 81.

45. Lisan ul-Mulk Sipihr, *Nāsikh ut-Tavārīkh-i Salāṭīn-i Qājārīyeh,* ed. Muhammad Baqīr Bihbūdī, 4 vols. (Tehran: Islāmīyeh, 1344/1965), 1:5.

46. During the first half of his reign Nāsir ed-Dīn Shah feared his brother, ʿAbbās Mīrzā. When he felt secure enough to invite ʿAbbās Mīrzā back to Tehran, the shah began to fear his older son, Zill us-Sultān, governor of Isfahan.

47. Watson, *Persia,* p. 14. Although the shah did not lose his throne in traveling to Europe, his sadr-i aʿzam, Mīrzā Huseyn Khān, lost his post.

48. Dr. J. E. Polak, *Persien, das Land und Seine Bewohner,* 2 vols. (Leipzig: J. U. Brodhaus, 1865), 2:39–40.

49. Muhammad Hasan Khān Iʿtimād us-Saltaneh, *Al-Maʾāsir-u val Āsār* (Tehran, 1307/1888), p. 9

50. Polak, *Persien,* 2:3.

51. Ibid.

52. Ibid., p. 37.

53. Ibid. See also Mihdi Bāmdād, *Tārīkh-i Rijāl-i Irān dar Qurūn-i 12, 13, va 14 Hijrī,* 5 vols. (Tehran, 1347–50/1968–73), 2:222.

54. Polak, *Persien,* 2:37.

55. Ibid.

56. Polak, Wills, and Amīn ud-Dowleh, among others, have remarked on how handsome he was.

57. Nāsir ed-Dīn Shah to Mīrzā Huseyn Khān, n.d., Farhād Collection, Tehran, Iran.

58. *Persien,* 2:38.

59. Ibid.

60. Adamiyat, *Amīr Kabīr,* provides the most exhaustive study of the man and his period.

61. Ibid., p. 652.

62. Ibid., p. 672.

63. Polak, *Persien,* 2:38.

64. Ibid.

65. Amīn ud-Dowleh, *Khāṭirāt,* p. ·14.

66. Piggot, *Persia,* p. 109.

67. Amīn ud-Dowleh, *Khāṭirāt,* p. 15.

68. Polak, *Persien,* 2:38.

69. For a more detailed account, see Hafiz Farman Farmayan, "The Forces of Modernization in Nineteenth Century Iran," in W. R. Polk and R. Chambers, *Beginnings of Modernization in the Middle East* (Chicago: University of Chicago Press, 1968).

70. Adamiyat, *Amīr Kabīr,* p. 53.

71. Ibid.

72. Jaʿfar Khān Mushīr ud-Dowleh, *Risāleh-yi Tahqīqāt-i Sarhaddīyeh,* ed. Muhammad Mushīrī (Tehran: Bunyād-i Farhang-i Irān, 1348/1969), p. 38.

73. Adimayat, *Amīr Kabīr*, p. 53.

74. One of the most interesting works about the movement is written by Prince Iʿtizād us-Saltaneh, the shah's great uncle, who had witnessed the birth of the movement and was suspected of being a Babi. Iʿtizād us-Saltaneh, ʿAlīqulī Mīrzā, *Fitneh-yi Bāb*, ed. ʿAbdul Huseyn Navāʾī (Tehran, 1333/1954). Another detailed account appears in M. le Comte de Gobineau, *Les religions et philosophies dans l'Asie centrale* (Paris: Ernest Leroux, 1900).

75. Watson, *Persia*, pp. 385–88.

76. Adamiyat, *Amīr Kabīr*, pp. 383–90.

77. Ibid., p. 348.

78. I am grateful to Professor Inalcik for drawing my attention to this important fact. See also Bernard Lewis, *The Emergence of Modern Turkey*, 2d ed. (London: Oxford University Press, 1968), pp. 113–14.

79. ʿAbbās Mīrzā's Nizām-i Jadīd (military reform in the 1820s), Amīr Kabīr's Dār ul-Funūn, Malkam's "Majlis-i Tanzīmāt," and many terms employed by Mīrzā Huseyn Khān and his programs witness this fact.

80. Khān Malik Sāsānī, *Sīyāsatgarān-i Dowreh-yi Qājār*, 2 vols. (Tehran: Tahūrī, 1337–45S/1958–66), 1:17.

81. Adamiyat, *Amīr Kabīr*, p. 745.

82. Mushīr ud-Dowleh, *Tahqīqāt-i Sarhaddīyeh*, p. 12. It should be mentioned that there was no relationship between Mīrzā Jaʿfar Khān Mushīr ud-Dowleh and Mīrzā Huseyn Khān, who bore the title Mushīr ud-Dowleh after Mīrzā Jaʿfar Khān's death. Qajar titles were either attached to a post (e.g., mustowfi to a financial bureau) or honorific, passing either from father to son or, as in this case, to a total stranger.

83. Bāmdād, *Tārīkh-i Rijāl*, 1:242–43.

84. Polak, *Persien*, p. 37.

85. Malkam Khan, *Risāleh-yi Usūl-i Tamaddun*, ed. Muhīt-i Tabātabāʾī (Tehran: 1325/1946), pp. 201–2.

86. Bāmdād, *Tārīkh-i Rijāl*, 1:243.

87. *Vaqāyiʿ-i Ittifāqīyyeh*, 21 Rabīʿ us-Sanī 1276/16 November 1859, Adamiyat Collection, Tehran.

88. Malkam, *Risāleh*, pp. 213–17.

89. Sāsānī, *Sīyāsatgarān*, 1:146. The Faramūshkhāneh was dissolved on 18 October 1861. See Hamid Algar, *Mīrzā Malkum Khān* (Berkeley: University of California Press, 1973), p. 38.

90. Sāsānī, *Sīyāsatgarān*, 1:147.

91. Mīhdīqulī Hidayat, *Khātirāt va Khatarāt* (Tehran: Zavvār, 1344/1965), p. 53.

92. Ibid., p. 20.

93. Mushīr ud-Dowleh, *Tahqīqāt-i Sarhaddīyeh*, p. 13.

94. Amīn ud-Dowleh, *Khātirāt*, p. 24.

95. Ibid., p. 28.

96. Ibid., p. 26.

CHAPTER 2

1. Iʿtimād us-Saltaneh, *Sadr ut-Tavārīkh* Tehran, 1349/1970), p. 266.

2. At least three of those who opposed him, Zill us-Sultān, Majd al-Mulk, and Iʿtimād us-Saltaneh, referred to him as the grandson of the masseur.

3. Adamiyat, *Amīr Kabīr*, p. 23.

4. I'timād us-Saltaneh, *Sadr ut-Tavārīkh*, p. 262. Farahanī refers to the fact that Amīr Kabīr came from Farahan.

5. Ibid.

6. Ghani Collection, Yale University Library, New Haven, Connecticut. This collection consists of fifty-seven letters written by Mīrzā Huseyn Khān to Nasīr ed-Dowleh. They are not dated, but reference to other matters indicates they were written in the last years of his life, 1879–80.

7. Watson, *Persia*, p. 19.

8. I'timād us-Saltaneh, *Sadr ut-Tavārīkh*, pp. 280–81.

9. Id., *Khalseh-yā Khābnāmeh-yi I'timād us-Saltaneh* (Tehran, 1348/1969), p. 46.

10. Bāmdād, *Tārīkh-i Rijāl*, 4:436.

11. Carla Serena, *Hommes et choses en Perse* (Paris, 1883), p. 110.

12. Ibid, p. 113.

13. Gobineau, *Les religions et philosophies dans L'Asic Centrale*, pp. 132–33.

14. Issawi, *Economic History*, p. 23. Iran began sending students to Europe in 1811. Only two students were in the first group, five in the second in 1815, and five in the third in 1844.

15. Watson, *Persia*, pp. 19–20.

16. I'timād us-Saltaneh, *Sadr ut-Tavārīkh*, p. 263.

17. Adamiyat, *Amīr Kabīr*, p. 543.

18. Farhād-Mu'tamid, *Sipahsālār*, p. 9. Mīrzā Huseyn Khān had succeeded in displaying the Iranian flag at the entrance to the building of the Iranian mission in Bombay.

19. Fereydoun Adamiyat, *Andīsheh-hā-yi Mīrzā Fath-'Alī Akhundzādeh* (Tehran: Kharazmi, 1349/1971), pp. 10–14.

20. Fath-'Ali Akhundzādeh, *Tamsīlāt*, trans. J. Qarajidaghi (Tehran: Andisheh Pub. Co., 1349S/1970), p. 7.

21. These two themes run through most of Akhundzādeh's writing, especially the short novel *Sitārigān-i Farībkhurdeh*, in the *Tamsīlāt*, and his various correspondence. For the latter, see id., *Alifbā-yi Jadīd va Maktūbāt*, ed. H. Muhammadzādeh and H. Araslī (Baku, 1963).

22. Mīrzā Fath-'Alī to Mīrzā Yūsuf Khan Mustashār ud-Dowleh, n.d., Fereydoun Adamiyat Collection, Tehran, Iran.

23. This point is discussed more extensively in ch. 3 on judicial reform.

24. Sāsānī, *Sīyāsatgarān*, 1:60.

25. Mahmūd Farhād-Mu'tamid, *Tārīkh-i Ravābit-i Sīyāsī-yi Īrān va Usmānī* (Tehran, 1327/1948), pp. 26–37.

26. Mushir ud-Dowleh, *Tahqīqāt-i Sarhaddīyeh*, pp. 34–35.

27. Farhād-Mu'tamid, *Tārīkh*, p. 47.

28. Khān Malik Sāsānī, *Yādbūhā-yi Safar-i Islāmbul* (Tehran, n.d.), p. 52.

29. I'timad us-Saltaneh, *Sadr ut-Tavārīkh*, p. 261.

30. Sāsānī, *Sīyāsatgarān*, 1:67.

31. Mīrzā Huseyn Khān to Mīrzā Sa'īd Khān, Iranian foreign minister, cited in Fereydoun Adamiyat, *Fikr-i Āzādī va Muqaddameh-yi Nihzat-i Mashrūtīyat* (Tehran: Sukhan, 1340/1951), p. 63.

32. Ibid., pp. 63–64.

33. Ibid., pp. 64–65.

34. 19 Ziqa'deh 1283/26 April 1867, Archives, Ministry of Foreign Affairs, Tehran, Iran.

35. Ibid., 24 Rabī' ul-Avval 1286/16 July 1869.

36. Ibid.
37. Ibid.
38. Ibid., 8 Rabīʿ ul-Avval 1286/20 June 1869.
39. Sāsānī, Sīyāstgarān, 1:67–68.
40. Ibid., p. 68.
41. Ibid., p. 69.
42. File 11, 19 Ziqaʿdeh 1283/26 April 1867, Archives, Ministry of Foreign Affairs, Tehran, Iran.
43. Ibid.
44. Ibid.
45. Sāsānī, Sīyāsatgarān, 1:66.
46. See ch. 6 for a full treatment of the Reuter concession.
47. Farhād-Muʿtamid, Tārīkh, pp. 32–33.
48. Watson, Persia, p. 340.
49. Ibrāhīm Teymūrī, ʿAsr-i Bīkhabarī yā Tārīkh-i Imtiyāzāt dar Īrān (Tehran, 1332S/1954), p. 33.
50. Ibid., p. 35.
51. Ibid., p. 33.
52. Masʿūd Mīrzā Zill us-Sultān, Tārīkh-i Sarguzasht-i Masūdī (Tehran, 1325/1907), pp. 210–11.
53. Sāsānī, Sīyāsatgarān, 1:104.
54. Ibid., 1:106–7.
55. Nāsir ed-Dīn Shah to Mīrzā Huseyn Khān, cited in Teymūrī, ʿAsr-i Bīkhabarī, p. 102.
56. Ibid., p. 2.
57. Bertold Spuler, "Central Asia: The Last Centuries of Independence," in F. R. C. Bagley, trans. and ed., The Muslim World: A Historical Survey (Leiden, 1969), pt. 3, p. 251.
58. Ibid., p. 247.
59. Ibid., p. 255.
60. Nāsir ed-Dīn Shah to Mīrzā Huseyn Khān, n.d. (probably 1874), Farhād Collection, Tehran, Iran.
61. Ibid.

CHAPTER 3

1. Irān, 11 Rabīʿ us-Sānī 1289/17 June 1872.
2. S. G. W. Benjamin, Persia and the Persians (Boston: Ticknor & Co., 1887), pp. 439–40.
3. Ibid., p. 440.
4. Algar, Religion and State, p. 13.
5. Farhād-Muʿtamid, Sipahsālār, pp. 39–43.
6. Amīn ud-Dowleh, Khātirāt, pp. 19–20.
7. Alison to Granville, 9 March 1871, FO 60/333, Public Record Office, London, England.
8. Ibid.
9. Vaqāyiʿ-i ʿAdlīyeh, Muharram 1288/March-April 1871, Hisām ud-Dīn Khurumī Collection, Tehran, Iran.
10. W. T. Thompson to Granville, 15 October 1873, FO 60/351, Public Record Office, London.

11. Houtum-Schindler places this number at 125,000 out of a total population of 7 million. *Encyclopaedia Britannica*, 10th ed., s.v. "Persia," 31:619.

12. This point is treated more fully in ch. 6.

13. This point is treated more fully later in this chapter.

14. Mīrzā Huseyn Khān to Mustashār ud-Dowleh, 16 Jamadi ul-Avval 1282/8 October 1865, Adamiyat Collection, Tehran.

15. Mīrzā Huseyn Khān to Nāsir ed-Dīn Shah, cited in Teymūrī, *'Asr-i Bīkhabarī*, p. 44.

16. *Vaqāyi'-i 'Adlīyeh*, Zī Hajjeh 1288/ March 1871, Khurumī Collection, Tehran.

17. C. J. Wills, *Persia as It Is* (London: Sampson, Low, Marston, Searle & Rivington, 1886), p. 46.

18. *Vaqāyi'-i 'Adlīyeh*, Zī Hajjeh 1288/March 1871, Khurumī Collection, Tehran.

19. Ibid., p. 5.

20. Ibid.

21. Ann K. S. Lambton, *Landlord and Peasant in Persia* (London: Oxford University Press, 1953), p. 164.

22. V. Minorsky, *Encyclopedia of Islam*, 1st ed. (1913–38), s.v. "Tiyul," 4:799–801.

23. Lambton, *Landlord and Peasants in Persia*, p. 155.

24. Hājjī Sayyāh, *Khātirāt-i Hājjī Sayyāh*, ed. Hamīd Sayyāh (Tehran, 1346/1967), pp. 137–38.

25. *Rūznāmeh-yi Dowlat-i 'Alīyyeh-yi Irān*, 2 Jamādī ul-Avval/20 July 1871.

26. Ibid.

27. I'timād us-Saltaneh, *Sadr ut-Tavārīkh*, p. 267.

28. Yūsuf Khān Mustashār ud-Dowleh, *Yik Kalimeh* (Tehran, 1287/1870), p. 16.

29. *Irān*, 11 Rabī' ul-Avval 1289/17 June 1872.

30. Ibid.

31. Thompson to Darby, 25 March 1875, FO 60/370, Public Record Office, London.

32. Ibid.

33. "Kitābcheh-yi Tanzīmāt Hasaneh-yi Dowlat-i 'Alīyēh va Mahrūsēh-yi Iran" (1292/1875), Senate Library, Tehran, p. 9.

34. For a full discussion of the code, see ch. 5.

35. *Tanzīmāt-i Hasaneh*, p. 9.

36. Ibid., p. 11.

37. Ibid., pp. 16–17.

38. The fate of the code will be discussed more fully in ch. 6.

39. Amīn ud-Dowleh, *Khātirāt*, p. 62.

40. I'timād us-Saltaneh, *Al-Ma'āsir-u val-Āsār*, p. 108.

41. Muhammad Taqī Dāmghānī, "Sad Sāl-i Pīsh az Īn," *Huqūq-i Mardum* (Fall 1345S/Fall 1966), p. 16.

CHAPTER 4

1. *Mirrīkh*, 29 Zīqa'deh 1293/16 December 1876.

2. *Irān*, 20 Rajab 1288/5 October 1871.

3. Adamiyat, *Amīr Kabīr*, p. 286.

4. Ibid., p. 294.

5. George N. Curzon, *Persia and the Persian Question*, 2 vols. (London: Longmans, Green & Co., 1892), 1:600.

6. Watson, *Persia*, p. 24.

7. *Irān*, 20 Rajab 1288/5 October 1871.

8. Ch. 5 considers Mīrzā Huseyn Khān's prime ministry.

9. Farhād-M'tamid, *Sipahsālār*, p. 631.

10. Ibid., p. 65.

11. Ibid., p. 66.

12. Mīrzā Mūsā to Nāsir ed-Dīn Shah, n.d., Farhād Collection. Mīrzā Yahyā Khān Mu'tamid ul-Mulk, Mīrzā Huseyn Khān's younger brother, was married to Nāsir ed-Dīn Shah's sister, 'Izzat ud-Dowleh.

13. Ibid.

14. Adamiyat, *Amīr Kabīr*, pp. 289–90.

15. Farhād-Mu'tamid, *Sipahsālār*, p. 90.

16. Mīrzā Huseyn Khān to Nāsir ed-Dīn Shah, n.d., but probably 1289 or 1290/ 1872 or 1874, Farhād Collection.

17. Ibid.

18. *Irān*, 27 Rabī' us-Sānī 1289/4 January 1872.

19. Curzon, *Persia*, 1:608.

20. Mīrzā Huseyn Khān to Nāsir ed-Dīn Shah, n.d., Farhād Collection.

21. Ibid.

22. Ch. 5 discusses the Shah's attitude more fully.

23. Mīrzā Huseyn Khān to Nāsir ed-Dīn Shah, n.d., probably 1291/1874, Farhād Collection.

24. See ch. 6.

25. Hājjī Sayyāh, *Khātirāt*, p. 136.

26. Mīrzā Huseyn Khān to the shah, n.d., probably 1292/1874, Farhād Collection.

27. Mary Lawrence Sheil, *Glimpses of Life and Manners in Persia* (London: John Murray, 1856), pp. 333–34.

28. Mīrzā Huseyn Khān to the shah, n.d., but probably 1289/1872, Farhād Collection.

29. Id., several letters written between 1291–92/1874–75, ibid.

30. Nāsir ed-Dīn Shah to Mīrzā Huseyn Khān, 1292/1874, ibid.

31. Muhammad Hasan Khan Sanī' ud-Dowleh (later I'timād us-Saltaneh), *Mir'āt ul-Buldān*, 4 vols. (Tehran, 1295/1878), 3:196.

32. Mīrzā Huseyn Khān to Nāsir ed-Dīn Shah, n.d., Farhād Collection. This was a reply written by the shah in the margin of Mirza Huseyn Khan's letter, which was returned to him instead of a separate letter. The shah occasionally followed this practice.

33. Ibid.

34. Ibid.

35. See ch. 6 for more detail.

36. Mīrzā Huseyn Khān to Nāsir ed-Dīn Shah, 1297/1879, Farhād Collection.

37. Nāsir ed-Dīn Shah to Mīrzā Huseyn Khān, 1297/1879, ibid.

38. The military newspapers frequently reported prompt payment.

39. The full text appears in *Rūznāmeh-yi Nizāmī*, 19 Muharram 1294/4 January 1877.

40. Ibid.

41. 'Abbās Mīrzā Mūlk Ārā, *Sharh-i Hāl-i 'Abbās Mīrzā Mūlk Ārā* (Tehran, 1325/ 1946), p. 98.

42. Curzon, *Persia*, 1:587.

43. *Mirrīkh*, 5 Muharram 1296/30 December 1878.

44. Ibid.

45. Ibid., 26 Rajab 1296/17 July 1879.

46. Firuz Kazemzadeh, "The Origins and Early Development of the Cossack Brigade," *American Slavic and East European Review* 15 (October 1956):351–63.

47. Ibid.

48. *Mirrīkh*, 21 Muharram 1296/15 January 1879.

49. Ibid.

50. Ibid., 5 Rabīʿ ul-Avval 1296/27 February 1879.

51. Ibid., 8 Jamādī ul-Avval 1296/30 May 1879.

52. Mūlk Ārā' *Sharh-i Hāl*, p. 87.

53. Ibid., p. 88.

54. Sāsānī, *Sīyāsatgarān*, 1:92.

55. Curzon, *Persia*, 1:604.

56. Ibid., p. 602.

57. Several letters to Krupp about the purchase of arms may be found in the Farhād Collection.

58. Amīn ud-Dowleh, *Khātirāt*, pp. 57–58.

59. *Mirrīkh*, 18 Rabīʿ ul-Avval 1297/29 February 1880.

60. Curzon, *Persia*, 2:602.

61. Iʿtimād us-Saltaneh, *Al-Ma'āsir-u val Āsār*, p. 120.

62. Zill us-Sultān, *Tārīkh*, p. 831.

63. Curzon, *Persia*, 1:589.

CHAPTER 5

1. Preamble to the Edict of the Darbar-i Aʿzam, *Irān*, 4 Ziqaʿdeh 1289/4 January 1873.

2. Ibid.

3. Amīn ud-Dowleh, *Khātirāt*, p. 8.

4. Among those killed by Karīm Khan was Huseyn Qulī Khan, the elder brother of Āghā Muhammad Khān.

5. The most notable of these was Mīrzā Ibrāhim Kalāntar, the sadr-i aʿzam, who had served the Zand dynasty in many ways.

6. Watson, *Persia*, pp. 139–40.

7. Ahmad Mīrzā ʿAzd ud-Dowleh, *Tārīkh-i ʿAzudī* (Tehran, n.d.), p. 12.

8. *Irān* 53, 8 Ramazān 1288/22 November 1871.

9. Ibid.

10. Ibid.

11. Ibid.

12. The work of the council was covered in several issues of *Irān*, beginning with 25 Ramazān 1289/9 December 1871.

13. Ibid.

14. Farhād-Muʿtamid, *Sipahsālār*, p. 120.

15. *Irān*, 4 Jamādī ul-Avval 1289/12 August 1872.

16. Roderic H. Davison, *Reform in the Ottoman Empire, 1856–1876* (Princeton: Princeton University Press, 1963), p. 159.

17. Ibid., p. 147.

18. Ibid., p. 148.

19. *Irān*, 4 Jamādī ul-Avval 1289/12 August 1872.

20. This was a method used by most Iranians who advocated reform. They either mentioned the Ottoman Empire, as in this instance, or tried to present their

reforms as being in harmony with the Qur'an and the Sharīʿa, as in the case of Mustashār ud-Dowleh in *Yik Kalimeh*. See ch. 3.

21. *Irān*, 4 Zīhajjeh 1289/1 January 1873.

22. Ibid.

23. See below, pp. 82–83.

24. Mīrzā Huseyn Khān to Muhsin Khān Muʿīn ul-Mulk, 29 Zīhajjeh 1289/22 February 1873, Ghanī Collection.

25. Amīn ud-Dowleh, *Khātirāt*, p. 94.

26. Polak, *Persien*, 2:1–15.

27. Farhād Collection, Tehran. All information about this edict is taken from an original copy that once belonged to Prince Farhād Mīrzā, the deputy prime minister at the time.

28. For a stimulating discussion of this topic, see Professor Petroshevsky's article in *Cambridge History of Iran*, vol. 5, and his two-volume work on the history of Iranian agriculture.

29. Mīrzā Huseyn Khān to the foreign minister, 14 Ziqaʿdeh 1286/16 February 1870, Archives, Ministry of Foreign Affairs.

30. See ch. 3 on judicial reform.

31. Iʿtimād us-Saltaneh, *Al-Ma'āsir-u val Āsār*, p. 128.

32. The circular was read by Mirza Huseyn Khan during a public audience with the shah; its text was printed in *Irān*, 12 Ziqaʿdeh 1288/22 January 1872.

33. Ibid.

34. Ibid.

35. Ibid.

36. Ibid.

37. Shah to Mīrzā Huseyn Khān, n.d. (probably 1288 or 1289), Farhād Collection.

38. Zill us-Sultān, *Tārīkh*, p. 217.

39. Iʿtimād us-Saltaneh, "Sadr ut Tavārīkh," Adamiyat Collection, p. 20.

40. Sāsānī, *Sīyāsatgarān*, 1:119.

41. Ibid.

42. Mīrzā Huseyn Khān to Muʿīn ul-Mulk, Zīhajjeh 1289/26 February 1873, Ghanī Collection.

43. Id., 1 Ziqaʿdeh 1289/1 January 1873, ibid.

44. Malkam Khan to Mīrzā Huseyn Khān, 26 Jamādī ul-Avval 1289/4 August 1872, Archives, Majlis Library, Tehran.

45. Bernard Lewis, *The Emergence of Modern Turkey* (London: Oxford University Press, 1968), p. 127.

46. I have arrived at this approximate figure by adding the number of students sent abroad (about 60, according to Issawi's *Economic History*) to the number of graduates of Dar-ul-Funūn, founded in 1852, with 150 students and a 6- to 8-year program.

47. Farhād-Muʿtamid, *Sipahsālār*, p. 149.

48. For a detailed account of the Reuter Concession, see ch. 2 in Firuz Kazemzadeh's *Russia and Britain in Persia, 1864–1915* (New Haven: Yale University Press, 1968). See also ch. 7 below.

49. Amīn ud-Dowleh, *Khātirāt*, p. 52.

50. Bāmdād, *Tārīkh-i Rijāl*, 4:271.

51. S. G. W. Benjamin, *Persia and Persians*, pp. 440–41.

52. In Istanbul, Mīrzā Huseyn Khān had been a follower of Hājjī Mīrzā Safā, a well-known Sufi leader. Sāsānī, *Sīyāsatgarān*, 1:60–67.

53. Teymūrī, *ʿAsr-i Bīkhabarī*, pp. 124–26.

54. Mīrzā Huseyn Khān to the shah, cited ibid., p. 44. Mīrzā Huseyn Khān points out that during the famine of 1871–72, he had helped Mīrzā Sālih ʿArab with donations of cash and grain.

55. Iʿtimād us-Saltaneh, "Sadr ut-Tavārīkh," ms. ed., Adamiyat Collection, p. 9. The published ed. is slightly different.

56. Ibid.

57. W. G. Abbott to the foreign minister, F.O. 60/351, Public Record Office, London.

58. Ibid.

59. The text of this letter is cited in Teymūri, *ʿAsr-i Bīkhabarī*, pp. 124–26. Malkam, who at the time was ambassador to Great Britain, was a vocal advocate of the contract and was influential in arranging it.

60. W. T. Thompson to Granville, 19 September 1873, F.O. 60/351, Public Record Office, London.

61. Iʿtimād us-Saltaneh, "Sadr ut-Tavārīkh," p. 9.

62. Amīn ud-Dowleh, *Khātirāt*, pp. 48–49.

CHAPTER 6

1. *Irān*, 10 Shaʿbān 1290/3 October 1873, p. 1.

2. Sāsānī, *Sīyāsatgārān*, 1:150.

3. Iʿtimād us-Saltaneh, "Sadr ut-Tavārīkh," Adamiyat Collection, p. 9.

4. Nasir ed-Dīn Shah to Mīrzā Huseyn Khān, 1290/1873, Farhād Collection.

5. Ibid.

6. Kazemzadeh, *Russia and Britain in Persia*, p. 116–17.

7. *Irān*, 19 Ramazan 1290/10 November 1873.

8. This refers to a Russian request for permission to build railways after the abrogation of the Reuter Concession. See Kazemzadeh, *Russia and Britain in Persia*, pp. 135–36.

9. Nasir ed-Dīn Shah to Mīrzā Huseyn Khān, n.d., Farhād Collection.

10. Ibid.

11. Kazemzadeh, *Russia and Britain in Persia*, p. 115.

12. *Irān*, 27 Shavvāl 1291/8 December 1874.

13. W. T. Thompson to Granville, 22 November 1874, F.O. 60/365, Public Record Office, London.

14. "Kitābcheh-yi Tanzīmāt-i Hasaneh," Senate Library, Tehran.

15. M. Churchill to W. T. Thompson, 8 May 1875, F.O. 60/374, Public Record Office, London.

16. Abdullāh Mustowfī, *Sharh-i Zindigānī-yi Man yā Tārīkh-i Ijtimāʿī va Idārī-yi Dowreh-yi Qājārīyeh*, 2 vols. (Tehran, 1321sh/1942–43), 1:101.

17. *Irān*, 26 Ziqaʿdeh 1291/5 January 1875.

18. Ibid., 23 Zīhajjeh 1291/1 February 1875.

19. According to Amīn ul-Mulk in 1297/1879, for instance, following the death of Shīr ʿAlī Khān, the amir of Afghanistan, the British government showed a willingness to allow Iran established suzerainty over the city of Herat. Mirza Huseyn Khan, who was chiefly responsible for the negotiations with the British, encouraged the shah to seize the opportunity and accept the British proposal, which demanded the British right to maintain a garrison in that city in exchange for recognition of Iranian control. The plan met with failure, however, because of opposition from

Zill us-Sultān, who feared that its success would restore Mirza Huseyn Khan to the shah's favor.

20. W. G. Abbot to W. T. Thompson, 31 March 1875, F.O. 60/375, Public Record Office, London.

21. Mustowfī, *Sharh-i Zindigānī*, 1:141.

22. See ch. 2.

23. *Irān*, 18 Zīqad'eh 1292/17 December 1875.

24. Ibid.

25. *Irān*, 6 Zīhajjeh 1292/4 January 1876.

26. Ibid.

27. Amīn ud-Dowleh, *Khātirāt*, p. 95.

28. Zill us-Sultān, *Tārīkh*, p. 95.

29. Mīrzā Huseyn Khān to Nāsir ed-Dīn Shah, 1297/1879, Farhād Collection.

30. The Ghanī Collection, Yale University Library, holds about fifty such letters. In many of them Mīrzā Huseyn Khān pleads with Nasīr ud-Dowleh not to abandon him. But Nasīr ud-Dowleh did in fact join his enemies and even supplied some damaging evidence that was used against him.

31. I'timād us-Saltaneh, *Rūznāmeh-yi Khātirāt-i I'timād us-Saltaneh*, ed. Iraj Afshar (Tehran, 1345/1966), pp. 140–41.

32. Ibid.

33. Mūlk-Ārā, *Sharh-i Hal*, p. 88.

34. The Farhād Collection contains several letters in which Mīrzā Huseyn Khān complains bitterly about Malkam Khān and his attitude toward himself and Nāsir ed-Dīn Shah.

35. Amīn ud-Dowleh, *Khātirāt*, p. 43.

36. Hājjī Sayyāh, *Khātirāt*, p. 97.

37. Amīn ud-Dowleh, *Khātirāt*, p. 47.

38. Ibid.

39. Ibid., p. 56.

40. Ibid., pp. 30–32.

41. Hājjī Sayyāh, *Khātirāt*, p. 200.

42. Amīn ud-Dowleh, *Khātirāt*, p. 61.

43. Ibid., pp. 61–62.

44. Ibid., p. 62.

45. Mūlk-Ārā, *Sharh-i Hal*, pp. 65–66.

46. I'timad us-Saltaneh, *Rūznāmeh*, p. 140.

47. Zill us-Sultān, *Tārīkh*, p. 236.

48. Mīrzā Huseyn Khān to Nāsir ed-Dīn Shah, 1297/1879, Farhād Collection.

49. For a detailed study of the rebellion, see I. Ghūrīyanus, *Qīyām-i Shaykh 'Ubiydullāh Shimzīnī dar 'Ahd-i Nāsir ed-Dīn Shāh* (Tehran: Danish, 1336/1957).

CHAPTER 7

1. According to Issawi, *Economic History*, p. 114, the total revenue from silk was £409,582 in 1859, £351,000 in 1863, and £502,000 in 1864; whereas the figure suddenly dropped to £65,000 in 1867, to £80,000 in 1868, and to £136,400 in 1869.

2. Ibid.

3. Ibid., p. 364.

4. Ibid., p. 30.

5. Mustowfī, *Sharh-i Zindigānī*, 1:564–70.
6. Ibid.
7. Ibid.
8. Ibid.
9. Sāsānī, *Sīyāsatgarān*, 1:149.
10. Mustowfī, *Sharh-i Zindigānī*, 1:153.
11. Ibid., pp. 153–54.
12. Ibid., p. 154.
13. *Irān*, 12 Zīqaʿdeh 1288/23 February 1872.
14. Ibid.
15. Iʿtimād us-Saltaneh, *Sadr ut-Tavārīkh*, p. 268.
16. Ibid.
17. Sāsānī, *Sīyāsatgarān*, 1:120.
18. Farhād-Muʿtamid, *Sipahsālār*, p. 131.
19. Ibid.
20. Zill us-Sultān, *Tārīkh*, p. 215.
21. This was discussed in more detail in ch. 5.
22. *Irān*, 18 Ramazān 1289/8 December 1872.
23. Sheil, *Life and Manners in Persia*, p. 387.
24. Ibid., p. 392.
25. Piggot, *Persia*, p. 303.
26. Ibid.
27. Sheil, *Life and Manners in Persia*, pp. 381–88.
28. Muhammad Khān Majd ul-Mulk, *Risāleh-yi Majdīyeh* (Tehran, 1321/1940), pp. 68–69.
29. Sheil, *Life and Manners in Persia*, p. 388.
30. Farhād-Muʿtamid, *Sipahsālār*, p. 103.
31. Mīrzā Huseyn Khān to Nāsir ed-Dīn Shah, 1292/1874, Farhād Collection.
32. *Irān*, 12 Jamādī ul-Avval 1290/8 July 1873.
33. "Kitābcheh-yi Tanzīmāt-i Hasaneh," Senate Library, Tehran, p. 1.
34. Ibid., p. 4.
35. *Encyclopaedia Britannica*, 10th ed., s.v. "Persia," 31:620; Curzon, *Persia*, 2:470.
36. See ch. 6.
37. See ch. 4.
38. R. F. Thomson to Granville, 8 May 1880, F.O. 60/428, Public Record Office, London.
39. Mīrzā Huseyn Khān to Nāsir ed-Dīn Shah, n.d., Farhād Collection.
40. Nāsir ed-Dīn Shah to Mīrzā Huseyn Khān, ibid.
41. Ibid.
42. R. F. Thomson to Granville, 8 May 1880, F.O. 60/420, Public Record Office, London.
43. Iʿtimād us-Saltaneh, *Al-Ma'āsir-u val Āsār*, p. 110.
44. M. Muhtasham, "Ta'sīs-i Bānk," *Majalleh-yi Bānk-i Sipah* (Tehran, Autumn 1341S/1962), p. 29.
45. Ibid. (Winter 1341S/1963), p. 30.
46. Ibid., pp. 36–37.
47. Ibid., p. 38.
48. Ibid., 33.
49. Ibid., p. 37.
50. Ibid. (Spring 1342S/1964), p. 13.

51. Malkam Khan to Mīrzā Huseyn Khān, n.d., Archives, Majlis Library, Tehran. Karbala was a holy shrine.

52. Issawi, *Economic History*, p. 346.

53. Recent work by economists and economic historians is beginning to reveal that the Iranian economy was much healthier in the last two decades of the nineteenth century than was previously believed. For more detail on these studies, see the works of F. Nowshiravani and my own forthcoming article on the proceedings of a conference on State Society and Economy in Nineteenth-Century Iran during the Ottoman Empire to be published by the Social Science Research Council.

54. Issawi, *Economic History*, pp. 78–79; Adamiyat, *Amīr Kabīr*, pp. 386–88.

55. Muhammad Muhsin Qaraguzlū, "'Ādāt ul-Mulūk," Adamiyat Collection, Tehran.

56. Sāsānī, *Sīyāsatgarān*, 1:68–69.

57. I'timād us-Saltaneh, *Sadr ut-Tavārīkh*, p. 267.

58. *Irān*, 10 Jamādī ul-Avval 1291/25 June 1874.

59. Mīrzā Yūsuf Khān Mustashār ud-Dowleh, cited in Adamiyat, *Fikr-i Azādī*, p. 184.

60. Mīrzā Huseyn Khān to the ministry, Archives, Ministry of Foreign Affairs, Tehran.

61. *Irān*, 10 Shavval 1289/12 December 1872.

62. Kazemzadeh, *Russia and Britain in Persia*, p. 108.

63. Ibid.

64. Malkam Khān, *Risāleh*, p. 15.

65. Kazemzadeh, *Russia and Britain in Persia*, p. 103.

66. Mīrzā Huseyn Khān to Mū'īn ul-Mulk, 9 Jamādī ul-Avval 1289/17 July 1872, Ghanī Collection.

67. Id. to Nāsir ed-Dīn Shah, n.d., probably July 1872, Farhād Collection.

68. Ibid.

69. Farhād-Mu'tamid, *Sipahsālār*, pp. 159–60.

70. F.O. 60/366, Public Record Office, London.

71. Mīrzā Huseyn Khān to Mirza Sa'īd Khān, 19 Zīqa'deh 1283/26 April 1867, Archives, Ministry of Foreign Affairs, Tehran.

72. Id. to Nāsir ed-Dīn Shah, n.d., probably 1289/1872, Farhād Collection.

73. *Irān*, 1 Rabī' us-Sānī 1292/7 May 1875.

74. The paper was the French-language *La Patrie*. See ch. 8, pp. 142–43.

75. "Avvalīn Risāleh-yi Rāh-Āhan dar Irān," *Majalleh-yi Bānk-i Sipah* 10–13 (Summer 1342S/1963).

76. Ibid. (Spring 1434S/1964).

77. Curzon, *Persia*, 1:616–23.

78. Ibid.

79. *Irān*, 27 Zīqa'deh 1292/26 December 1875.

80. Edward Stack, *Six Months in Persia*, 2 vols. (London: Sampson, Low, Marston, Searle, & Rivington, 1882), 2:191.

81. Serena, *Hommes et choses en Perse*, pp. 210–11.

82. See ch. 8, pp. 158–59.

83. Adamiyat, *Fikr-i Azādī*, p. 185.

84. Serena, *Hommes et choses en Perse*, p. 147.

85. *Irān*, 12 Rabī' ul-Avval 1292/18 May 1875.

86. *Rūznāmeh-yi 'Ilmīyeh va Adabīyeh*, 12 Muharram 1294/28 January 1877, Khurumī Collection, Tehran.

87. *Encyclopaedia Britannica,* 10th ed., s.v. "Persia," 31:620.
88. Ibid.
89. Curzon, *Persia,* 2:602.
90. *Irān,* 6 Zīhajjeh 1292/4 January 1876.

CHAPTER 8

1. Rajab 1276/February 1860, Archives, Ministry of Foreign Affairs, Tehran.
2. Mīrzā Huseyn Khān to Mīrzā Saʿīd Khān, 24 Rabīʿ ul-Avval 1286/5 July 1869, ibid.
3. Id. to Nāsir ed-Dīn Shah, Muharram 1284/May 1876, ibid.
4. Ibid.
5. Teymūrī, *ʿAsr-i Bīkhabarī,* p. 33.
6. *Irān,* 15 Ramazān 1289/17 December 1872.
7. Mīrzā Huseyn Khān to Nāsir ed-Dīn Shah, Ramazān 1289/December 1872, Suppléments Persans, Bibliothèque Nationale, Paris.
8. Iʿtimād us-Saltaneh, *Sadr ut-Tavārīkh,* p. 269.
9. Ibid., p. 270.
10. For details, see ch. 5, pp. 91–94.
11. Nāsir ed-Dīn Shah to Mīrzā Huseyn Khān, 1290/1873, Farhād Collection.
12. Amīn ud-Dowleh, *Khātirāt,* p. 49.
13. Sāsānī, *Sīyāsatgarān,* pp. 68–69.
14. 21 Safar 1287/24 May 1870, Archives, Ministry of Foreign Affairs, Tehran.
15. *Rūznāmeh-yi Dowlat-i ʿAlīyeh-yi Irān,* issues prior to 1287/1870.
16. See *Irān,* 20 Muharram 1288/12 April 1871, for a typical letter to the editor.
17. Stack, *Six Months in Persia,* 1:262; Arthur Arnold, *Through Persia by Caravan* (New York: Harper & Brothers, 1877), p. 225.
18. ʿAbbās Iqbāl, "Tārīkh-i Rūznāmehnigāri dar Irān," *Yādigār,* Isfand 1323 S/ February-March 1945, pp. 6–17.
19. Serena, *Hommes et choses en Perse,* p. 169. Mme Serena is the only source that gives a detailed account of what this newspaper was about.
20. Ibid., pp. 169–70.
21. *Mirrīkh,* 5 Muharram 1296/30 December 1878, p. 1.
22. Ibid., 5 Rabīʿ ul-Avval 1296/27 February 1879.
23. Ibid.
24. *Rūznāmeh-yi Dowlat-i ʿAlīyeh-yi Irān,* 2 Jamādī ul-Avval/20 July 1871.
25. *Mirrīkh,* 5 Rabīʿ ul-Avval 1296/27 February 1879.
26. Ibid.
27. Ibid.
28. Ibid.
29. Mīrzā Huseyn Khān to Mīrzā Saʿīd Khān, 23 Rabīʿ ul-Avval 1283/6 August 1866, Archives, Ministry of Foreign Affairs, Tehran.
30. Ibid.
31. Ibid., 2 Zīhajjeh 1286/6 March 1870.
32. Ibid.
33. Watson, *Persia,* p. 19.
34. Adamiyat, *Amīr Kabīr,* pp. 357–60.
35. Hidāyat, *Khātirāt va Khatarāt,* p. 92.
36. Mīrzā Huseyn Khān to Nāsir ed-Dīn Shah, 1289/1872, Farhād Collection.
37. *Rūznāmeh-yi Nizāmī, ʿIlmī va Adabī,* 11 Muharram 1295/16 January 1878.
38. See ch. 4.

39. Serena, *Hommes et choses en Perse*, p. 143.

40. Ibid.

41. *Rūznāmeh-yi Nizāmī-yi Dowlat-ī ʿAlīyyeh-yi Irān*, 6 Zīhajjeh 1293/24 December 1876.

42. Iʿtimād us-Saltaneh, *Al-maʾāsir-u val Āsār*, pp. 277–78.

43. *Irān*, 16 Rabīʿ ul-Avval 1289/25 May 1872.

44. Ibid.

45. Iʿtimād us-Saltaneh, *Sadr ut-Tavārīkh*, pp. 277–78.

46. Adamiyat, *Amīr Kabīr*, p. 165.

47. Ibid., p. 464.

48. Watson, *Persia*, p. 6.

49. Stack, *Six Months in Persia*, 2:77.

50. Mīrzā Huseyn Khān to Mīrzā Saʿīd Khan Ansarī, 24 Rabīʿ ul-Avval 1286/6 July 1869, Archives, Ministry of Foreign Affairs, Tehran.

51. *Mirrīkh*, 11 Rabīʿ ul-Avval 1296/19 March 1879.

52. *Irān*, 13 Rabīʿ ul-Avval 1289/21 May 1872.

53. Ibid.

54. Ibid.

55. Ibid.

56. Ibid.

57. Sheil, *Life and Manners in Persia*, pp. 83–84.

58. Iʿtimād us-Saltaneh, *Khalseh*, p. 47.

59. Muhsin Khān Qaraguzlū, "ʿĀdāt ul-Mulūk," Adamiyat Collection, Tehran.

60. Bāmdād, *Tārīkh-i Rijal*, 4:423–24.

61. Serena, *Hommes et choses en Perse*, p. 73.

62. Farhād-Muʿtamid, *Sipahsālār*, p. 86.

63. Ibid., p. 90.

64. *Irān*, 14 Safar 1288/6 May 1871.

65. Iʿtimād us-Saltaneh, *Al-Maʾāsir-u val Āsār*, p. 113.

66. Id., *Sadr ut-Tavārīkh*, pp. 19–20.

67. Hājjī Sayyāh, *Khātirāt*, p. 490.

68. *Irān*, 24 Muharram 1290/24 March 1873.

69. Iʿtimād us-Saltaneh, *Al-Maʾāsir-u val-Āsār*, p. 109.

70. *Irān*, 11 Zīqaʿdeh 1288/26 January 1872.

71. Curzon, *Persia*, 1:466.

72. Stack, *Six Months in Persia*, 1:218.

73. *Encyclopaedia Britannica*, 10th ed., s.v. "Persia," 31:625.

74. Ibid, pp. 635–36.

75. Ibid.

76. By Curzon's admission, Houtum-Schindler supplied him with most of the original material for *Persia and the Persian Question* (preface, p. xiii). He also says, "Few men so excellently qualified to write a first-rate book themselves would have lent such unselfish exertion to improve the quality of another man's work."

77. *Encyclopaedia Britannica*, 10th ed., s.v. "Persia," 31:626.

78. Ibid.

79. Curzon, *Persia*, 1:305.

80. Ibid.

81. Iʿtimād us-Saltaneh, *Al-Maʾāsir-u val Āsār*, p. 58.

82. James Bassett, *Persia, the Land of the Imams: A Narrative of Travels and Residence, 1871–1886* (New York: Charles Scribner's Sons, 1886), p. 108.

83. Ibid., p. 100.
84. Serena, *Hommes et choses en Perse*, p. 53.
85. Iʿtimād us-Saltaneh, *Sadr ut-Tavārīkh*, pp. 277–78.
86. Ibid., p. 279.

CHAPTER 9

1. Iʿtimād us-Saltaneh, *Kalseh*, pp. 47–48.
2. Mīrzā Huseyn Khān to Nāsir ed-Dīn Shah, n.d., Farhād Collection.
3. Mūlk-Ārā, *Sharh-i Hāl*, p. 66.
4. Lewis, *Emergence of Modern Turkey*, p. 128.
5. Adamiyat, *Akhundzādeh*, p. 104.
6. Amīn ud-Dowleh, *Khātirāt*, p. 43.
7. R. F. Thompson to Lord Granville, September 14, 1880, F.O. 60/428, Public Record Office, London.
8. Ibid.
9. Mūlk-Ārā, *Sharh-i Hāl*, p. 89.
10. Amīn ud-Dowleh, *Khātirāt*, p. 72.
11. Stack, *Six Months in Persia*, 2:300–301.
12. Muhammad Hasan Khan Sanīʿ ud-Dowleh, *Muntazam-i Nasīrī*, 3 vols. (Tehran, 1300/1882), 3:368–69.

APPENDIX

1. The documents of the Farhād Collection were salvaged by the father of the present owner from a grocery store, where they were waiting to be used as wrapping paper.
2. Teymūrī, *ʿAsr-i Bīkhabarī*, p. 1.
3. Ibid., p. 80.

INDEX